Reconstructing the Responsibility to Protect

This book revisits and interrogates the evolution of the Responsibility to Protect in search of the root cause of R2P's failure to date.

Employing a critical constructivist lens throughout, the book locates the origin of that apparent failure in the close association of R2P with humanitarian intervention. In returning to the ideational underpinnings and broader ambitions of R2P's architects, the analysis reveals that reducing R2P to little more than a "solution" to the long-standing problem(s) confronting humanitarian intervention betrayed its fundamental purpose: advancing a new norm of, and for, human security provision. Employing a modified version of the norm life-cycle model as a diagnostic tool, the author uncovers the underlying dynamics of R2P's normative stagnation over the past two decades. The book concludes with a prescriptive remedy in the form of a two-part blueprint for reconstructing and reanimating R2P's normative agenda for an international society confronted by mounting and existential threats to humanity.

This book will be of much interest to scholars and students of the Responsibility to Protect, human rights, security studies, and international relations in general.

Michael J. Butler is Associate Professor of International Relations and Chair of the Department of Political Science at Clark University in Worcester, Massachusetts. He is the author/co-author or editor of six books and over two dozen peer-reviewed journal articles. He is a member of Sweden's Folke Bernadotte Academy International Research Working Group on Dialogue, Mediation, and Peace Processes; a Senior Fellow at the University of Toronto's Canadian Centre for the Responsibility to Protect; and an affiliate with the Netherlands Institute for Advanced Study. He has served as co-editor of the *International Studies Intensives* book series (Routledge) since 2016.

Global Politics and the Responsibility to Protect
Series Editors: Alex J. Bellamy *University of Queensland,* Sara E. Davies, *Griffith University and* Monica Serrano *The City University of New York.*

The aim of this book series is to gather the best new thinking about the Responsibility to Protect into a core set of volumes that provides a definitive account of the principle, its implementation, and its role in crises, that reflects a plurality of views and regional perspectives.

Protecting the Global Civilian from Violence
UN Discourses and Practices in Fragile States
Timo Kivimäki

Covid-19 and Atrocity Prevention in East Asia
Edited by Mely Caballero-Anthony and Noel M. Morada

Advocacy Networks and the Responsibility to Protect
The Politics of Norm Circulation
Sarka Kolmasova

Regional Approaches to the Responsibility to Protect
Lessons from Europe and West Africa
Jochem Rietveld

Strengthening the Responsibility to Protect
A Transitional Cosmopolitan Approach
Richard Illingworth

Reconstructing the Responsibility to Protect
From Humanitarian Intervention to Human Security
Michael J. Butler

For more information about this series, please visit: https://www.routledge.com/Global-Politics-and-the-Responsibility-to-Protect/book-series/GPRP

Reconstructing the Responsibility to Protect

From Humanitarian Intervention to Human Security

Michael J. Butler

Routledge
Taylor & Francis Group
LONDON AND NEW YORK

First published 2025
by Routledge
4 Park Square, Milton Park, Abingdon, Oxon OX14 4RN

and by Routledge
605 Third Avenue, New York, NY 10158

Routledge is an imprint of the Taylor & Francis Group, an informa business

British Library Cataloguing-in-Publication Data
A catalogue record for this book is available from the British Library

Library of Congress Cataloging-in-Publication Data
Names: Butler, Michael J., author.
Title: Reconstructing the responsibility to protect : from humanitarian intervention to human security / Michael J. Butler.
Description: Abingdon, Oxon [UK] ; New York, NY : Routledge, 2024. | Series: Global politics and the responsibility to protect | Includes bibliographical references and index. |
Identifiers: LCCN 2024026162 (print) | LCCN 2024026163 (ebook) | ISBN 9781138095663 (hardback) | ISBN 9781032883557 (paperback) | ISBN 9781315105628 (ebook)
Subjects: LCSH: Responsibility to protect (International law) | Humanitarian intervention. | Humanitarian law. | Human security.
Classification: LCC KZ4082 .B88 2024 (print) | LCC KZ4082 (ebook) | DDC 341.5/84--dc23/eng/20240812
LC record available at https://lccn.loc.gov/2024026162
LC ebook record available at https://lccn.loc.gov/2024026163

ISBN: 978-1-138-09566-3 (hbk)
ISBN: 978-1-032-88355-7 (pbk)
ISBN: 978-1-315-10562-8 (ebk)

DOI: 10.4324/9781315105628

Typeset in Times New Roman
by SPi Technologies India Pvt Ltd (Straive)

Contents

Illustrations

Figure

Table

Preface and Acknowledgments

As this book goes to press, the world is rife with human suffering. We are well into the second year of a major interstate war in which a world power (Russia) is unabashedly employing a military strategy rooted in the perpetration of mass atrocities, crimes against humanity and ethnic cleansing against a nation (Ukraine) which it claims does not exist. A civil war in Yemen has pushed nearly 20 million to the brink of famine amid what is widely considered the biggest humanitarian crisis in the world. Last, but certainly not least, one is appalled by the violent besiegement of 2 million Palestinians confined within a 141-square-mile territory that has long been characterized as an open-air prison by such disparate figures as Noam Chomsky and David Cameron. This litany of tragedy blatantly exposes the stark and striking weakness of existing practices of civilian protection.

And the list, sadly, goes on. It includes situations of chronic and widespread human suffering and insecurity that are less directly related to armed conflict, if at all. A catastrophic earthquake in Türkiye and Syria, causing the deaths of tens of thousands, and the displacement of scores more in the spring of 2023 was in some sense one humanitarian crisis compounding another (the decade-long Syrian civil war). Gang warfare and political violence throughout Central America, caused by years of corruption and outside interference, has destroyed the economies and social fabric of the region and produced major out-migrations to the United States and other countries in search of sanctuary. The world continues to feel the reverberations of the metaphorically seismic impact of the global COVID-19 pandemic, which caused the death of millions, widespread disruptions to economic and social life, and similarly widespread disruptions to mental health, psychological well-being, and human development; a generalized sense of literal dis-ease. These and other significant threats and challenges to human security could be rendered irrelevant in light of the looming specter of what some fear could be an extinction-level event triggered by global climate change.

The level of misery and suffering on display in examples such as these is both beyond most people's depth of comprehension and outside their scope of consideration. With the exception of those directly engaged in the provision and/or assessment of humanitarian assistance, or those on the receiving end or in desperate need of it, the ubiquity of suffering and our perpetually under-developed and under-resourced tools for responding to and ameliorating it threaten to obscure it. For those (myself most certainly included) whose daily existence is defined by the privilege of safety, security, and opportunity, it is all too easy to begrudgingly accept or even actively ignore the plight of those experiencing acute humanitarian crises (whether natural or human-induced), as well as those confronted by the many chronic threats to human security. Real and perceived fears and anxieties about our immediate circle and often ourselves, in conjunction with (and perhaps caused by) a highly fragmented, profit-driven, and politically polarized media and informational landscape, direct our attention and our resources inwardly, while atrocities, catastrophes, and anxieties abound throughout the global system.

This diminished interest in and attentiveness to human suffering and vulnerability around the world has contributed in multiple and tangible ways to a declining capacity to respond to such circumstances. In some ways, it also represents a normalization. For example, in the early days of the war, debates raged over the need for and prospects of humanitarian intervention in Syria. A decade later, the prospect of doing anything more than attempting a minimalistic (and quickly abandoned) establishment of "humanitarian corridors" to facilitate the displacement of millions of Ukrainians in the face of the Russian onslaught was a non-starter. The humanitarian fund administered by the UN's Office for the Coordination of Humanitarian Affairs (OCHA) remains perpetually in the red, while the agency is reduced to begging major donor countries not to abandon their annual pledge amounts in the face of crises persisting, mounting, and new crises alike. Western and purportedly liberal states – among them some of the most rhetorically and performatively supportive advocates of human rights and international law – craft refugee and asylum policies and practices that discriminate against those fleeing violence and persecution on the basis of race, ethnicity, religion, gender, and sexuality and employ elaborate quota systems to (re)distribute them for the convenience of the receiving state. In some cases, these very states join their illiberal counterparts in engaging in overt exercises of biopower against the displaced or build massive and costly fortifications intended to exclude them completely.

The normalization and invisibility of human suffering among citizens and policymakers alike is a far cry from what was envisioned for – even expected of – the politics of the twenty-first century. Rather than a distressing normalization of human suffering, the prevailing assumption among leading scholar–activists working at the intersection of security studies, human rights, and development at the dawn of a new millennium was of the rise of a new norm of humanitarianism. One leading voice in this wilderness, Nicholas Wheeler, noted that while the dilemma of what to do about strangers subject to cruelty, atrocities, and disasters was not a new one, the normative context around that dilemma had changed markedly – establishing limits and empowering states, non-governmental organizations, and international organizations to scrutinize such situations and to act decisively to stop them and alleviate human suffering in the process. A solution to what Wheeler referred to as the problem of "saving strangers" was ostensibly at hand – with that solution embodied most definitively and concretely in the attempt at crafting a new doctrine to govern humanitarian intervention; namely, the Responsibility to Protect (R2P). What follows represents an attempt to uncover what happened in the intervening two decades, as the promise of a new norm of human security provision gave way to the age-old practice of officially sanctioned human suffering.

Before turning to that undertaking, I must acknowledge the contributions of those people without whom this book would have never been realized. This monograph has been (too) long in the making, having undergone significant twists and turns, both methodologically and ontologically, since its inception. These were, ultimately, necessary adjustments that reflected the critical evolution in my own thinking – an evolution spurred by both a deeper knowledge of the topic and a changed positionality toward it. Throughout it all, the continued support of my esteemed editor Andrew Humphrys at Routledge has been unflagging and deeply appreciated.

One positive externality of the prolonged germination and growth cycle of this project has been an opportunity to receive valuable research assistance from several outstanding students along the way, including Noor Almaslamani, Benjamin August, Camilo Botero-Alzate, Ethan Butler, and Charlene Kirongozi. All in their own way have left impressions on the final product. Additionally, I have been the beneficiary of constructive critique from many insightful chairs, discussants, and panelists when presenting various iterations of this research at numerous ISA conventions over the years, as well as conferences in Potsdam (Germany), Brussels, Wrocław, Ljubljana, and Barcelona. Among these, questions posed by Taylor Seybolt and Jennifer Welsh, former Special Adviser to the UN Secretary-General on R2P, at the Security, Intervention, and Humanitarianism Symposium at Institut Barcelona d'Estudis Internacionals (IBEI), proved to be especially pertinent and probing. Lastly, I would be remiss in not acknowledging my supportive colleagues in the Political Science department at Clark University and various associates at the Canadian Centre for the Responsibility to Protect for their insights along the way.

This book would not have been possible without the generous research support from the Marion and Jasper Whiting Foundation, as well as from the Francis A. Harrington Public Affairs Fund at Clark University. It also would not have been possible without the loving support of my family, to whom I am deeply indebted and by whom I am constantly amazed.

Introduction

R2P, R.I.P.?

The endorsement of the Responsibility to Protect (R2P) by the UN Security Council in April 2006 was hailed as a new dawn with respect to the international community's commitment to promoting and supporting human security (Bellamy, 2009a). As a formal codification of the notion that a state's sovereignty is contingent on its responsibility to its citizenry, UNSCR 1674 – like the World Summit Outcomes document approved by the UN General Assembly the previous year – was considered a watershed moment in the long, arduous struggle toward fashioning a more robust international ethic of human security via responsive governance (Evans, 2009).

Particularly groundbreaking in this regard was R2P's explicit concern with fostering the sense of a collective duty on the part of the international community to protect vulnerable populations in scenarios where states and their leaders proved unable or unwilling to attend to the well-being of those in their charge. Given this aim, R2P at base represented an effort to advance a new security norm, with individuals supplanting states at the center of security thinking and practice. To this point, as Thakur and Maley (2015: 10) assert,

> The R2P doctrine is fundamentally normative. It is offered as a set of proposals about what should be done in certain circumstances, namely those in which vulnerable people are faced by the threat of mass atrocity crime. It is directed at shaping the behavior of actors who might be called upon to engage in preventative action, or in reacting, or in rebuilding.

Yet nearly two decades after the international community officially endorsed this normative project, the R2P is stuck in the very same political quagmire that preceded and precipitated it (Holt and Berkman, 2006). From an ambitious and seemingly timely effort to drastically remake the policy guidelines and legal architecture of the international system regarding the duty to alleviate human suffering and insecurity, R2P has devolved to the point of irrelevance. What happened?

DOI: 10.4324/9781315105628-1

The "saving strangers" problem

One illustration of R2P's current peril is its fraught relationship with the practice of humanitarian intervention – understood here as "coercive action by one or more states involving the use of armed force in another state without the consent of its authorities, and with the purpose of preventing widespread suffering or death among the inhabitants" (Roberts, 2002: 4).[1] As subsequent chapters will reveal, the central position that humanitarian intervention has occupied in R2P discourse and practice is not only an illustration of the doctrine's current and continuing peril but also its primary cause. Indeed, from its very inception R2P has been saddled with what I characterize here as the "saving strangers problem" – a problem stemming from the intentional and close association of R2P with humanitarian intervention.

Framing R2P as a "solution" to the persistent problem of intervening in crisis situations in order to alleviate widespread human suffering (often politically motivated) has undermined R2P's ability to effect what was envisioned as a radical change to security policy and practice. Instead, the close association of R2P with humanitarian intervention – to the point of near-equivalency – has reduced R2P to little more than an effort to legitimate third-party intervention (Graubart, 2015). The chief consequence of this strategic move has been a derailing of R2P's maturation and diffusion as a security norm.

To be sure, R2P was never intended to be a blank check for humanitarian intervention; in fact, in some formulations, it was viewed as a successor to it (Henderson, 2020). Yet in practice the fundamental association of R2P with humanitarian intervention since its initial inception over two decades ago is beyond debate (Finnemore, 2003). As Ramesh Thakur – a member of the International Commission on Intervention and State Sovereignty (ICISS) which fashioned R2P in 2001 – argued, "R2P is not solely about military intervention, but if it is to have any meaning at all, it must include that option" (Thakur, quoted in Bajoria and McMahon, 2013). In no small part this stems from the prevailing notion among R2P's early architects and champions that it could serve as a remedy for the paralysis that characterized the debate over humanitarian intervention in the 1990s (Thakur and Maley, 2015). As a result, R2P was explicitly tied to scenarios in which political authorities proved unable or unwilling to respond to the threat or actual occurrence of large-scale loss of life, widespread forced displacement, and systematic and egregious violations of human rights (i.e., humanitarian crisis). As Terry Nardin (2013) noted:

> As articulated in UN documents such as the 2005 World Summit Outcome (UNGA A/60/L.1 2005) and a subsequent report of the Secretary-General (UNGA A/63/677 2009), each state has a responsibility to protect those it governs against crimes against humanity. If it fails to do so, that responsibility passes to the international community, which may resort to armed intervention if voluntary measures are ineffective.

In acknowledging then-UN Secretary-General Ban Ki-Moon's point that the coercive aspects of R2P were reflected in only one of R2P's three "pillars," Roland Paris (2014: 572) nonetheless asserted that "...this pillar looms over the others: armed intervention is the last-resort emergency option to prevent mass atrocities if all non-military measures fail."

To some extent a linkage of R2P and humanitarian intervention was unavoidable, in part due to R2P's overriding objective: to elicit a comprehensive mechanism for decisively responding to acute threats. These threats include discrete episodes of mass suffering and acts of harm imposed upon individuals and social groups by political authorities responsible for their well-being. Yet, as we will see, in its original codification by the ICISS R2P fully reflected a broader human security impetus beyond the parameters of the "saving strangers" problem. The primary contention of this research is that R2P represents, at base, a fundamentally normative enterprise. It was constructed with the goal of transforming security provision in order to improve the protection of civilians and foster enhanced human security and well-being. Critically, the subsequent decision to emphasize the international community's responsibility to react – only one of three areas of responsibility delineated by the ICISS – proved a fateful one not only with respect to R2P's influence on security policy and practice but also for the broader normative transformation its architects envisioned.

R2P: A dead letter?

The relative dearth of support for humanitarian intervention within the international community since the mid-2000s can be attributed to a multitude of causes (Binder, 2017; Hehir, 2013). Yet whatever the confounding factors, it is inarguable that R2P itself has proven inadequate for the task of facilitating the provision of humanitarian intervention. One need look no further than the fate of the UN Security Council Resolution (UNSCR 1674), offering explicit Security Council endorsement for R2P in 2006. Like the endorsement of gender mainstreaming in UNSCR 1320 (2000), as a thematic resolution UNSCR 1674 articulated clear support for infusing R2P principles into all subsequent Security Council deliberations and decisions.

At the time UNSCR 1674 was viewed by R2P's advocates as a policy triumph that would facilitate capacity building and responsiveness with respect to humanitarian crises in which civilian protection and atrocity prevention were imperative (Bellamy, 2009a). The acceptance of "sovereignty as responsibility" within international society seemed to be at hand with R2P even characterized as an "embodiment of today's ambitious normative international landscape" (Serrano, 2011: 425–426). Such triumphalism seems quaint in light of the declining frequency of and support for humanitarian intervention in the years following R2P's endorsement.

In reality, R2P has had minimal impact on the responsiveness of the international community to humanitarian crisis, or – by extension – on the strict adherence to state sovereignty via the non-interference principle that impedes such responses. One measure of R2P's impact in that regard comes through references to R2P and its underlying concepts and principles in UN Security Council Resolutions and Presidential Statements. To that end, the Global Centre for the Responsibility to Protect (2023) has identified 93 instances of "R2P references" – a seemingly impressive figure which nonetheless amounts to only 8.5% (93/1086) of all UNSC Resolutions issued since the introduction of R2P in April 2006. Furthermore, investigation of this subset of resolutions and presidential statements reveals only four instances of direct references to UNSCR 1674 itself (see Table 0.1) and no direct mentions of humanitarian intervention.

Explicit reference to UNSCR 1674 or R2P principles in a UNSC resolution is only one standard for assessing impact, and a limited one at that. As Bellamy (2011: 196) contends, "RtoP's ultimate test is not the number of resolutions that endorse it, but the number of graveyards that stand empty because tragedy was averted." To that point, a rudimentary content analysis of the text of all Security Council resolutions issued between the endorsement of UNSCR 1674 (28 April 2006) and the end of calendar year 2023 utilizing the search terms "responsibility" and "protect" provides further confirmation of R2P's lack of traction as an animating mechanism for alleviating or preventing human suffering. Though the yield is somewhat greater, only 29% (322/1086) of all resolutions approved by the UNSC following UNSCR 1674 even reference "responsibility" and "protect." Even by this generous standard, fewer than one-third of all resolutions passed since the UNSC endorsement of R2P could plausibly be said to reflect the basic concerns of R2P.[2] Among these, perhaps the most notable – and most explicit – is UNSCR 1973 (17 March 2011), which provided authorization under Chapter VII of the UN Charter for direct intervention in Libya for the purposes of civilian protection and the alleviation of human suffering, only to see both persist and even increase in the years following that intervention.[3]

As more systematic analyses confirm, it is not only the provision but also the very possibility of humanitarian intervention itself that has diminished drastically. The juxtaposition between a proliferation of complex political emergencies[4] in which human rights are systematically violated and civilian

Table 0.1 UNSC Resolutions Directly Referencing UNSCR 1674 (2006–2023)

Resolution	*Date*	*Scope/Focus*
1706	31 August 2006	Report of the Secretary-General on the Situation in Sudan (Darfur)
2187	25 November 2014	Report of the Secretary-General on the Situation in Sudan/South Sudan
2223	28 May 2015	Extending UN Mission (UNMISS) in South Sudan
2241	9 October 2015	Resolution of conflict in Republic of South Sudan

protection desperately needed (in Gaza, Ukraine, Yemen, Syria, Myanmar, and Venezuela, among others) and the failure of the UN Security Council and, by extension, the international community to marshal an effective response to them affirms the persistence of a bleak reality which R2P was intended to address. The fact that this evaporation of political support for, and even contemplation of, humanitarian action has occurred contemporaneously with the institutionalization of R2P is damning. Indeed, in May 2023 UN Secretary-General Antonio Guterres bluntly stated that "the world is failing to live up to its commitments to protect civilians; commitments enshrined in international humanitarian law" (France24, 2023). Not long thereafter, in July 2023, Special Adviser to the UN Secretary-General on R2P George Okoth-Obbo resigned after little over a year on the job, largely due to the generalized stagnancy surrounding R2P both as a concept and as a policy tool (Barber, 2023).[5]

Once considered indicative of an emergent norm of humanitarian action, R2P today is essentially a dead letter. This characterization of R2P is especially hard to refute if one accepts the widely held proposition that R2P's main purpose was (and is) to foster greater support for humanitarian intervention among prominent states and international organizations. Yet the chief harbinger of R2P's failure is not its inability to elicit broad support for humanitarian intervention as a practice, or to trigger UN Security Council endorsement for direct action in response to specific crisis events (though a compelling case to that effect can be, and has been, made; see Mennecke and Stensrud, 2021). Make no mistake about it – R2P has failed. Yet that failure is broader in scope and more fundamental, and stems from R2P's divergence from its original purpose: advancing a new norm of and for security provision in the international arena.

Problem v. purpose

Given the close association of R2P with humanitarian intervention, it is understandable that the efficacy of the former might be evaluated primarily on the status of the latter. Yet to evaluate R2P on these grounds would be a mistake. Humanitarian intervention is an epiphenomenal manifestation of what was fundamentally a deeply ambitious, even revolutionary, normative project (Thakur and Maley, 2015). Understood in this way, circumventing the paralytic humanitarian intervention debate is merely a positive externality of that normative project (Serrano, 2011). The ultimate significance of R2P's inability to elicit greater support for or provision of humanitarian intervention lies not in that deficiency itself, but in what that deficiency tells us about the norm shift that R2P sought to engender (Keranen, 2016). Consequently, a full understanding of why the core idea(s) of R2P have fallen out of favor requires not only an attentiveness to state interests and behavior, but to social norms and context.

If we consider both the degree of political resistance that greeted R2P upon arrival (Evans, 2008) as well as the deficit of humanitarian intervention persisting two decades after its introduction (Gromes and Dembinski, 2019), we would be hard-pressed to conclude that R2P has attained normative status in international society. The new humanitarian ethic bound up within and represented by R2P has failed to manifest itself behaviorally; for all intents and purposes, what was at one time considered an emergent norm has now become something of an afterthought.[6] The consequences of this failure are profound. They suggest the interruption and possibly even disintegration of the underlying purpose (as opposed to superficial objective) of R2P: the transformation of international norms with respect to the prevailing understanding of moral responsibility, as well as the transference of political authority and decision-making over security provision from the domain of sovereign states to that of the international community.

In taking into account R2P's antecedents (such as the notion of "sovereignty as responsibility"; see Cohen and Deng, 1998) as well as its impetus and initial formulation by the ICISS in 2001, it is abundantly clear that the architects of R2P had something bigger than just the provision of humanitarian intervention in their sights. That something was a desire to usher in a post-Westphalian conception of, and approach to, security provision (Newman, 2013). In the words of the historian Sir Martin Gilbert, R2P was "the most significant adjustment to national sovereignty in 360 years" (2007). This assessment is borne out not only in the work of the international commission tasked with finding a solution to the humanitarian intervention problem (with that problem conjoined with the principle of state sovereignty in its very name!), but in the larger context of human security in which R2P was situated. In such an "adjustment", the presumptive "international community" would inevitably supplant states as the primary source of, and authority for, security action (transference), and individuals would naturally supplant states as the primary referent in security thinking (transcendence).

This fundamental and double-edged purpose for R2P is borne out not only in the ideology of its early principal architects, but also in the subsequent steps employed to implement it. Take, for example, R2P's early orientation around the "three pillars" of responsibility (Bellamy, 2015). The Three Pillars reflects a basic presumption on the part of R2P's proponents that the answer to the state-centric machinations that dominated humanitarian intervention and human security provision lie in elevating the issue to the level of mutually shared obligation (Bellamy, 2023). The practical result of this "elevation" would be a transference of sovereign authority from the state to the global level. At the same time, the ICISS explicitly drew from emergent arguments favoring the recalibration of security policy around the concept of human security and the well-being of the individual, a framing of R2P clearly indicative of a desire to transcend existing Westphalian norms (Hampson, 2012; Slaughter, 2005; Paris, 2001).

As originally constructed, R2P engaged the problem of humanitarian intervention – as thorny and vexing as it was – as but a symptom of a bigger and more fundamental problem in international society. That problem was the continued strict adherence to the Westphalian paradigm, and the implications of that strict adherence for attending to the security needs of those at greatest risk (Western, 2011). Recognizing this feature of R2P's underlying and fundamental purpose is crucial to properly appraising not only what ultimately went wrong with respect to R2P, but also how it might be salvaged (Illingworth, 2024).

Reconstructing R2P

It is tempting to seek a greater understanding of R2P's unraveling by focusing entirely on how and why R2P failed to achieve the objective of generating greater support and capacity for humanitarian intervention. However, doing so would be putting the proverbial cart before the horse. The present research "flips the script," instead seeking to chronicle how and why humanitarian intervention has ultimately failed R2P – and what, if anything, can be done to salvage it.

R2P's advocates are at least partly to blame for R2P's unraveling, by advancing a version of R2P which contributed to its stagnation as a new norm of human security. The effort to promote R2P as a corrective to the humanitarian intervention deficit delimited R2P's scope and potential while also subjecting it to the intractable and interminable debates over that contentious practice. As a result, R2P began to drew fire both from those who viewed it as a vehicle for unchecked liberal internationalism (Graubart, 2013), and from those who considered it an insufficient means for responding to the pervasive scourge of humanitarian crises deserving of, if not demanding, the involvement of the international community (Friberg-Fernros and Brommesson, 2013).

Examples reflecting both critiques abound. On the former score, NATO's invocation of R2P as grounds for military intervention in Libya in 2011 did little to alleviate human suffering in the short run, and even less after that, as the political vacuum that emerged following the ouster of Muammar Qaddafi has devolved into a perpetual state of violence and lawlessness. In this way, the Libyan debacle was a close facsimile of the failure of R2P as a mechanism for protection in Darfur half a decade earlier (de Waal, 2007). The widespread human suffering and dislocation that continues to characterize Libya long after NATO's exit does little to support a humanitarian rationale for the 2011–2012 intervention, but lends compelling support to those who view R2P as merely a pretext for regime change and political chicanery orchestrated by the West (Graubart, 2015), or as a palliative for the "do something syndrome" (von Hippel and Clarke, 1999). From the opposite side of the ledger, as prominent crises in Ukraine, Gaza, Yemen, Syria, Myanmar, and Venezuela among others demonstrate, the absence of support for (and even contemplation of) the provision of humanitarian intervention in response to the frequent occurrences of complex political emergencies[7] which by definition necessitate such a response support the claim that R2P is an inadequate mechanism for eliciting international humanitarian response.

Using Wheeler's (2000) terminology, the problem(s) of "saving strangers" – a problem which R2P was ostensibly introduced to fix – proved to be a Gordian knot so enduring and vexing that it bound R2P up within it. Proof of this lies in the fact that when confronted by the reality of the failure of R2P to elicit greater support for humanitarian intervention, some of R2P's most vocal and prominent proponents sought to decouple it from humanitarian intervention altogether (Chandler, 2015). This stark about-face contradicts the initial response of R2P's proponents to the UN Security Council's endorsement in 2006 as a *cause* célébré. Given that body's ostensible authority in security matters, UNSCR 1674 was considered a breakthrough – alleviating, if not obviating, long-standing obstacles to humanitarian intervention and, by extension, an indication of R2P's emerging normativity (Nardin, 2013; Bellamy and Wheeler, 2008; Evans, 2008). However, the persistence of debates over the legitimacy of sovereignty-transgressing actions predicated on R2P – not to mention the staunch opposition to such actions within and beyond the P-5 itself, opposition which has allowed mass atrocities to continue unabated – following that endorsement suggests quite the opposite result (Paris, 2014).

Recognizing that mounting opposition to interventions predicated on humanitarian grounds in the aftermath of operations such as those in Kosovo and Iraq was infecting R2P, the effort was quickly made to insert daylight between the two (Bellamy, 2009b). Accordingly, within five years after its endorsement by the UN some of R2P's most vocal interlocutors were engaged in propagating the claim that R2P was never intended as a "red flag" galvanizing the international community to react to humanitarian crisis (Bellamy, 2010), and that it was always directed toward prevention rather than reaction (Evans, 2012). Others subsequently advanced even more creative arguments following the related debacles of the Libya intervention and the Syria non-intervention, including that R2P ultimately did "solve" the humanitarian intervention problem by supplanting it as an ideational notion (Crossley, 2018; Gierycz, 2010), and that R2P was never fundamentally concerned with humanitarian intervention (Chesterman, 2021).

Representations of R2P that disclaim the central importance of the humanitarian intervention deficit in evaluating R2P's overall impact provide something of a *camera obscura* portrait. The fact that R2P has encountered such resistance on the path to normativity due to its association with humanitarian intervention is vitally important. It is a dynamic that demands scrutiny rather than apology, engagement rather than denial. To this end, the two chapters following this one (Chapters 1 and 2) work together as a piece, providing a historiography of sorts: of humanitarian intervention, R2P, and especially the fusion of the two in the policy imagination of R2P's proponents and critics alike. Doing so reveals the way(s) in which R2P was expressly delineated as a "solution" to several key facets of the persistent problem of humanitarian intervention.

From there, Chapter 3 offers a diagnosis and critique of what, exactly, went wrong with that "solution." Specifically, I draw on constructivist and critical theory in order to uncover how and why the assignation of R2P to humanitarian intervention proved consequentially limiting for its broader potential as a norm. Advancing a critical revision to the ubiquitous norm life cycle model (Finnemore and Sikkink, 1998), Chapter 3 provides a picture of a normative enterprise in stagnation, as the core idea(l)s of R2P ran headlong into a social environment that was neither receptive to a doctrine designed to elicit a highly contentious and contested form of international political behavior (humanitarian intervention), nor to the "saving strangers" ethos at the heart of it.

However, the argument advanced here embraces the proposition of R2P as an aspirational norm, locating its "failure to launch" primarily in attempts at translating and implementing it that strayed from its core ideational propositions concerning both responsibility and protection. As such, R2P's demise – revealed through critical interrogation – is not, and should not be taken as, a *fait accompli*. As Chapter 3 concludes, the ultimate consequence of R2P's effective equivalence with humanitarian intervention has been, to date, its stagnation as an emerging security norm. This stagnation is a by-product of two closely related disconnects: one between international society and the highly circumscribed version of R2P (focused almost exclusively on reaction to discrete crisis events) that prevails today, and the other between that limited version of R2P (what Thomas Weiss dubbed "R2P-lite") and the fuller, authentic version introduced by the ICISS.

Having demonstrated the extent and implications of the stagnation of R2P as a normative project, Chapters 4 and 5 proceed to sketch out a potential remedy to this stagnation in the form of a reimagined and reconstructed R2P. This reconstruction unfolds in two parts, both drawing extensively and explicitly from a concept which shares R2P's objective of fostering new (post-Westphalian) security arrangements and its aspiration to introduce new norms to govern international security thinking and practice: namely, the notion of human security. In revisiting R2P's ideational alignment with the human security agenda, Chapter 4 thoroughly examines the prevailing notion of responsibility at R2P's core – returning to the cosmopolitan ethic at the heart of both R2P and human security. Likewise, Chapter 5 repositions R2P as an instrumental vehicle of and for protection on a broader scale, moving far beyond the operational and cultural limits of "saving strangers" through discrete responses to humanitarian crises. Instead, Chapter 5 documents R2P's potential for proactively engaging with and ameliorating chronic and transnational security threats that universally impact humanity on an existential level. From an ontological position, the overriding emphasis on the responsibility to react (i.e., intervene) has proven to be a limiting factor not only because of R2P's inability to elicit more and better humanitarian intervention but also because it has come at the expense of the effective advancement of the other two areas of responsibility (prevention and rebuilding) expressly embedded within R2P's ethic of protection (Keranen, 2016; Rosenberg, 2009).

The reconstruction of R2P proposed here is underwritten by a recognition of larger normative ambitions of R2P's architects, and an argument for returning to those ambitions. The original purpose motivating R2P's framers was the transfer of political and policy authority over security matters, and the transcendence of traditional security norms in light of the abject and abysmal failure of the state as a security actor. In reconstructing R2P through this return to its original impetus, this book seeks to uncover a path for productive and effective action on transnational security threats and their consequences for individuals and society.

Notes

1 "Humanitarian intervention" is an undeniably broad term encompassing a wide range of potential actions undertaken by a similarly wide range of potential actors. Some aspects of humanitarian intervention are consistent regardless of the form of action entailed. For example, humanitarian intervention by definition is primarily motivated by the goal of arresting and/or alleviating human suffering in a crisis situation; likewise, intervention necessarily entails action(s) undertaken by external third-parties. While acknowledging that humanitarian intervention in some translations can be (and sometimes is) undertaken by various NGOs (domestic and/or international) and can be (and sometimes is) non-military in nature, the focus of this research is on examining the provision of humanitarian *military* intervention, and the relationship between the provision of that particular form of humanitarian action by actors disposed to provide it (states and IGOs) and the Responsibility to Protect. As such, the term "humanitarian intervention" in this book should be understood in all cases as referring to humanitarian military intervention, undertaken on a multilateral or collective basis or with multilateral or collective support, wherein the action undertaken may not be fully or necessarily humanitarian in character, but can be humanitarian in outcome (Seybolt, 2008).

2 A content analysis was conducted on the population of UNSC Resolutions passed between 28 April 2006 and 31 December 2023, utilizing the full-text repository available on the UNSC website: https://www.un.org/securitycouncil/content/resolutions.

3 Qualitatively, it is worth noting a trend in recent years toward "looser" allusive references to the concepts and logic of R2P (if not to UNSCR 1674 itself), with most such references coming in relation either to thematic resolutions – such as those pertaining to reaffirmations of the Women, Peace & Security (WPS) agenda – or in conjunction with UNSC support for "human rights," broadly defined.

4 The UN defines complex political emergencies as events constituted by "a humanitarian crisis in a country, region, or society where there is a total or considerable breakdown of authority resulting from internal or external conflict which requires an international response that goes beyond the mandate or capacity of any single agency and/or the ongoing UN country programme." *INTER-AGENCY STANDING COMMITTEE WORKING GROUP XVITH MEETING*, edited by United Nations Department of Humanitarian Affairs [Meeting minutes, Inter-Agency Standing Committee Working Group XVI, 30 November 1994]. Available: https://interagencystandingcommittee.org/sites/default/files/migrated/2014-12/WG16_4.pdf. Last accessed 1 February 2024.

5 This is a pattern, not an outlier; as Barber (2023) also notes, Okoth-Obbo's predecessor, Karen Smith of South Africa, lasted two and a half years while her predecessor, Ivan Šimonović of Croatia, resided in the position only two years.

6 As Doyle (2011) has argued, the fact that R2P has any claim to normativity at all is itself reflective of an increasing normative and ethical pluralism in international relations, which in turn equates to a messy and "confused" normative and ethical landscape with respect to humanitarianism (Barnett, 2011).

7 The 1994 Working Paper by an Inter-agency Standing Committee of the UN Department of Humanitarian Affairs defines complex political emergencies as events constituted by "a humanitarian crisis in a country, region, or society where there is a total or considerable breakdown of authority resulting from internal or external conflict which requires an international response that goes beyond the mandate or capacity of any single agency and/or the ongoing UN country programme."

Bibliography

Bajoria, Jayshree, and Robert McMahon. 2013. *The Dilemma of Humanitarian Intervention*. New York: Council on Foreign Relations.

Barber, Rebecca. 2023. "The UN Should Increase Support for the Responsibility to Protect," *Just Security* (17 August 2023). Available online: https://www.justsecurity.org/87571/the-un-should-increase-support-for-the-responsibility-to-protect. Last accessed 30 March 2024.

Barnett, Michael. 2011. *Empire of Humanity: A History of Humanitarian Intervention*. Ithaca, NY: Cornell University Press.

Bellamy, Alex J. 2023. "The Responsibility to Protect," in Paul D. Williams and Matt McDonald (eds.), *Security Studies: An Introduction* (4th ed.) (pp. 268–283). London/New York: Routledge.

Bellamy, Alex J. 2015. "The Three Pillars of the Responsibility to Protect," *Pensamiento propio* 41(20): 35–64.

Bellamy, Alex J. 2011. *Global Politics and the Responsibility to Protect: From Words to Deeds*. New York: Routledge.

Bellamy, Alex J. 2010. "The Responsibility to Protect – Five Years On," *Ethics & International Affairs* 24(2): 143–169.

Bellamy, Alex J. 2009a. *Responsibility to Protect: The Global Effort to End Mass Atrocities*. Cambridge: Polity Press.

Bellamy, Alex J. 2009b. "Realizing the Responsibility to Protect," *International Studies Perspectives* 10(2): 111–128.

Bellamy, Alex J., and Nicholas J. Wheeler. 2008. "Humanitarian Intervention in World Politics," *The Globalization of World Politics* 5: 479–496.

Binder, Martin. 2017. *The United Nations and the Politics of Selective Humanitarian Intervention. Basingstoke: Palgrave Macmillan.*

Chandler, David. 2015. "The R2P is Dead, Long Live the R2P: The Successful Separation of Military Intervention from the Responsibility to Protect," *International Peacekeeping* 22(1): 1–5.

Chesterman, Simon. 2021. "R2P and Humanitarian Intervention: From Apology to Utopia and Back Again," in Robin Geiß and Nils Melzer (eds.), *The Oxford Handbook on the International Law of Global Security* (pp. 808–820). New York: Oxford University Press.

Cohen, Roberta, and Francis M. Deng. 1998. *Masses in Flight: The Global Crisis of Internal Displacement*. Washington, DC: Brookings Institution Press.

Crossley, Noele. 2018. "Is R2P Still Controversial? Continuity and Change in the Debate on 'Humanitarian Intervention'," *Cambridge Review of International Affairs* 31(5): 415–436.

Doyle, Michael W. 2011. "International Ethics and the Responsibility to Protect," *International Studies Review* 13(1): 72–84

de Waal, Alex. 2007. "Darfur and the Failure of the Responsibility to Protect," *International Affairs* 83(6): 1039–1054.

Evans, Gareth. 2012. "Gareth Evans on 'Responsibility to Protect' after Libya," (An interview with Gareth Evans by Alan Philips). *The World Today* (October 2012). London: Chatham House.

Evans, Gareth. 2009. "The Responsibility to Protect: From an Idea to an International Norm," in R.H. Cooper and J.V. Kohler (eds.), *Responsibility to Protect: The Global Moral Compact for the 21st Century* (pp. 15–30). Basingstoke/New York: Palgrave Macmillan.

Evans, Gareth. 2008. "The Responsibility to Protect: An Idea Whose Time Has Come… and Gone?" *International Relations* 22(3): 283–298.

Finnemore, Martha. 2003. *The Purpose of Intervention: Changing Beliefs about the Use of Force*. Ithaca: Cornell University Press.

Finnemore, Martha, and Kathryn Sikkink. 1998. "International Norm Dynamics and Political Change," *International Organization* 52(4): 887–917.

France24. 2023. "World 'Failing' to Protect Civilians Caught in Conflicts, UN Chief Says," (24 May). Available online: https://www.france24.com/en/americas/20230523-world-failing-to-protect-civilians-caught-in-conflicts-un-chief-says. Last accessed 15 September 2023.

Friberg-Fernros, Henrik, and Douglas Brommesson. 2013. "The Responsibility to Protect—An Incoherent Doctrine?" *International Politics* 50: 600–622.

Gierycz, Dorota. 2010. "From Humanitarian Intervention (HI) to Responsibility to Protect (R2P)," *Criminal Justice Ethics* 29(2): 110–128.

Gilbert, Sir Martin. 2007. "The Terrible 20th Century," *The Globe and Mail* (31 January). Available online: https://www.theglobeandmail.com/opinion/the-terrible-20th-century/article17990016/. Last accessed 14 May 2023.

Global Centre for the Responsibility to Protect. 2023. "UN Security Council Resolutions and Presidential Statements Referencing R2P," (19 December). Available online: https://www.globalr2p.org/resources/un-security-council-resolutions-and-presidential-statements-referencing-r2p/. Last accessed 1 February 2024.

Graubart, Jonathan. 2015. "War is Not the Answer: The Responsibility to Protect and Military Intervention," in R. Thakur and W. Maley (eds.), *Theorising the Responsibility to Protect* (pp. 200–220). Cambridge: Cambridge University Press.

Graubart, Jonathan. 2013. "R2P and Pragmatic Liberal Interventionism: Values in the Service of Interests," *Human Rights Quarterly* 35(1): 69–90.

Gromes, Thorsten, and Matthias Dembinski. 2019. "Practices and Outcomes of Humanitarian Military Interventions: A New Data Set," *International Interactions* 45(6): 1032–1048.

Hampson, Fen Osler. 2012. "Human Security," in Paul D. Williams (ed.), *Security Studies: An Introduction* (pp. 301–316). London/New York: Routledge.

Hehir, Aidan. 2013. "The Permanence of Inconsistency: Libya, the Security Council, and the Responsibility to Protect," *International Security* 38(1): 137–159.

Henderson, Stacey. 2020. "Humanitarian Intervention and R2P," *Journal of International Peacekeeping* 22(1–4): 325–343.

Holt, Victoria K., and Tobias C. Berkman. 2006. *The Impossible Mandate? Military Preparedness, the Responsibility to Protect and Modern Peace Operations*. Washington, DC: Henry L. Stimson Center.

Illingworth, Richard. 2024. *Strengthening the Responsibility to Protect: A Transitional Cosmopolitan Approach*. London/New York: Routledge.

Keranen, Outi. 2016. "What Happened to the Responsibility to Rebuild?" *Global Governance* 22(3): 331–348.

Mennecke, Martin, and Ellen E. Stensrud. 2021. "The Failure of the International Community to Apply R2P and Atrocity Prevention in Myanmar," *Global Responsibility to Protect* 13(2–3): 111–130.

Nardin, Terry. 2013. "Humanitarian Intervention," in H. LaFollette (ed.), *International Encyclopedia of Ethics* (pp. 2477–2486). Hoboken, NJ: Wiley-Blackwell.

Newman, Edward. 2013. "The United Nations and Human Security: Between Solidarism and Pluralism," in *Routledge Handbook of Human Security* (pp. 245–258). London/New York: Routledge.
Paris, Roland. 2014. "The 'Responsibility to Protect' and the Structural Problems of Preventive Humanitarian Intervention," *International Peacekeeping* 21(5): 569–603.
Paris, Roland. 2001. "Human Security: Paradigm Shift or Hot Air?" *International Security* 26(2): 87–102.
Roberts, Adam. 2002. "The So-Called 'Right' of Humanitarian Intervention," in *Yearbook of International Humanitarian Law 2000*, vol. 3 (pp. 3–51). The Hague: T.M.C. Asser.
Rosenberg, Sheri P. 2009. "Responsibility to Protect: A Framework for Prevention," *Global Responsibility to Protect* 1: 442–477.
Serrano, Mónica. 2011. "The Responsibility to Protect and its Critics: Explaining the Consensus," *Global Responsibility to Protect* 3: 425–437.
Seybolt, Taylor B. 2008. *Humanitarian Military Intervention: The Conditions for Success and Failure*. Oxford: Oxford University Press.
Slaughter, Anne-Marie. 2005. *A New World Order*. Princeton, NJ: Princeton University Press.
Thakur, Ramesh, and William Maley. 2015. "Theorising Global Responsibilities," in R. Thakur and W. Maley (eds.), *Theorising the Responsibility to Protect* (pp. 3–15). Cambridge: Cambridge University Press.
von Hippel, Karin, and Michael Clarke. 1999. "Something Must Be Done," *The World Today* 55(3): 4–7.
Western, Jon. 2011. "Protecting States or Protecting Civilians: The Case for R2P," *The Massachusetts Review* 52(2): 348–357.
Wheeler, Nicholas J. 2000. *Saving Strangers: Humanitarian Intervention in International Society*. New York: Oxford University Press.

1 The persistent problem(s) of humanitarian intervention

The overriding concern of this book lies with gaining a better understanding of why and how R2P lost its way on the path toward attaining the status of a behavior-inducing norm. Doing so requires one to consider the interface between the idea of R2P and the social context in which it was introduced. To that end, and despite *ex post facto* efforts to the contrary, R2P's origin story cannot be told without affording a major leading role to the confounding and persistent problem(s) of humanitarian intervention. Although, as we will see, the intention of R2P's architects was neither solely nor primarily the resuscitation of humanitarian intervention, a clear and compelling relationship between R2P and humanitarian intervention undoubtedly existed from its very inception (Badescu, 2011).

This relationship is reflected in R2P's endorsement by the United Nations. Indeed, a key driver of that endorsement was R2P's status as an apparent solution to the puzzle of humanitarian intervention. The UN's 2004 High-Level Panel on Threats, Challenges, and Change went as far as to advocate for R2P in a chapter on "collective security," under the heading of "use of force" (Bellamy, 2009a). As such, gaining a comprehensive understanding of why and how R2P has unraveled – failing to attain the twin objectives of transferring authority over security matters from states to the international community, and transcending the normative strictures of the Westphalian states-system in the process – requires fully acknowledging the impact of the problem(s) of humanitarian intervention on R2P's genesis and evolution (Sarkin, 2009). In this we would do well to remember that solving this problem was a clearly stated objective by R2P's architects, the International Commission on Intervention and State Sovereignty (ICISS): an international commission tasked with "re-conceptualizing humanitarian intervention" (ICISS, 2001: 9) in order to move the international community beyond the "pitched battles of humanitarian intervention" (Weiss, 2016: 19).

A brief history of humanitarian intervention

The introduction of the concept of humanitarian intervention to the political lexicon is widely attributed to the English lawyer William Edward Hall in 1880,

DOI: 10.4324/9781315105628-2

with antecedents dating to the 19th century, if not earlier (Badescu, 2011; Chesterman, 2002). Indeed, the concern with alleviating human suffering has had some bearing on state (and later, institutional) behavior and decision-making for decades, if not centuries. Consequently, the political, legal, and ethical dilemmas associated with humanitarian intervention have long been of significance to scholars, jurists, and statespersons alike.

Given its universalist and theological underpinnings, arguments for humanitarian intervention can be discerned in the antecedents of the natural law tradition, including Hebrew, Greek, and Roman law (Murphy, 1996). Likewise, conceptions of humanitarian "duties" can be found in natural law tributaries such as just war theory, as reflected in the writings of Francisco de Vitoria concerning the duties of the "civilized" world to intervene in the "New World" to end practices such as human sacrifice (Butler, 2012). Opposition to humanitarian intervention grew after the Treaty of Westphalia (1648), with the codification of state sovereignty (itself reflecting the tenet of *cuius regio, eius religio*, or "whose realm, his religion") and the emergence of positive law and the doctrine of non-interference (Gray, 2018). Through the prism of history, it seems evident that the tension between the principles of human rights and state sovereignty residing at the forefront of contemporary debate concerning humanitarian intervention has long and deep roots (Murphy, 1996).

In his seminal work on the laws of war, Ian Brownlie (1963) argues that the notion of humanitarian intervention as a "right" – however vague and contentious – gained traction with most legal scholars by the end of the 19th century. However, the resonance of the concept at what was arguably the apex of positive law undoubtedly stemmed in part from its utility as a covering rationale for self-interested undertakings by powerful states.[1] As Weiss (2005) notes, the situation concerning humanitarian intervention at the time was ambiguous. Though undoubtedly invoked for self-interested reasons by the European great powers of the late 19th and early 20th centuries, the concerted effort to construct legal and moral arguments in service of framing interventions in contested colonial lands or on the European-Ottoman fault line of the late 19th century as "quasi-judicial police measures" (Chesterman, 2002: 36–37) were indicative of the increasing relevance of the concept.

The cataclysmic nature of the two world wars and the great political and economic dislocations that defined the interwar period made provision of humanitarian intervention irrelevant, in the process rendering arguments for and against humanitarian intervention moot. At the same time, the widespread and appalling atrocities pervasive in both wars and, even more acutely, the horrors of the Holocaust combined to resuscitate natural law, and the notion of universal rights and responsibilities central to it (Walzer, 1977). Reflected in post-war international legal instruments such as the 1948 Universal Declaration of Human Rights (UDHR), the 1948 Convention on the Prevention and Punishment of the Crime of Genocide, and even the United Nations Charter itself, the resurgence of natural law in the second half of the 20th century ultimately led to a return to the fore of humanitarian intervention as a concept

(Hehir, 2010). Though largely hortatory in function, the fundamental position of human rights in the post-war international legal architecture paved the way for reconsideration of when and how such rights and their abrogation might demand redress. Yet, as these very same legal instruments (including, and perhaps especially, the UN Charter) reflected, long-standing tension between the universalistic (natural law) impulses of human rights advocacy and protection and the particularistic (positive law) emphasis on state sovereignty remained unresolved.

The conceptual and legal dilemma posed by the twin mandates to respect state sovereignty while promoting and protecting individual human rights reflected in the UN Charter – what Badescu (2011) refers to as "the humanitarian intervention conundrum" – were only exacerbated by the contentious international political environment of the Cold War period (Weiss, 2016). Whatever the likelihood of humanitarian intervention, most political and legal scholars agree that the Charter did not (and does not) permit the use of force for the protection of populations from humanitarian crisis by states acting at their own discretion (Holzgrefe and Keohane, 2003). Instead, authority for any such action (independent of the merits of such an action, which require additional and separate deliberation) resides with the UN Security Council (Holzgrefe and Keohane, 2003). For its part, the International Court of Justice rejected the possibility that a right of intervention by force could be consistent with international law. In its landmark 1949 *Corfu Channel* judgment, the ICJ ruled that the right of intervention by force has no basis in international law, given that "respect for territorial sovereignty is an essential foundation of international relations" (ICJ, 1949).

With inchoate legal arguments reinforced by the dueling Security Council vetoes of the Cold War superpowers, it is hardly surprising that humanitarian intervention was rarely observed during the Cold War – or that the debate surrounding it remained largely stultified. To that end, Weiss (2005) notes that there was not even a single mention of humanitarian concerns by the Security Council during the period from 1945 until the Six Day War of 1967. One empirical study of intervention during the Cold War concluded that there were no cases of military intervention primarily motivated by humanitarian causes during the period 1946–91, nor any cases of legal arguments for such behavior solely reliant on humanitarian grounds (Beck and Arend, 1993). Findings such as these provide empirical support to arguments that intervention during the Cold War era was an instrument dedicated entirely to strategic ends rather than humanitarian ones (Ayoob, 2002).[2]

At the same time, empirical studies introducing finer distinctions of what constitutes "humanitarian intervention" as well as those more sensitive to the idea of mixed motives for intervention suggest that, in point of fact, humanitarian intervention during the Cold War was not the total non-factor that some scholars have made it out to be. Prominent, if aberrational, cases of humanitarian outcomes arising from military interventions during the Cold War – such as India's intervention in East Pakistan (1971), Vietnam's incursion to halt the

Khmer Rouge genocide in Cambodia (1978), and Tanzania's campaign to overthrow Idi Amin in Uganda (1979) – have been well-chronicled (Walzer, 1977).

Further contradicting Beck and Arend's (1993) claim, the combined International Military Intervention dataset (Pearson and Baumann, 1993; Pickering and Kisangani, 2009) depicts an empirical landscape in which humanitarian considerations, while far from commonplace, are discernable. Of the total sum of cases (n = 1112) meeting the established definitional criteria for military intervention during the period 1947–2005, 273 (24.5%) featured verifiable evidence of a humanitarian motive.[3] If one were to include military interventions employed to protect a socio-ethnic minority group in the target state as also constituting humanitarian intervention, then 28.4% of all military interventions (301/1112) occurring during the period 1947–2005 could be characterized as featuring a humanitarian dimension.[4]

Humanitarian intervention after the Cold War

The longer-term legacy of humanitarian intervention notwithstanding, it is beyond contention that humanitarian intervention took on much greater significance and importance in the post–Cold War era – constituting what Bellamy and McLoughlin (2018: xii) have characterized as a "minor revolution." As Barnett and Weiss (2008: 29) contend, in the post–Cold War era "… humanitarianism has become institutionalized, internationalized, and prominent on the global agenda. It is an orienting feature of global social life that is used to justify, legitimate, and galvanize action." Reasons for this "revolution" abound. Structural changes in the distribution of power in the international system (and their ramifications for the UN and other international and regional organizations), an upwelling of numerous intra-state conflicts marked by mass atrocities and extensive human rights violations, and the emergence of the 24-hour news cycle and various forms of new media all propelled humanitarian crises and action higher on the global policy agenda (Hehir, 2010). This was especially evident in the debates over, and deployment of, UN peace and security operations throughout the 1990s, as the Security Council expanded the notion of what constitutes a threat to international peace and security as well as the basis for authorizing third-party intervention (Weiss, 2016).

The Gulf War precedent

As in myriad other ways, the Gulf War proved a crucial point of demarcation for humanitarian intervention. As Bellamy (2004) argues, the Bush Administration's utilization of a generalized humanitarian rationale alongside the more obvious legal one (pertaining to Iraq's abrogation of Kuwait's sovereignty) in fashioning a broad coalition force and ultimately launching *Operation Desert Storm* via the UN Security Council was precedent-setting. In emphasizing the illegitimacy of Saddam's regime based on its treatment of civilians both in Iraq and in occupied Kuwait, the United States was effectively advancing a humanitarian exception to the doctrine of non-intervention, and in the process infusing humanitarian and human rights concerns into the Security Council's "international peace and security" mandate (Teson, 1996).

This argument was only intensified in the aftermath of the "100-hour war" as the United States and its coalition partners engaged in deliberations over how to respond to the Iraqi government's heinous crackdown on Shia and Kurdish uprisings originally fomented by the Bush Administration (Diamond, 1996). Though ultimately the U.S.-led coalition forces did little to prevent Saddam's regime from brutalizing Iraqi civilians (beyond belatedly establishing a "no-fly zone" in northern Iraq through UNSCR 688 on 5 April 1991), the Bush Administration's self-congratulatory proclamations of a "New World Order" – defined by a greater regard for, and willingness to enforce, human rights and international law – in the aftermath of Iraq's withdrawal from Kuwait represented a catalyst for the emergence to the fore of humanitarian intervention as a concept and as a practice (Weiss, 2016).

The UN Security Council's authorization of a Chapter VII action in the form of *Operation Desert Shield / Storm* (via UNSCR 678, 29 November 1990) proved pivotal in this regard. Not only did that resolution establish a precedent for a "humanitarian exception" to the non-interference clause, it also suggested the possibility of a transformed Security Council that would serve as a more activist decision-making body. As van Baarda (1994) argued, whereas the Security Council afforded little attention to the humanitarian aspects of armed conflict during the Cold War, the early and mid-1990s were a different story altogether. With respect to the Security Council's agenda, Weiss (2004) views this period as something of a *tabula rasa*, with twice as many resolutions passed between 1990 and 1995 as between 1945 and 1990. A not-insignificant number of these resolutions explicitly defined humanitarian crisis as a threat to international peace and security, further expanding the Security Council's remit (Weiss, 2004). Unfolding in parallel with the expansion of international humanitarian law through the establishment of tribunals (ICTY, ICTR) and, ultimately, the Rome Statute and the ICC, the tilt toward human security and the expansion of concern with the rights of the individual relative to those of states was patently evident (Badescu, 2011; Meron, 1995).[5]

UN peace operations and the "humanitarian exception"

Nowhere was the spirit of activism relative to threats to international peace and security posed by the internal affairs of states and societies greater than in the office of UN Secretary-General Boutros Boutros-Ghali. This was best evinced in his effort, via the *Agenda for Peace* (June 1992), to redefine UN peace operations in ways that would expand the authority of the UN and by extension enhance the capacity of the international community to act frequently and decisively – with force, when necessary – in response to humanitarian crises (Butler, 2009). The vision of the document was one in which long-standing constraints of consent and impartiality, themselves by-products of a strict adherence to state sovereignty, would be jettisoned in pursuit of a more expansive mandate: "peace enforcement." Boutros-Ghali viewed such an arrangement, defined by relaxed or even suspended concerns with consent and impartiality as well as more coercive rules of engagement, as a moral imperative in large part due to the perceived need for civilian protection (Weiss, 2016). Such changes were indicative of a "UN with teeth," with peace enforcement affording the organization a mechanism through which it could ***create*** the conditions of peace where they did not entail – and where, by extension, human security and human rights were imperiled.

This turn toward an "assertive multilateralism" advanced by the UN Secretariat in concert with major Western powers (especially the United States) was put to the test by the contemporaneous outbreak of several prominent and pivotal cases of political, security, and humanitarian crises – including and especially those in Somalia, Bosnia, and Rwanda. The full details of these multifaceted and complex events are beyond the scope of the present discussion. With respect to humanitarian intervention, each of these crises had a profound effect on prevailing thought concerning human rights and security within scenarios of intra-state conflict and state incapacity – or what the UN's Department of Humanitarian Affairs dubbed "complex political emergencies" (Inter-agency Standing Committee, 1997). These crises also revealed that the most immediate challenges to implementing the "humanitarian exception" through the novel concept of peace enforcement were themselves hardly novel at all: namely, constraints on available and appropriate resources within the UN organization, a lack of political will on the part of key member-states, and the challenge of coordinating an efficacious response (Butler, 2009).

While operations in Somalia (UNOSOM I and II), Bosnia and Herzegovina (UNPROFOR), and Rwanda (UNAMIR) all revealed different facets of the problematic nature of peace enforcement, they resided on a common continuum. Having received a peace enforcement mandate via UNSCR 794 in Somalia, UNOSOM II failed to realize its humanitarian objectives due to its inability to alter the lawlessness and chaos of a failed state. Subsequently, when authorization for peace enforcement was needed in Bosnia it was elusive and partial— resulting in, among other things, the disastrous safe areas policy. Twice bitten, the UN Security Council refused to commit a meaningful military presence to Rwanda, thereby indirectly facilitating genocide.

Forced to confront the legacy of these failed operations and their mounting humanitarian and security consequences, Boutros-Ghali responded with the *Supplement to an Agenda for Peace* in January 1995. The *Supplement* took great pains to downplay peace enforcement, acknowledging the hazards of undertaking such expansive operations given the UN's insufficient capacity. As a result, the term peace enforcement as well as the "humanitarian exception" underpinning it were almost completely absent, with the former meriting only a single mention as one among "many instruments for controlling and resolving conflicts between and within states" (Boutros-Ghali, 1995).

If the *Supplement to an Agenda for Peace* sought to curtail the expansion of UN peace operations, once again events conspired against that objective. Regardless of its intent, complex and profound intra-state conflicts typified by mass atrocity events and widespread humanitarian dislocation continued apace. As such, the pendulum swung once again in the direction of a more activist UN, with four increasingly expansive operations authorized by the UNSC in 1999 (UNTAET, in East Timor; MONUC, in the Democratic Republic of the Congo; UNAMSIL, in Sierra Leone; and UNMIK, in Kosovo). The individual and collective size of the force authorizations (which more than doubled the total number of active UN peacekeepers), as well as the fact that they were all commissioned within the span of a year served notice of another reversal of course for UN peace operations (Bellamy et al., 2010).

The Brahimi Report

This additional about-face was fully codified in an independent review of peacekeeping operations conducted in 2000, in conjunction with the UN's Millennium Summit and authorized by new Secretary-General (and former head of the Department of Peacekeeping Operations [DPKO]) Kofi Annan. Stressing that peace operations were the "yardstick with which the [UN] Organization is judged," the so-called "Brahimi Report" (so named for its chair, prominent Algerian diplomat and UN official Lakhdar Brahimi) asserted that "over the last decade, the United Nations has repeatedly failed to meet the challenge, and [it] can do no better today" (Brahimi, 2000: paragraph 1). In doing so, the panel asserted the need for the UN and its member-states to revisit the possibilities inherent in more expansive peace enforcement-style operations, detailing a number of recommendations for such a revised and robust approach intended to enhance the protection of civilians (Bellamy, 2015). And, while conceding the necessity for discrimination in undertaking new operations, the Brahimi Report identified the top priority for action with respect to improving the provision of a more robust form of peace operations to be that of insufficient institutional capacity.

Perhaps the major contribution of the Brahimi Report with respect to the persistent problem of humanitarian intervention was not the identification of the capacity problem per se, but the manner in which the panel sought to address it. Correctly diagnosing the roots of the UN's capacity problems in the structural realities of its status as a member-state organization, the Brahimi Report sought to galvanize member-states to act more quickly and decisively in responding to humanitarian and security crises with appropriate force through moral suasion. The Report traced a direct line from institutional incapacity to a deficiency in political will on the part of member-states. Accordingly, its distinguishing feature was a direct appeal to member-states to recognize the foremost obstacle to a more expansive and responsive peace and security mandate for the UN – namely, strict adherence to a Westphalian conception of state sovereignty. Brahimi prevailed upon states to dispense with this in favor of a shared obligation to the maintenance of international peace and security (including and especially the security of civilians).

The overriding legacy of the Brahimi Report was this insistence that considerations of consent, impartiality, and self-defense following from (and contributing to) the reification of state sovereignty should not continue to inhibit international responses to humanitarian crisis. In the view of the Brahimi panel, unyielding adherence to state sovereignty not only contributed to the capacity shortfalls of the DPKO and other UN agencies involved in the provision of peace and security, but also had a pernicious effect on the deliberative agenda of the UN itself with respect to when, whether, and how to respond to security and humanitarian crises. Especially noteworthy were those cases in which sovereignty concerns and a vestigial adherence to impartiality trumped considerations of the alleviation of human suffering. In the language of the report itself, "no failure did more to damage the standing and credibility of United Nations peacekeeping in the 1990's than its reluctance to distinguish victim from aggressor and act accordingly" (Brahimi, 2000). Even more pointedly, the Brahimi Report characterized continued adherence to restrictive notions of sovereignty and impartiality as causing a dereliction of duty relative to civilian protection that was tantamount to "complicity with evil" (Brahimi, 2000). Informed by the calamitous failures of UN peacekeepers in Rwanda and Bosnia, the Brahimi Report argued that UN personnel witnessing violence being perpetrated against civilians should be "presumed to be authorized to stop it, within their means" (quoted in Bellamy, 2015: 39). In this, the Brahimi Report can be properly understood as setting the table for the ICISS.

The humanitarian intervention deficit

Following its initial resurgence in the 1990s, support for humanitarian intervention along with the political will and institutional capacity to provide it has significantly waned (Weiss, 2016). Contrary to the forecast of numerous scholars and practitioners (Bellamy, 2011; Bellamy and Williams, 2011; Evans, 2009; Finnemore, 2003; Luck, 2008; Weiss, 2012), the new millennium has been defined by diminished rather than increased support for interventions to alleviate human suffering. Even long-standing supporters of international humanitarian action have conceded that as the 21st century has worn on "...the moral necessity of humanitarian action is no longer self-evident" (Smillie and Minear, 2004). As *Financial Times* columnist Philip Stephens noted well over a decade ago, "...on both sides of the Atlantic, the impulse to engage is giving way to an inclination to retreat" (quoted in Evans, 2006). Such characterizations ring even truer today, amid resurgent nationalism, democratic backsliding, and a tilt toward *Realpolitik* even in the face of major transnational security problems for which individual states have no clear answer.

The evident decline in political support for humanitarian intervention over the past two decades stands in profound contradiction to the many ongoing humanitarian crises that have commanded the attention of policymakers, the media, and the public since the end of the Cold War (O'Hanlon and Singer, 2004). One particularly stark display of this incongruence in humanitarian intervention's demand and supply curves was the protracted dithering within and outside the confines of the UN Security Council over fashioning some humanitarian response to the egregious violence and systematic human rights violations in the midst of the Syrian civil war. As the Syria example aptly illustrates, rationales for intervention in humanitarian crises have declined in their appeal at the national and global level even as the crises themselves have intensified and proliferated (Weiss, 2016).

While the dynamics and scale of the humanitarian crisis caused by the Syrian civil war may be outliers, the scope and causes of the crisis are not. Humanitarian crises triggered by political and social unrest, rooted in contested and/or collapsed state authority, and defined by systematic and violent incidences of human rights violations up to and including mass atrocity events continue apace (Seybolt, 2008). Despite the shift in strategic priorities among many states (and most especially the United States) toward terrorism and counterterrorism, the "facts on the ground" that made humanitarian crises so prominent during the 1990s (civil wars, failing states, climate events) have persisted (O'Hanlon and Singer, 2004). Moreover, some of the critical arenas where terrorism and counterterrorism played out (Afghanistan, Iraq, Syria, and Yemen) have further revealed and underscored the links between strategic interests and humanitarian challenges. The scope and level of suffering and brutality on display in these types of situations, and the recurrent and blatant incidence of one-sided violence that typifies them, makes humanitarian crisis seem almost ubiquitous – a claim that the High Commissioner of the UNHCR advanced in October 2012 (UNHCR, 2012).

Since the end of the Cold War, then, humanitarian intervention has proven to be something of a conundrum. It is a form of international political behavior that has been (and remains) evidently and acutely needed, yet one for which material and political support has been (and remains) fleeting. What are the underlying reasons for this conundrum – referred to here as the "humanitarian intervention deficit"? Why has support for humanitarian intervention within the international community proven so elusive, and provision so infrequent – particularly given the litany of instances in which, prima facie, it would seem warranted? In looking back at the political and discursive context surrounding humanitarian intervention during the tumultuous decade of the 1990s, one can discern the intensification of three major (and long-standing) problems that have long plagued the provision of humanitarian intervention. It is these three problems, discussed below, that individually and collectively provided the impetus for the development of R2P.

The problem of legality

The first challenge confronting humanitarian intervention, introduced briefly above, is its dubious standing in international law (Hehir, 2010). Indeed, the shaky legal ground on which humanitarian intervention resides is largely a function of the long-standing dilemma over how to strike a workable balance between notions of popular sovereignty and the rights of the individual with state sovereignty and the principle of sovereign equality. There is quite possibly no more fundamental debate in international law, and perhaps no other more contentious battleground for that debate than that of humanitarian intervention (Gray, 2018).

The unresolved (if not unresolvable) nature of this debate is on full display within the UN Charter itself (Teson, 1997). One need look no further than the stark contrast between clauses reaffirming sovereign equality (Article 2[1]) and non-interference (Article 2[7]), and prohibiting the use of force in all cases other than self-defense (Article 2[4], Article 51), and those, such as Articles 55 and 56, prevailing upon UN members to respect the principle of "equal rights" for all peoples and called for members' "universal respect for, and observance of, human rights and fundamental freedoms for all." As Henkin (1999: 824–825) notes, while the principles of law, and the interpretations of the UN Charter, generally prohibit unilateral humanitarian intervention, this should not be taken to reflect a conclusion that the "sovereignty of the target state stands higher in the scale of values of contemporary international society than the human rights of its inhabitants to be protected from genocide and massive crimes against humanity."

From this contemporary starting point of legal ambiguity, then, it is hardly surprising that the reanimation of the humanitarian intervention debate (as a function of the renaissance of UN peace and security operations) in the 1990s similarly reanimated questions about humanitarian intervention's legality. Of particular concern are two recurring questions: first, what (if any) entity has legal competence to authorize humanitarian intervention; and second, what are the prevailing criteria (again, if any) by which humanitarian intervention might be considered lawful.

Competent authority

With regard to the first question, it is still widely accepted that despite its flaws, the most appropriate entity for authorizing such action has been and remains the UN Security Council. In the "thin" version of this argument, the legitimacy or competency of the UNSC is a relative condition, compared to the complete inadmissibility of unilateral humanitarian intervention (Chesterman, 2002). A "thicker" version points to the appropriateness of the UNSC to the task at hand. As Henkin (1999: 827) asserts, "…the authority of the Security Council recognizes that the Charter prohibition on the use of force does not apply to the use of force "in the common interest"; it also recognizes that intervention authorized by the Security Council affords the strongest safeguard against abuse of humanitarian intervention that the contemporary political system provides." In large part this stems from the intention of the UN's architects to embed within the Security Council the "competent" or legitimate authority of a sovereign, as well as the evident need for any such action to reflect a collective, rather than unilateral, will (Falk, 1968). Identifying a "competent" or legitimate authority was crucial to, and consistent with, the resurgence of natural law thinking in the post-war international legal environment (Claude, 1961; Nardin, 1992).[6]

If we accept the premise of the Security Council as the entity best disposed to serve as a legitimate authority, we would be well-advised to consider the particular source of its authority as residing in Chapter VII of the UN Charter (Gray, 2018). Like peace enforcement (and unlike traditional peacekeeping), humanitarian intervention involves some component of coercive military force in service of remedial action, rendering it a qualitatively different type of third-party intervention than peacekeeping, mediation, and the like. In this regard, and in light of the shift toward (re)defining intra-state conflicts and state failure and the threats they pose to civilians as threats to international peace and security (Henkin, 1999), Articles 41 and 42 of the UN Charter would seem especially pertinent to humanitarian intervention:

> The Security Council may decide what measures not involving the use of armed force are to be employed to give effect to its decisions, and it may call upon the Members of the United Nations to apply such measures. These may include complete or partial interruption of economic relations and of rail, sea, air, postal, telegraphic, radio, and other means of communication, and the severance of diplomatic relations.
>
> (UN Charter, Chapter VII, Article 41)

> Should the Security Council consider that measures provided for in Article 41 would be inadequate or have proved to be inadequate, it may take such action by air, sea, or land forces as may be necessary to maintain or restore international peace and security. Such action may include demonstrations, blockades, and other operations by air, sea, or land forces of Members of the United Nations.
>
> (UN Charter, Chapter VII, Article 42)

An important wrinkle here with respect to the premise of the UNSC serving as a competent source for authorizing humanitarian intervention is that, like peace enforcement, humanitarian intervention typically involves external intervention using coercive force in the internal affairs of (ostensibly) sovereign states. As such, the legal authority of the UNSC relative to humanitarian intervention must contend with counter-arguments that endorsement for such action must necessarily be provided by the political authority of the state/society in question, either directly or in concert with the UNSC. This is tricky business given the tendency for most contemporary (post–Cold War) humanitarian crises to occur in what Jackson (1993) dubbed "quasi-states"; that is, to be intertwined with complex political emergencies in which there is no functioning and/or widely recognized political authority to confer such an endorsement.

This was precisely the challenge anticipated by Boutros-Ghali in fashioning the concept of peace enforcement in the *Agenda for Peace* (Bellamy et al., 2010).

Returning to face the challenge of consent head on at the dawn of the new millennium, the Brahimi Report elected to prioritize the UN's responsibility to provide peace and security over its responsibility to uphold the norm of non-interference by introducing the notion of "managed consent" (Butler, 2009). Presenting the former responsibility as a moral obligation, the Brahimi Report downplayed the long-standing debate over consent. While consent from political authorities in the target society was not inconsequential, it would be better to procure it ex post facto from some source of authority in the society in question – even if the authority of that leader, group, or institution is dubious in the eyes of some segments of the population – than to delay in responding to a security and humanitarian crisis at a critical juncture.

Not surprisingly, with respect to humanitarian intervention (as well as peace enforcement) this approach to "managing" consent has proven wholly inadequate in addressing the concerns of those who contend that humanitarian intervention cannot be considered lawful unless it corresponds with the will of the effected population. Numerous cases of controversial, sovereignty-defying interventions predicated on managed consent that resulted in regime change (the US-led coalition in Iraq; NATO in Libya), were predicated on support for an aggrieved minority population (Russia in Donbas) or were launched for territorial and strategic gain (Russia in Crimea) only further contributed to the inadequacy of managed consent as a "solution" to this problem.

An additional challenge to the legitimacy of the UN Security Council as a (the?) primary source for authorizing humanitarian intervention stems not from those reluctant or opposed to humanitarian intervention (particularly in the absence of consent from political authorities in the target society), but rather – and perhaps counterintuitively – from those who strongly support it. Here, the case study of NATO's military operation in Kosovo is instructive. With humanitarian rationales residing at the forefront of justifications for military action by the US and UK governments throughout late 1998 and early 1999, authorization by the UNSC was considered secondary in importance, compared to the compelling need to respond to atrocities deemed by then US Secretary of State Madeleine Albright as akin to the Holocaust (Isaacson, 1999). This diminished emphasis on Security Council authorization was largely a reflection of a likely veto of military action by members of the P-5 (Russia and China). However, the longer-term implication of NATO's 78-day air war against Serbia in the spring of 1999 was its revelation of the fallacy that the Security Council authorized effective legal jurisdiction over humanitarian intervention.[7] While the Kosovo campaign, commenced without UNSC authorization, fueled well-chronicled ongoing criticism over the politicized nature of humanitarian intervention, from a legal standpoint it served to further muddy the waters with respect to the locus of legal authority for such undertakings.

Humanitarian exceptions?

A second key dimension of the long-standing debate over the legality of humanitarian intervention concerns the prevailing conditions that might make it actually or potentially lawful for external parties to intervene forcibly in the internal affairs of a sovereign entity. In other words, what are the minimal criteria necessary to render a situation of sufficient danger to international peace and security and to human well-being such that the principle of sovereign equality – and the related norm of non-interference – might be suspended? Here, again, the highly elusive "sweet spot" between sovereign equality and human rights comes into play via the so-called "humanitarian exception."

Making a case for humanitarian intervention requires development and articulation of a set of (positive) criteria which, if satisfied, would justify invoking the so-called humanitarian exception. In this regard, Chesterman (2002) offers a helpful set of "common themes" derived from the literature that help determine whether an intervention sufficiently clears the minimal threshold to be considered humanitarian in character. Three of these common themes are especially instructive for our purposes – two pertaining to the situation itself, and one to the motives and intentions of the intervener(s). First, and perhaps foremost, with respect to situational criteria is the requirement that the ongoing human rights abuses are severe, systematic, documented, and compelling. Though not strictly speaking a legal distinction, the phrase "acts shocking to the conscience of mankind" – employed by the UN General Assembly in reference to the emerging genocide convention in 1946, and repeatedly since, characterizes the nature of the harm(s) necessary to justify action (International Commission of Jurists, 1972).[8] Greater international recognition of basic or fundamental human rights in the ensuing decades seemingly does – or should – provide greater clarity concerning the nature and type of abuses justifying external intervention. As reflected in the thinking of the ICISS, satisfaction of this first criterion may be realized whether the authorities in the target state are directly perpetrating the harm(s) in question, or contributing to a permissive environment through an inability or unwillingness to act in order to prevent or arrest it (them).

A second criterion related to the "situation on the ground" is that, for an act of intervention to be plausibly considered humanitarian in character it must and should be undertaken only when the situation clearly allows for no other alternative (Chesterman, 2002). In this we can draw a parallel between the humanitarian exception and the just war concept of last resort; both speak to a scenario in which the use of force is permissible because all other alternatives short of it have been exhausted (Hehir, 2010; Walzer, 1977). This criterion can be satisfied either as a result of repeated – and failed – attempts at non-coercive (or in the case of economic sanctions, less coercive) remediation, or in instances where the nature of the situation itself in concern with the severity of the harm(s) being perpetrated (see above) makes it patently evident that means short of intervention are inadmissible (Hehir, 2010; Walzer, 1977).

The third instructive criterion for determining the admissibility of the "humanitarian exception" relate not to the situation itself, but rather to the intentions and motivations of the external actor(s). For starters, in order for that exception to plausibly entail, in general terms the intervention itself must necessarily not be aimed at undermining the territorial integrity or political independence of the target state (Weiss, 2016). Yet beyond that basic, if not obvious, consideration, the intervention must also be calibrated so as to involve and employ the minimal degree of coercion and interference necessary to end the systematic and compelling human rights abuses, and to prevent further violations – but no more (Chesterman, 2002). As with the second criterion, there is an overlap with just war thinking and language – here, with regard to the just war principles of reasonable chance of success and proportionality (Walzer, 1977).

The logic is parallel; whether in the short or the longer-term, the intervention cannot meet the threshold for humanitarian action if, in service of alleviating harm, it would instead result in (or seem likely to result in) harm that meets or exceeds that precipitating the initial action, in the plausible advance estimation of the intervener(s) and/or their supporters (Walzer, 1977). Further extending this line of reasoning, the intervener(s) should exhibit a degree of "disinterest" (Chesterman, 2002) with regard to the political affairs of the target state/society, apart from how they may relate to the humanitarian situation. Though, as Weiss (2016) helpfully reminds us, humanitarian interventions in point of fact are almost always (if not always) prompted by a mix of motives, in order for the humanitarian exception to be invoked it would seem reasonable that the humanitarian objective(s) eliciting intervention be paramount (Scheffer, 1991).

The problem of (in)capacity

Debates over the legality of humanitarian intervention notwithstanding, in the view of one leading scholar of the subject, the essential challenge confronting humanitarian intervention today is operational (Weiss, 2016). Irrespective of whether humanitarian intervention is justified in a given circumstance, perhaps the greater constraint on its provision is the fact that no actor in the international system possesses the appropriate resources necessary to do the job effectively on a consistent basis (Paris, 2014). In the words of O'Hanlon and Singer (2004: 79), "if humanitarian intervention were to be conceptualized as a market, there remains a glaring gap between the demand and the supply of capable peacekeeping forces that the international community can mobilize."

In some ways, this deficiency obviates the interminable debates over whether or not humanitarian intervention is or can be legal. Even if (or when) such a mandate exists, effectively acting on that mandate has repeatedly proven to be, and remains, a most vexing challenge. As Mills and O'Driscoll (2010) note, legal debates have in some ways crowded out consideration of what might be the most appropriate and effective methods for humanitarian intervention, and the practical challenges associated with undertaking such action.

One aspect that makes the problem of (in)capacity so vexing is the reality that the actual provision of humanitarian intervention does not clearly fall under the remit of any actor in the international system. If we are to accept the premise that the UN Security Council remains the most prominent and plausible source of legal authorization for humanitarian intervention, then it would stand to reason that some UN agency (or agencies) would be the institutional actor(s) most likely to implement said action, once authorized. In so doing, such action would most logically be embedded within the mandate of some form of peace operation (most likely multidimensional peacekeeping or peace enforcement), thereby making the DPKO the UN agency most appropriate to the task of humanitarian intervention provision. That being said, provisions in the UN Charter concerning military enforcement powers (see esp. Art 43) presume the existence of a standing agreement with member-states writ large to make standing forces available for UN operations upon request by the UNSC, to be dispatched in conjunction with the DPKO (Weiss, 2016).

With such agreements never coming to full fruition (the SHIRBRIG experiment notwithstanding), the entire history of UN peace operations has been typified by a cumbersome and irregular process of knitting together troop and financial contributions from member-states on an ad-hoc, incremental, and voluntary basis. Whether constituted in service of a humanitarian mandate or not, the chief outcomes of this process are three: one, DPKO-led multinational operations deployed directly under UN command; two, unilateral and/or multilateral coalition operations proceeding with Chapter VII authority extended to them by the UNSC; or three, operations carried out by regional organizations and/or "pivotal states" with authority delegated to them by the UN under the auspices of Chapter VIII (Butler, 2009). Regardless of the trajectory an operation follows, the existing architecture reminds us that like peace operations, humanitarian intervention remains a practice greatly influenced by states, either directly or through the intermediary of international and regional governmental organizations. This is true not only with respect to when or if humanitarian intervention will occur, but how it will be provided, and what its objectives and limits are.

There is more than a small element of path-dependency here. While the 21st century is one in which complex political emergencies and humanitarian crises transpiring in a void of state authority are ubiquitous, efforts to respond to such events remain fundamentally bound to states. Even so, it bears repeating that the problem of (in)capacity relative to humanitarian intervention is, as Weiss (2016) contends, chiefly an operational rather than philosophical one. Though we would be well advised not to conflate the two, allowing UN peace operations to serve as a rough proxy of sorts for humanitarian intervention helps provides a grasp of the dimensions of this problem (Farrell, 2010). As of the time of this writing (February 2024) there are 12 active DPKO-led UN peace operations, with approximately 80,000 personnel deployed (DPKO, 2023). Though the number of active operations and associated personnel assuredly varies over time and in conjunction with events, both figures have held more or less constant over the past decade (DPKO, 2023).

This is striking, in that systematic estimates advanced nearly two decades ago suggested that the supply of available peacekeepers should minimally consist of approximately 200,000 personnel, with an ideal of three times that figure when factoring in the need for troop rotations (O'Hanlon, 2004).[9] The datedness of this estimate only underscores the conservatism of this figure, in the process bringing into broad relief the apparent stagnation of UN peace operations over the past decade. This stagnation is, again, at least somewhat suggestive by proxy of similar supply-side problems in terms of the international community's capacity to respond to humanitarian crisis.

Isolating on the purely operational aspects of the capacity problem requires one to take the existing architecture of the international community with respect to the provision of humanitarian and peace operations as a given. From this point of origin, there are two main alternatives for those interested in capacity building. The first accepts the state-centric status quo outlined above concerning the provision of force by third parties in the service of humanitarian and/or peace operations. Accordingly, this approach seeks to bolster and more fully utilize national military capacities in order to enhance the provision of humanitarian intervention both in a quantitative and qualitative sense (O'Hanlon and Singer, 2004). Arguments for this approach hinge largely on efficiency; as national armies are already paid, trained, and equipped, building on and re-purposing existing capacity is considered preferable to starting "from scratch" (O'Hanlon and Singer, 2004).

From this vantage point, the key function for the UN and other multilateral institutions is largely the coordination of command and control, logistics, and equipment provision. This particular diagnosis of the capacity problem points toward a need to recalibrate efforts in the direction of states with significant military capabilities. Existing institutional and political parameters for humanitarian intervention provision would remain more or less unchanged. The appropriate "solution" would largely revolve around efforts to mobilize states with the capabilities to both commit and project (not the same thing) forces to humanitarian intervention (i.e., the United States), to do so more often. Simultaneously, and in parallel, this approach also requires persuading states lacking in the capacity to engage in humanitarian interventions but with the potential to do so (i.e., smaller NATO states, other non-western powers) to bolster their military commitments and logistics and projection capabilities (O'Hanlon and Singer, 2004).

The second alternative differs from the first, in seeking to circumvent the state-centric status quo embedded within that architecture, at least with respect to enhancing operational capacity. Though also falling far short of a drastic departure from the existing international political and legal architecture relative to third-party intervention, this approach seeks to constitute and realize a truly independent standing UN force for coercive humanitarian action (Pattison, 2008). Retaining the basic tenets of UN authorization or operational command, this second alternative does allow for some reform with respect to decisions about when and where to deploy such a force (O'Hanlon and Singer, 2004). However, the main point of departure is a fundamental rejection of the premise that the solution to the supply-side problem with respect to humanitarian intervention lies in further drawing on the military capabilities of individual member-states.

To the contrary, with respect to humanitarian intervention the track record of states with sufficient military capabilities has long been poor – not solely due to self-interest, but also as a function of the orientation of their military forces and technologies, as well as real and perceived credibility problems relative to the target state/society (Ayoob, 2001; Pattison, 2008). Well-chronicled deficiencies of military and strategic planning in the UN, NATO, and major Western military powers relative to operations designed to use force to protect civilians within the context of humanitarian and peace operations only add to and compound these problems (Bellamy, 2009a; Holt and Berkman, 2006). Accordingly, any approach to the problem of (in)capacity that doubles down on member-states has a low probability of success; as such, it seems more advisable to pursue realization of the original intent embedded in Chapter VII of the UN Charter to fashion a standing, integrated, and professional "cosmopolitan force" under UN auspices (Pattison, 2008). Such a force would be oriented solely toward preventive humanitarian intervention, with an emphasis on early and rapid response through improved projection capabilities and technologies. Additional gains in this regard would entail from the standing character of such a force, which would eliminate the need for protracted campaigns of "begging" for troop and financial contributions (Pichat, 2004).

Of course, any "cosmopolitan force" would prove a significant departure from standing practice. Such a concept has been proposed on multiple occasions, and even realized to a limited degree under the guise of SHIRBRIG (1996–2009), but has never received much support from the P-5 or other states essential to its realization and long-term success. Even among its proponents, debates have raged over the appropriate size of such a force, as well as how to ensure its credibility and legitimacy both at the decision-level and on the ground – challenges that would require the force to have some tangible degree of autonomy from member-states (Pattison, 2008).

Ultimately the crucial difference revealed in this potential solution to the (in)capacity problem lies in the very different manner in which that problem is conceived. Whereas typically the problem of (in)capacity with respect to humanitarian and peace operations is considered to be a by-product of insufficient material power, here it is viewed as the outgrowth of bureaucratic dithering. This difference in diagnosis not surprisingly produces a difference in terms of the nature of the cure. Rather than prevailing hopefully upon member-states to dramatically increase their commitments of troops, equipment, and/or money to prolonged and multifaceted UN-authorized deployments constituted by an amalgam of troop contributing countries (TCCs), instead a small elite force might be developed and positioned to act quickly and nimbly to triage a situation before it develops into a full-blown humanitarian crisis.

The objective here being to plug a hole in the international political and legal architecture relative to humanitarian action rather than to rebuild its very foundation.

As Bellamy (2009b: 121) notes, "Though it has become commonplace for UN peace operations to be tasked with civilian protection, much less progress has been made towards developing the necessary capacities and doctrines. It is hard to see how the problem of capacity is likely to be resolved in the short-term." There are, of course, other avenues by which the (in)capacity problem plaguing humanitarian intervention provision could be addressed – avenues which would involve more significant departure from existing institutional strictures and processes. One such approach would be to consign humanitarian intervention provision entirely to individual states, essentially leaving it to the aforementioned "pivotal states" (Brosig, 2019) best positioned and inclined to intervene on humanitarian grounds to do so as and when they see fit. There is precedent for such action, dating back some decades (e.g., India's intervention in East Pakistan in 1971; Tanzania in Uganda in 1979). Such an approach could be seen as an extreme version of the national capacity argument outlined above, and would certainly circumvent the cumbersome operational architecture of the United Nations – thereby reducing or eliminating "market inefficiencies" associated with the existing process of fashioning such an operation under UN auspices.

Still, whatever efficiencies might be had from such an approach would seemingly be vastly outweighed by the obvious perils associated with it. Of particular concern here is the utilitarian opportunism that would almost certainly ensue, as well as the gross manipulation of humanitarian rationale(s) for self-regarding behavior that would more or less negate the possibility for legitimate humanitarian action going forward (Hehir, 2010). Here, solving one problem (insufficient capacity) would only produce other, more pernicious ones. One need look no further than humanitarian justifications for the US invasion of Iraq, Russia's annexation of Crimea, or the rationales provided by various external actors for their engagements in the Syrian civil war for examples. Such impulses and their deleterious effects would be even more acute and egregious in the event that outsourcing humanitarian and peace operations to private military security contractors was employed *en masse* as a "solution" to the (in) capacity problem (Avant, 2004; Pattison, 2010).

Ultimately, irrespective of who the primary actor(s) on the supply-side side of the humanitarian intervention equation might be, operational capacity remains a major obstacle. Further compounding the problem is the reality that humanitarian crises compete with other security challenges for the attention of policymakers and citizens. The fact that humanitarian crises have been pushed down the security agendas of major states and international and regional organizations as a result of the intensive securitization of terrorism, migration, climate change, and other issues in recent years has only further exacerbated the problem of incapacity (Butler, 2019; Weiss, 2016).

The problem of political will

The ability of militarily capable states to credibly signal their willingness to intervene for humanitarian purposes can be vital in alleviating human suffering and preventing mass atrocities (Davies and Johns, 2016). Yet in the words of one leading scholar, the biggest impediment to the provision of humanitarian intervention is simply that states choose not to undertake them (Chesterman, 2003: 54). Whereas the inviolability of state sovereignty is a frequently cited cause, Weiss (2016) argues that this is largely a smokescreen masking the sheer lack of motivation and will to act. Such claims only gain further traction when one considers the many and varied instances when sovereignty concerns were easily cast aside, as reflected in Krasner's (1999) critique of the organized hypocrisy embedded within the concept.

As Barnett (2011) argues, the dilemma with regard to humanitarian intervention has always come down to striking a balance between ethical and political considerations. As a result, humanitarian intervention is often "limited to situations in which states had the political will to bear substantial financial and human costs" (Weiss, 2016: 62), such as the United States in *Operation Restore Hope* in Somalia, or Australia in INTERFET in East Timor (Seybolt, 2008). To the contrary, the failure of the international community to intervene in the Rwandan genocide was in Ramesh Thakur's estimation the by-product of a failure of "civic courage" and "collective conscience" (Thakur, 2018) – or, as the ICISS report would describe it when fashioning R2P, as "a failure of international will" (ICISS, 2001: 1).

However, ascribing the problem of the lack of political will solely to the rational self-interested nature of states and, by extension, the international community they help comprise without unpacking the nature of the calculus undertaken tells us little. A crucial link in the causal chain rendering humanitarian intervention provision "irrational" from the standpoint of external actors is the risk and associated costs attendant in providing physical protection to civilians trapped in a complex political emergency typically involving a breakdown of established social order punctuated by violence. To be effective in such a context requires external actors to take on the provision and maintenance of public security, physical safety, and general social order. Such mandated responsibilities in turn typically dictate expanded rules of engagement (ROE) and the requisite use of coercive force against any parties opposed or resistant to these objectives.

Accordingly, operations of this type require the deployment of significant numbers of well-trained military personnel supplied with adequate weaponry and backed with appropriate logistical, communications, and transport capabilities – all of which, by extension, demand a high degree of commitment and political will on the part of interveners. As Seybolt (2008: 276) notes, "if a government does not have the political will to devote substantial military capabilities and to risk its soldiers' lives, it should not choose such a challenging type of intervention, even if the needs on the ground warrant it. The chance of success … while acting 'on the cheap' is low."

Humanitarian interventions in complex and socially disordered environments featuring violence and widespread human rights violations and mass atrocity events often closely approximate "traditional" military operations in terms of resource requirements, unpredictability in outcomes, the likelihood of encountering lethal force in opposition, and the like. Those actors responsible for human rights violations or atrocities against civilian populations may very well reject the premise that the intervener(s) has (have) the commitment and/or capability to act effectively to stop such activities, in which case it becomes even more incumbent upon the intervener(s) to marshal and demonstrate political will and military capacity and to act quickly and forcefully (Seybolt, 2008). The crucial distinctions between humanitarian intervention and war are the absence of material gains or "spoils of war," in lieu of a more generalized commitment to alleviating human suffering. As with peace operations, the "enemy" in any humanitarian intervention is the continued perpetuation of the acts precipitating the intervention. Thus, by design, the orientation of the operation defaults toward implementing the humanitarian mandate in an even-handed fashion, with coercive force applied with regard to the compliance (or non-compliance) of the parties with the mandate which the operation has been tasked to implement.

To this end, humanitarian interventions entail many, if not most, of the same risks as war, yet in service of attempting to fix all varieties of domestic political and social disorder and widespread human suffering. In so doing they conjoin those risks to outcomes that are not only difficult to obtain, but even to ascertain (Lu, 2007). Even if states embarking on humanitarian interventions restrict themselves to the highly circumscribed objective of staving off major humanitarian disaster – a challenging enough proposition, to be sure – there is little to say that, absent alteration of the domestic and/or external conditions precipitating that disaster, it will not persist or recur (Lu, 2007).

Considering the marriage of high risks, other-regarding objective(s), and dubious probability of success that together typify humanitarian intervention, it is not hard to understand how and why states are often reluctant to engage in such activity. This combination of factors works together to effectively nullify the prospect of doing so for all but a few states with the material capabilities needed to offset or bear the risks and costs. Those that do possess those capabilities (major military powers) are increasingly disinclined to commit to humanitarian intervention not only because of the risks and costs involved, but also due to existing, long-term, and costly commitments (Afghanistan, Syria, the Western Balkans), clear reluctance to subject their military forces to UN or other command structures, and perceptions of strategic insignificance (Bellamy, 2009b; Weiss, 2016).

In the absence of political will on the part of one or more major powers, international interventions with a credible humanitarian rationale will almost certainly suffer from deficient resources (Bellamy and McLoughlin, 2018). This deficiency in turn typically translates into ineffectual operations (Keating, 2012). Yet when the degree of political will necessary to elicit something approximately humanitarian intervention does materialize on the part of major military powers, as Lu (2007) demonstrates, humanitarian interests are typically secondary, or worse. An examination of international responses to politically induced humanitarian crises since the end of the Cold War shows at best a "pursuit of modest moral ambitions within strict political constraints," as in East Timor or Sierra Leone – with authority for such action officially extended by the UN Security Council, but for all intents and purposes dictated by the will of major military powers (Lu, 2007). As a consequence, more common scenarios include the instrumental manipulation of humanitarian justifications for self-interested actions (Iraq, Crimea), or non-intervention in the face of evident and undeniable humanitarian atrocities when strategic interests are either deemed insufficient, as in Rwanda, or too significant, as in Syria.

In this sense, we could conclude that the practices of *Realpolitik* have infused and commandeered considerations of human rights and human security, rather than the other way around (Menon, 2016). However, it would be hazardous to consider the impact of political will (or the absence thereof) on humanitarian intervention provision without taking into account the impact of domestic political audiences as a factor within the intervening (potentially intervening) society. Bearing in mind that myth of "depoliticized humanitarianism" (Weiss, 2016), we must acknowledge that mobilized public opinion is a crucial component in generating national and international support for humanitarian interventions (Macfarlane et al., 2004). In lieu of such support, decision-makers are typically not inclined to intervene, or to commit to a sustained intervention if mass support materializes initially, but later wanes (Davies and Johns, 2016). There is a potential signaling effect involved here too, in that significant and sustained popular support for humanitarian action within an intervening (or potentially intervening) society not only contributes to catalyzing and sustaining that action, but also conveys the commitment and resolve of the intervening party (or parties) to those responsible for human rights violations and mass atrocities in the target society (Davies, 2012; Pattison, 2007).

Here we are reminded that the phenomenon of political will is somewhat ephemeral. And certainly its relationship with the provision of humanitarian intervention is non-linear. As Wallace (2019) has shown, if political will can be marshaled, it can actually offset the constraints of (in)capacity. While concerns over the risks and costs of provision are real, a perception within the public that the humanitarian motive is real and legitimate – best signaled by UN authorization for action – has the potential to outweigh other material considerations in ways that can elicit greater domestic support, and possibly political will, for humanitarian intervention (Wallace, 2019).

Westphalia rules

Though hardly the only obstacles to the provision of humanitarian intervention, the three issues discussed at length here – legal authority, capacity, and political will – have long been among the most vexing. If anything, these issues where magnified in significance during the post–Cold War period, in conjunction with the heightened potential (and need) for humanitarian intervention. As the preceding discussion suggests, each poses distinct challenges on a discrete basis, while at the same time overlapping and reinforcing one another. It is not hard to see where, for instance, a lack of political will could lead decision-makers opposed to intervening to cite legal obstacles or capacity shortfalls or, conversely, where challenges to the legal basis for action could explain why capacity and/or political will to act remains insufficient. We can see evidence of the interrelationship of these three problems not only in the abstract, but manifest in particular cases where humanitarian intervention seems warranted and justifiable, but does not materialize (Rwanda in the former instance, Syria in the latter).

The interactive and overlapping nature of these pivotal problems for humanitarian intervention provision in turn reveals a common taproot: the concept of state sovereignty in its pure, unadulterated Westphalian form. The singular constant running through the philosophical and ideational problem of legal authority and the more practical and operational problems of (in)capacity and political will is, undoubtedly, the strict adherence to non-interference. To the extent that state sovereignty is considered sacrosanct and inviolable, it stands to reason that from a default position humanitarian intervention would have to clear an extremely high legal bar – the so-called "humanitarian exception" – without the presence of an actor or set of actors ready, willing, and able to meet the burden of proof necessary to do so. And, in an international political architecture whose chief cornerstone has long been and continues to be state sovereignty, it makes abundantly good sense that states and their leaders would necessarily devote their material capabilities to the core task(s) of self-preservation, with their foreign policy orientations and the inclinations of both decision-makers and citizens similarly directed.

Ultimately, it is the central animating condition of Westphalian sovereignty that has long been, and remains, the core problem for the provision of humanitarian intervention – with debates over legal authorization, chronic shortfalls in capacity, and weak and fleeting commitments from potential "senders" following from this animus. Yet in the same way that the end of the Cold War revealed both a greater need for humanitarian intervention as well as the major challenges to doing so, it also opened a window of opportunity for re-conceptualizing sovereignty in ways that could not only help facilitate humanitarian intervention provision, but more fundamentally re-orient international law and society. It is to that endeavor, and its translation through the development of the Responsibility to Protect (R2P), that we now turn.

Notes

1 This is a defining feature of humanitarian intervention, which some contend persists even today (Menon, 2016).

2 As Weiss (2016) notes, this was a particularly pernicious problem identified by the ICISS Research Directorate; namely, that during the Cold War the rhetoric of

humanitarianism was relied upon most heavily in cases where actual humanitarian motives were weak in comparison to other, more pragmatic considerations.

3 Defined by the IMI codebook to include the saving of lives, relief of widespread suffering, distribution of foodstuffs to prevent starvation, and the like.

4 Similarly, if one were to adjust the denominator (total population of cases) to remove from consideration those cases of military intervention in which no coding determination relative to humanitarian cause or action is possible, the overall proportion of humanitarian interventions without regard for protection of minority groups in the target state would increase from 24.5% to 27% (273/960), as would the figure for all humanitarian interventions including those focused on the protection of minority groups within the target state, from 28.4% to 31.4% (301/960).

5 To this end, as Bellamy (2015: 36) contends, in the case *Bosnia v Serbia* (2007), the ICJ "...found that states have a legal responsibility to do what they can, within existing law, to prevent genocide. Specifically, the court found that states had a responsibility to take positive action to prevent genocide when they have prior knowledge about its likely commission and the capacity to influence the suspected would-be perpetrators."

6 The explicit attempt by the UN's framers to confer what just war theory refers to as 'competent authority' regarding the decision to use military force on the Security Council diverges from the traditionally statist orientation of international law. However, since the international agreement establishing the United Nations Organization had recognized legal status, and since the principles espoused by the UN Charter concerning the use of force were not manifestly unjust, than in just war terms that body can be said to possess the right to serve as a legitimately recognized authority able to sanction acceptable uses of force and prohibit unacceptable ones. In light of the foundational role that just war theory has played in informing contemporary international law concerning the use of force, then, it seems eminently plausible to accept the premise of the UNSC as a competent or legitimate authority in this regard (Butler, 2012; Chesterman, 2002).

7 Chesterman (2002) offers an instructive anecdote here, relative to then US Deputy Secretary of State Strobe Talbott's February 1999 speech in Bonn, wherein Talbott included the UNSC among a number of entities (including NATO and the Contact Group) that had "pooled their energies and strengths on behalf of an urgent common cause." As Chesterman stresses, Talbott acknowledged the UN lending its political and moral authority to the Kosovo campaign, with no mention of legal authority – thereby undermining the legal primacy of the UN Charter.

8 See UNGA Res 96(1) (1946) preamble. Cf. Reservations to the Genocide Convention [1951] ICJ Rep 15, 23).

9 This estimate was based on *extant* needs of 10,000–20,000 troops per deployment, the typical minimum duration of deployments of two years, as well as reasonable projections of new deployments (O'Hanlon, 2004).

Bibliography

Avant, Deborah. 2004. "The Privatization of Security and Change in the Control of Force," *International Studies Perspectives* 5(2): 153–157.

Ayoob, Mohammed. 2002. "Humanitarian Intervention and State Sovereignty," *International Journal of Human Rights* 6(1): 81–102.

Ayoob, Mohammed. 2001. "Humanitarian Intervention and International Society," *Global Governance* 7(3): 225–230.

Badescu, Christina Gabriela. 2011. *Humanitarian Intervention and the Responsibility to Protect: Security and Human Rights*. London/New York: Routledge.

Barnett, Michael. 2011. *Empire of Humanity: A History of Humanitarian Intervention*. Ithaca, NY: Cornell University Press.

Barnett, Michael, and Thomas G. Weiss (eds). 2008. *Humanitarianism in Question: Politics, Power, Ethics*. Ithaca, NY: Cornell University Press.

Beck, Robert J., and Anthony Clark Arend. 1993. "Don't Tread on Us: International Law and Forcible State Responses to Terrorism," *Wisconsin International Law Journal* 12: 153.

Bellamy, Alex J. 2015. "The Three Pillars of the Responsibility to Protect," *Pensamiento propio* 41(20): 35–64.

Bellamy, Alex J. 2011. *Global Politics and the Responsibility to Protect: From Words to Deeds*. New York: Routledge.

Bellamy, Alex J. 2009a. *Responsibility to Protect: The Global Effort to End Mass Atrocities*. Cambridge: Polity Press.

Bellamy, Alex J. 2009b. "Realizing the Responsibility to Protect," *International Studies Perspectives* 10(2): 111–128.

Bellamy, Alex J. 2004. "Motives, Outcomes, Intent and the Legitimacy of Humanitarian Intervention," *Journal of Military Ethics* 3(3): 216–232.

Bellamy, Alex J., and Stephen McLoughlin. 2018. *Rethinking Humanitarian Intervention*. Basingstoke: Palgrave Macmillan.

Bellamy, Alex J., and Paul D. Williams. 2011. "The New Politics of Protection? Cote d'Ivoire, Libya, and the Responsibility to Protect," *International Affairs* 87: 825–850.

Bellamy, Alex J., Paul D. Williams, and Stuart Griffin. 2010. *Understanding Peacekeeping*. London: Polity.

Boutros-Ghali, Boutros. 1995. *Supplement to an Agenda for Peace* (position paper of the Secretary-General on the occasion of the 50th anniversary of the United Nations). New York: UN (25 Jan 1995).

Brahimi. 2000. "Report of the Panel on United Nations Peace Operations," A/55/305-S/2000/809 (21 August 2000). Available online: http://www.un.org/peace/reports/peace_operations/docs/a_55_305.pdf. Last accessed 24 July 2018.

Brosig, Malte. 2019. "Ten Years of BRICS: Global Order, Security and Peacekeeping," *International Peacekeeping* 26(5): 521–526.

Brownlie, Ian. 1963. *International Law and the Use of Force by States*. Oxford: Oxford University Press.

Butler, Michael J. (ed.). 2019. *Securitization Revisited: Contemporary Applications and Insights*. London/New York: Routledge.

Butler, Michael J. 2012. *Selling a 'Just' War: Framing, Legitimacy, and U.S. Military Intervention*. Basingstoke: Palgrave Macmillan.

Butler, Michael J. 2009. *International Conflict Management*. London/New York: Routledge.

Chesterman, Simon. 2003. "Blue Helmet Blues," *Security Dialogue* 34(3): 369–379.

Chesterman, Simon. 2002. *Just War Or Just Peace?: Humanitarian Intervention and International Law*. Oxford: Oxford Monographs in International Law.

Claude, Inis L. 1961. "The Management of Power in the Changing United Nations," *International Organization* 15(2): 219–235.

Davies, Graeme A.M. 2012. "Coercive Diplomacy Meets Diversionary Incentives: The Impact of US and Iranian Domestic Politics during the Bush and Obama Presidencies," *Foreign Policy Analysis* 8(3): 313–331.

Davies, Graeme A.M., and Robert Johns. 2016. "R2P from Below: Does the British Public View Humanitarian Interventions as Ethical and Effective?" *International Politics* 53(1): 118–137.

Department of Peacekeeping Operations (DPKO), United Nations. 2023. "Global Peacekeeping Data," (30 November). New York: United Nations. Available online: https://peacekeeping.un.org/en/data

Diamond, Howard. 1996. *The One Hundred Hour War*. Pew Case #234. Washington, DC: Georgetown University Institute for the Study of Diplomacy.

Evans, Gareth. 2009. "The Responsibility to Protect: From an Idea to an International Norm," in R.H. Cooper and J.V. Kohler (eds.), *Responsibility to Protect: The Global Moral Compact for the 21st Century*, pp. 15–30. Basingstoke/New York: Palgrave Macmillan.

Evans, Gareth. 2006. "Crimes against Humanity: Overcoming Global Indifference," *Journal of Genocide Research* 8: 325–339.

Falk, Richard A. 1968. *Legal Order in a Violent World*. Princeton, NJ: Princeton University Press.

Farrell, Theo. 2010. "Humanitarian Intervention and Peace Operations," *Strategy in the Contemporary World* 2: 313–334.

Finnemore, Martha. 2003. *The Purpose of Intervention: Changing Beliefs about the Use of Force*. Ithaca: Cornell University Press.

Gray, Christine. 2018. *International Law and the Use of Force* (4th ed). New York: Oxford University Press.

Hehir, Aidan. 2010. *Humanitarian Intervention: An Introduction*. Basingstoke: Palgrave Macmillan.

Henkin, Louis. 1999. "Kosovo and the law of 'humanitarian intervention'," *American Journal of International Law* 93(4): 824–828.

Holt, Victoria K., and Tobias C. Berkman. 2006. *The Impossible Mandate? Military Preparedness, the Responsibility to Protect and Modern Peace Operations*. Washington, DC: Henry L. Stimson Center.

Holzgrefe, Jeff L., and Robert O. Keohane. 2003. *Humanitarian Intervention: Ethical, Legal and Political Dilemmas*. Cambridge: Cambridge University Press.

Inter-agency Standing Committee, United Nations Department of Humanitarian Affairs. 1997. "Working Paper on the Definition of Complex Political Emergency (December 1994)," in *Humanitarian Report 1997*. New York: United Nations.

International Commission of Jurists. 1972. "The Review," no. 8 (June 1972). Available online: https://www.icj.org/wp-content/uploads/2013/07/ICJ-Review-8-1972-eng.pdf. Last accessed 21 December 2018.

International Commission on Intervention and State Sovereignty (ICISS). 2001. *The Responsibility to Protect*. Ottawa: International Development Research Centre.

International Court of Justice (ICJ). 1949. Judgement: *Corfu Channel (United Kingdom of Great Britain and Northern Ireland*. ICJ Reports.

Isaacson, Walter. 1999. "Madeleine's War," *Time* (10 May 1999). Available online: https://www.cnn.com/ALLPOLITICS/time/1999/05/10/albright.html

Jackson, Richard H. 1993. *Quasi-states: Sovereignty, International Relations and the Third World* (Vol. 12). Cambridge: Cambridge University Press.

Keating, Tom. 2012. "Generating the Political will to Act," in W. Andy Knight, Frazer Egerton (eds.), *The Routledge Handbook of the Responsibility to Protect*, pp. 115–125.

Krasner, Stephen. 1999. *Sovereignty: Organized Hypocrisy*. Princeton: Princeton University Press.

Lu, Catherine. 2007. "Humanitarian Intervention: Moral Ambition and Political Constraints," *International Journal* 62(4): 942–951.

Luck, Edward C. 2008. "Introduction: The Responsible Sovereign and the Responsibility to Protect," in *Annual Review of United Nations Affairs 2006/2007*. New York: Oxford University Press, Vol. 1, pp. xxxiii–xliv.

Macfarlane, S. Neil, Carolin J. Thielking, and Thomas G. Weiss. 2004. "The Responsibility to Protect: Is Anyone Interested in Humanitarian Intervention?" *Third World Quarterly* 25(5): 977–992.

Menon, Rajan. 2016. *The Conceit of Humanitarian Intervention*. New York: Oxford University Press.

Meron, Theodore. 1995. "International Criminalization of Internal Atrocities," *American Journal of International Law* 89: 554–577.

Mills, Kurt, and Cian O'Driscoll. 2010. "From Humanitarian Intervention to the Responsibility to Protect," in Robert A. Denemark (ed.), *The International Studies Encyclopedia*, pp. 2532–2552. London: Wiley-Blackwell.

Murphy, Sean D. 1996. *Humanitarian Intervention.* Philadelphia: University of Pennsylvania Press.

Nardin, Terry. 1992. "International Ethics and International Law," *Review of International Studies* 18(1): 19–30.

O'Hanlon, Michael E. 2004. *Expanding Global Military Capacity for Humanitarian Intervention.* Washington, DC: Brookings Institution Press.

O'Hanlon, Michael E., and Peter W. Singer. 2004. "The Humanitarian Transformation: Expanding Global Intervention Capacity," *Survival* 46(1): 77–100.

Paris, Roland. 2014. "The 'Responsibility to Protect' and the Structural Problems of Preventive Humanitarian Intervention," *International Peacekeeping* 21(5): 569–603.

Pattison, James. 2010. *Humanitarian Intervention and the Responsibility to Protect: Who Should Intervene?* Oxford: Oxford University Press.

Pattison, James. 2008. "Humanitarian Intervention and a Cosmopolitan UN Force," *Journal of International Political Theory* 4(1): 126–145.

Pattison, James. 2007. "Humanitarian Intervention and International Law: The Moral Importance of an Intervener's Legal Status," *Critical Review of International Social and Political Philosophy* 10(3): 301–319.

Pearson, Fredric S., and R.A. Baumann. 1993. *International Military Intervention, 1946–1988.* Inter-University Consortium for Political and Social Research, Data Collection No 6035. Ann Arbor: University of Michigan.

Pichat, Stephen Kinloch. 2004. *A UN 'legion': Between Utopia and Reality.* London: Routledge.

Pickering, Jeffrey, and Emizet F. Kisangani. 2009. "The International Military Intervention Dataset: An Updated Resource for Conflict Scholars," *Journal of Peace Research* 46(4): 589–599.

Sarkin, Jeremy. 2009. "The Role of the United Nations, the African Union and Africa's Sub-regional Organizations in Dealing with Africa's Human Rights Problems: Connecting Humanitarian Intervention and the Responsibility to Protect," *Journal of African Law* 53(1): 1–33.

Scheffer, David J. 1991. Toward a Modern Doctrine of Humanitarian Intervention. *University of Toledo Law Review*, 23: 253.

Seybolt, Taylor B. 2008. *Humanitarian Military Intervention: The Conditions for Success and Failure.* Oxford: Oxford University Press.

Smillie, Ian, and Larry Minear. 2004. *The Charity of Nations: Humanitarian Action in a Calculating World.* Bloomfield, CT: Kumarian Press.

Teson, Fernando R. 1997. *Humanitarian Intervention: An Inquiry into Law and Morality.* Irvington, NY: Transnational Publishers.

Teson, Fernando R. 1996. "Collective Humanitarian Intervention," *Michigan Journal of International Law* 17(1995–1996): 323–370.

Thakur, Ramesh. 2018. *Reviewing the Responsibility to Protect: Origins, Implementation, and Controversies.* London/New York: Routledge.

United Nations High Commission on Refugees (UNHCR). 2012. "High Commissioner's Opening Statement to the 63rd Session of ExCom," delivered at the Palais des Nations, Geneva (1 October 2012). Available online: http://www.unhcr.org/506987c99.html. Last accessed 2 March 2018.

van Baarda, T.A. 1994. "The Involvement of the Security Council in Maintaining International Humanitarian Law," *Netherlands Quarterly of Human Rights* 12(2): 137–152.

Wallace, Geoffrey P.R. 2019. "Supplying Protection: The United Nations and Public Support for Humanitarian Intervention," *Conflict Management and Peace Science* 36(3): 248–269.

Walzer, Michael. 1977. *Just and Unjust Wars: A Moral Argument with Historical Illustrations*. New York: Basic Books.
Weiss, Thomas G. 2016. *Humanitarian Intervention* (3rd ed.). Cambridge: Polity.
Weiss, Thomas G. 2012. *Humanitarian Intervention: Ideas in Action* (2nd3 ed.). London: Polity.
Weiss, Thomas G. 2005. *Military–Civilian Interactions: Humanitarian Crises and the Responsibility to Protect*. Lanham, MD: Rowman and Littlefield.
Weiss, Thomas G. 2004. "The Sunset of Humanitarian Intervention? The Responsibility to Protect in a Unipolar Era," *Security Dialogue* 35(2): 135–153.

2 The R2P "solution"

As the international community slouched toward a new millennium, the heady and naïve optimism of a prematurely declared "New World Order" was being exposed. This naïveté was profoundly evident with respect to humanitarian intervention. Continued adherence to a strict Westphalian conception of sovereignty, as well as the tributary dilemmas it spawned in the legal, institutional, and political realms, represented a clear and profound roadblock to any attempt at facilitating more and more effective responses to humanitarian crises and mass atrocity events. In a concrete attempt to surmount this obstacle, the Responsibility to Protect was born. Though R2P's leading proponents have sought to put space between it and humanitarian intervention in recent years, from its inception R2P expressly sought to "embed nonconsensual force within the broader continuum of measures aimed at preventing and halting genocide and mass atrocities" (Bellamy, 2009b: 117).[1]

While it is superficially accurate to characterize R2P's chief concern as "solving" the problem(s) of humanitarian intervention, the underlying purpose as well as the problem it sought to remedy were in fact far more profound. While the Responsibility to Protect was always about humanitarian intervention, from the very earliest its architects and proponents in and around the International Commission on Intervention and State Sovereignty (ICISS) diagnosed the ills plaguing humanitarian intervention (legality, capacity, and political will) as mere symptoms of a bigger life-threatening condition: the overwhelming dominance of the state in the international security arena. Accordingly, R2P sought to rectify the problem(s) of the "humanitarian intervention deficit" in the only way possible: by explicitly seeking to alter the political and ethical relationship between and among the international community, the sovereign state, and the individual (Thakur and Maley, 2015). Accomplishing this goal would, in turn, require a total overhaul of the prevailing notion of both the rights and responsibilities ascribed to all three. In this way, the introduction of R2P was tantamount to a shot across the bow of the very structure of international society.

DOI: 10.4324/9781315105628-3

The birth of R2P

At the most basic level the Responsibility to Protect represents a "normative and moral undertaking requiring a state to protect its own citizens" (Pace and Deller, 2005: 25). In formulating the concept of R2P around that undertaking over a period of roughly 16 months (September 2000 to December 2001), the ICISS considered the fruit of their labors both an important breakthrough as well as a culmination. On the latter score, R2P was in many ways an extension of an ideational movement concerning the principle of state sovereignty and its limits and conditions that had been building throughout the 1990s. Prior to the establishment of the ICISS by Lloyd Axworthy and the Canadian government, the apex of that movement was the principle of sovereignty as responsibility.

"Sovereignty as responsibility" and the ICISS

The ambiguity and tension at the heart of deliberations concerning intervention of all types – and especially humanitarian intervention – throughout the post–Cold War period are indicative of the inchoate emergence of, and resistance to, a post-Westphalian system (Bellamy et al., 2010). Within this *milieu* we can also locate the direct conceptual antecedent to R2P, the ideational notion of "sovereignty as responsibility" (Cohen and Deng, 1998; Deng et al., 1996). The discrete idea of sovereignty as responsibility was itself a direct by-product of the security and humanitarian challenges extant in weak and failing states and/or prolonged intra-state and regional conflicts. Focusing on cases where the welfare of individuals was at risk due to displacement or statelessness, or where a strict adherence to state sovereignty proved to compromise the well-being of citizens, the proponents of "sovereignty as responsibility" – most notably Francis Deng and Roberta Cohen – introduced the concept as a means of highlighting the duties attendant in state sovereignty as well as the rights or benefits associated with it (Cohen and Deng, 1998, 2016).

Out of concern with the dynamics and implications of population displacement in the midst of situations such as the Sudanese civil war, Deng, Cohen, and their colleagues were drawn to the need to reframe state sovereignty as a condition that entails if, and only if, the agents of the state are willing and able to carry out attendant obligations to their citizens (Deng et al., 1996).[2] Simply put, state sovereignty is contingent on the ability and willingness of the state to fulfill its obligations to the governed. Drawing on the notion of the social contract at the heart of liberal theory, sovereignty as responsibility conceded that the condition of sovereignty does confer rights to its holders – including and especially the "right" to non-interference as stipulated in the UN Charter, and elsewhere. However, the rights associated with sovereignty were themselves a function of the ability and willingness of the holder of those rights (i.e., states and their agents) to deliver on the responsibility to govern effectively, fairly, and judiciously and in ways that afford and provide for the well-being of citizens.

Squarely in the crosshairs of Deng and Cohen's attempt to revise the prevailing understanding of state sovereignty was the relationship between the state and its own population – and by extension the credibility of the international community's commitment to protecting basic human rights and security. As such, it is nearly impossible to disentangle the notion of sovereignty as responsibility from concurrent debates concerning the provision of humanitarian intervention, or larger contemporaneous efforts to introduce and promote the concept of human security (UNDP, 1994). With respect to humanitarian intervention, the principle of "sovereignty as responsibility" had two significant implications. First, strict adherence to state sovereignty should not be allowed to serve as a legal and political "trump card" preventing external interference irrespective of prevailing conditions on the ground. Second, sovereignty should not be relaxed to the point of irrelevance, lest those conditions be used as a pretext for abrogating political independence on an ad hoc and capricious basis. Though seemingly contradictory claims, these ideas could be and were reconcilable through the reformist orientation of sovereignty as responsibility – which was an argument for recasting rather than negating state sovereignty.

The touchpoint between sovereignty as responsibility and the "humanitarian intervention deficit" was the overdetermined emphasis on maintaining the ideal of the Westphalian state-system even in the face of contemporary security challenges disproportionately impacting individuals. The fetishization of the state as security actor pointed the international community in two directions, both effectively dead-ends: an inaction in the face of humanitarian crisis born of political and legal paralysis, or action taken arbitrarily and outside the bounds of accepted legal and political authority structures. The consequence of these equally problematic outcomes and the dilemmas they posed were outlined by then-Secretary-General Kofi Annan in his 1999 Address to the UN General Assembly (Annan, 1999). Drawing on the then-recent examples of Rwanda (in the former instance) and Kosovo (in the latter), Annan elaborated the twin perils of either extreme – namely, a willingness to act hamstrung by slavish devotion to established procedure, and a willingness to act without regard or respect for established procedure.

In seeking to rectify these problems and carve out a "middle way" between the two extremes, in September 2000 the government of Canada (at the recommendation of Foreign Minister Lloyd Axworthy) established an International Commission on Intervention and State Sovereignty (ICISS), endorsed by Annan.[3] If "sovereignty as responsibility" was R2P's ideational forebear, the ICISS (co-chaired by Gareth Evans and Mohammed Sahnoun) was its midwife. Intellectually speaking, the relationship between the two was seamless, with the Commission's mandate and efforts rightly understood as a direct extension of the intellectual and policy labors of Deng and Cohen, as well as related efforts embodied in the Pugwash Study Group meetings and the 2000 Constitutive Act of the African Union (Bellamy, 2009a; Cohen and Deng, 1998). At the same time, the ICISS explicitly drew from emergent arguments favoring the recalibration of security policy around the concept of "human security" and the well-being of the individual (Slaughter, 2005; Hampson, 2002; Booth, 1991).

The release of the ICISS' findings in the form of the landmark report *The Responsibility to Protect* in December 2001 was characterized as representing the "prevailing international state of mind" (Lewis, quoted in Weiss, 2012: 103). Annan himself endorsed the report wholeheartedly, describing it as "the most comprehensive and carefully thought out response we have seen to date" (Annan, 2002). In this sense the work of the ICISS was both synthetic as well as generative, building on preceding insights in fashioning a new concept and doctrine intended to unlock the paralyzed debate over intervention, and security provision more broadly. Indeed, it was the expressed goal of the ICISS to subvert the conventions of the prevailing debate (sovereignty *versus* intervention) and attendant arguments for and against a "right to intervene." This subversion was attempted through the bold stroke of norm generation, with the ICISS orienting R2P explicitly and expressly around the obligation of the international community writ large to ensure the well-being, security, and dignity of the human person. In this vein, the Secretary-General characterized the report as a landmark, heralding a "...new equation, with human life, human dignity, and human rights raised above the entrenched concept of state sovereignty" (Annan, quoted in Luck, 2008: 7).

Three pillars, three dimensions

In seeking to appeal to notions of legal obligation expressed in the UN Charter and other international conventions, a chief motivation of the ICISS was to reframe the response to humanitarian crisis, the prevention of mass atrocities, and by extension the promotion of human security through use of the discourse of collective responsibility. From the point of view of its architects, recalibrating the focus on the international community toward the point of view of those individuals rendered insecure, as well as situating the fraught and politically charged concept of humanitarian intervention within a larger continuum of humanitarian "engagement," were crucial strategic moves in the R2P approach (CCFPD, 2001; Cohen and Deng, 1998).

This strategy was exemplified in the "three pillars" approach underpinning the R2P. These "pillars" were first articulated in general terms in the ICISS report, later codified in paragraphs 138 and 139 of the 2005 World Summit Outcome Document, and further elaborated in the Secretary-General's 2009 Report on Implementing the Responsibility to Protect (A/63/677). Each of these pillars individually and collectively extends from and fleshes out the basic premise of sovereignty as responsibility:

1. The State carries the primary responsibility for protecting populations from genocide, war crimes, crimes against humanity and ethnic cleansing, and their incitement;

2. The international community has a responsibility to encourage and assist States in fulfilling this responsibility;
3. The international community has a responsibility to use appropriate diplomatic, humanitarian and other means to protect populations from these crimes. If a State is manifestly failing to protect its populations, the international community must be prepared to take collective action to protect populations, in accordance with the Charter of the United Nations. (A/RES/60/1, para 138–139).

The stakes of this strategy, like its end-game, were high. The ICISS and its chief supporters considered the transition to a post-Westphalian social order essential. Only through such a broad transformation could the problematic condition of strict adherence to state sovereignty at the expense of the "natural rights" of citizens be negated (Teson, 1997). It was this adherence which, in the view of R2P's chief proponents, was responsible both for *obstructionist* attitudes when the need for the provision of humanitarian engagement was widely accepted (as in the Rwandan genocide), and *non-compliant* attitudes when the need for the provision of humanitarian engagement was widely contested (as in the Kosovo crisis). Whether with respect to the former scenario (what Chesterman referred to as the problem of "in-humanitarian non-intervention"; see Hehir, 2012: 32) or the latter, roundly criticized as neo-imperial overreach (Bain, 2006; Fearon and Laitin, 2004), R2P was considered by its advocates as the best path forward in confronting the conceptual and political impasse of state sovereignty and humanitarian intervention due to its reliance on the notion of collective responsibility (Thakur, 2016; Slaughter, 2005).

Having articulated the logical progression of a collective responsibility to protect, the ICISS report also introduced gradated dimensions for implementation of that responsibility: the ***responsibility to prevent***, the ***responsibility to react***, and the ***responsibility to rebuild***. The first dimension of prevention was characterized as the priority objective; as such, while exceedingly elusive, it remains a litmus test of sorts in terms of demonstrating the efficacy of the entire premise of R2P (Bellamy and Williams, 2011; Luck, 2010). The third dimension – rebuilding – was in essence an expanded conception of responsibility that underscored the obligation to rebuild post-conflict societies and institutions in such a fashion as to stimulate political and economic (re)development, a return to (or introduction of) the rule of law, and general stability and security. As a precursor of future challenges, the ICISS offered little by way of operationalizing either of these concepts (prevention and rebuilding), or concrete provisions for implementation. Both the prevention and rebuilding dimensions of R2P represented something of an aspirational goal.

This was decidedly not the case with respect to the second articulated dimension, the responsibility to react (Bellamy, 2009b). In light of the underspecified nature of prevention and rebuilding, the reaction dimension vaulted to a position of relative prominence within the discourse surrounding R2P. At its core, reaction referred to the use of third-party intervention when and where appropriate to respond to situations characterized by a large-scale loss of life or other mass atrocities deliberately caused by the actions of states, or following from state inaction. In operationalizing reaction in this way, the ICISS purposefully harkened back to the long-standing problem(s) of humanitarian intervention, expressly seeking a solution to it (ICISS, 2001: 9). In doing so the ICISS also paved the way for what would prove to be a problematic phenomenon in the longer term: the close association, to the point of equivalency, between humanitarian intervention and R2P in the minds of opponents and supporters alike.

R2P as normative project

Emergence

A primary impetus for the establishment of the ICISS was a perceived need to re-engineer the polarizing and paralytic debates concerning collective security provision and humanitarian intervention prevailing at the time (Badescu, 2011). To this end, R2P was introduced with the express intention of altering the prevailing discourse surrounding intervention within venues like the UN Security Council (Thakur and Maley, 2015). Yet, as has been referenced previously, R2P had a far more ambitious purpose that generating enhanced political support for humanitarian intervention, or beyond that, "solving" the related problems of legality, capacity, and political will. Viewed in broad relief, R2P was (and remains) an ontological and discursive move intended to wrest decision-making authority on international security matters from the clutches of *Realpolitik* by introducing and articulating a prescriptive norm grounded in a reimagined conception of political community and ethical obligation (Gelpi, 1997).

In ascribing to the international community the ultimate responsibility to ensure that states fulfill their duties to their citizens, it is hard not to see R2P as a concerted attempt at norm-building (Glanville, 2016; O'Bannon, 2016).[4] Indeed, the efforts of norm entrepreneurs to elevate humanitarian engagement to the status of an obligation and broaden it to include the prevention of mass atrocities and the rebuilding of societies shattered by conflict – thereby transforming prevailing conceptions of state sovereignty – strongly support this characterization (Bailey, 2008). So too do assertions by R2P's supporters that it is grounded in a universal, enduring, and permanent moral responsibility (Bellamy, 2015).

R2P's fundamental appeal to collective responsibility in and of itself is reflective of the quality of "oughtness" that distinguishes norms from other types of rules (Finnemore and Sikkink, 1998). By extension, it is also hard not to see one of chief behaviors targeted in that norm-building enterprise to be humanitarian intervention. In the estimation of one of R2P's biggest proponents, from the beginning the ICISS was clearly more interested in reaction than in the prevention and rebuilding aspects of R2P (Bellamy, 2009b).[5] Further to this point, the ICISS went as far as to introduce an explicit and specific set of guiding principles or criteria for advancing the determination of whether and when to intervene with military force in response to humanitarian crises. The very fact that these criteria were themselves steeped in the norms of just war theory (highlighting, among other things, considerations of just cause, last resort, and proportionality of response) is strongly suggestive of the conflation of norm-building and humanitarian action evident within the ICISS and R2P's early proponents (Hehir, 2012).

Characterizing R2P as a normative project requires some consideration of the emergence and role of norms in society in general, and in international society in particular. At the most basic level, prescriptive norms such as R2P are concrete expressions of a "logic of appropriateness" intended to shape social behavior (March and Olsen, 1998). Indeed, in this sense prescriptive norms possess significant, if subtle, power not only in defining standards of appropriate behavior but by altering actor preferences and interests. This dynamic is captured by Alexander Wendt's pithy characterization of the logic of constructivism as "ideas all the way down" (Wendt, 1999). From a constructivist standpoint, considerations of norms have more impact on agents and their actions than do utility calculations (March and Olsen, 1998). In large part this impact comes from the intersubjectivity that is fundamental to a norm's very existence, and essential to its perpetuation (Wendt, 1999).

Whereas the internal dynamics and logic of intersubjective agreement are important to norm generation (see Guzzini, 2000; Wendt, 1992), the perpetuation of a prescriptive norm is largely contingent on the constant and continual process of definition and redefinition through (conforming) behavior. Simply put, normative standards rise and fall on the basis of whether agents engaged in intersubjective engagements (sufficiently cumulated) agree that a behavior prescribed by a norm is appropriate or not, with that agreement reflected in practice (Hoffmann, 2002; Katzenstein, 1996; Kratochwil, 1989). As Edna Ullmann-Margalit (2015: 8) noted, "Norms do not as a rule come into existence at a definite point in time, nor are they the result of a manageable number of identifiable acts. They are, rather, the resultant of complex patterns of behavior of a large number of people over a protracted period of time." When a sufficient critical mass of actors within a given society accept the specification of a particular behavior as appropriate such that behavioral change begins to manifest within that society, the social context becomes transformed. As a result, prevailing understandings borne of intersubjective exchanges going forward, between other actors in the society, are themselves changed as a wider segment of the population strives to act in a fashion consistent with a nascent norm (Hoffmann, 2002).

This feedback loop, when it materializes, has a profound socializing effect that helps explain norm generation and diffusion. A significant aspect of that profundity stems from the fact that agents are themselves part of the construction of norms via the intersubjective, interactive process of meaning-making. To the extent that actors in society themselves have some hand in creating (or recreating) the prevailing social structure via the emergence of a given norm, said norm has heightened potential for voluntary compliance. And, once sufficiently established, this self-enforcing character can ultimately lead to reification and, by extension, institutionalization of the norm. At this juncture, the strength of the prescriptive norm is found largely in its unconscious acceptance by the majority (Epstein, 2000). Finnemore and Sikkink (1998) describe this phenomenon within the parameters of the norm life cycle model as "internalization" – wherein conformity with a new norm is reflexive, even automatic.

As the preceding discussion suggests, if norm generation is contingent on the emergence of a proto-norm through intersubjectivity, so too is the perpetuation of that norm reliant on its embrace by norm entrepreneurs, as a means of promoting and facilitating the penetration of behavior by that emergent norm (Finnemore and Sikkink, 1998). Both elements of the process are evident in R2P's origin story. Indeed, the catalytic efforts of the ICISS (discussed previously) represented an initial and ambitious attempt to fashion a new norm. This venture benefited greatly from the strong support R2P received upon its introduction from UN Secretary-General Kofi Annan (Bellamy, 2015). One pivotal example of this entrepreneurship was the convention of the Secretary-General's High-Level Panel on Threats, Challenges, and Change in November 2003.

Annan elected to convene a global summit to consider proposals for UN reform in the security arena in the wake of the US-led invasion of Iraq, using the High-Level Panel to help shape the agenda for that summit. Providing further evidence of R2P's emerging normativity, the main determination of that panel – which included, among others, ICISS member Gareth Evans – was an explicit endorsement of R2P in conjunction with humanitarian intervention on normative grounds (Bellamy, 2015). The High-Level Panel report went as far as to explicitly acknowledge "the emerging norm that there is a responsibility to protect," in the process reaffirming the proposed ICISS criteria for the use of force, and prevailed upon the UNSC to curtail the use of the veto in cases of large-scale violence being perpetrated against civilians (UNGA, A/59/565; Blätter and Williams, 2011). The report of the High-Level Panel also embraced the fundamental principles of R2P, recognizing and supporting

> …a collective international responsibility, exercisable by the Security Council authorizing military intervention as a last resort, in the event of genocide and other large-scale killing, ethnic cleansing and serious violations of humanitarian law which sovereign governments have proved powerless or unwilling to prevent.
>
> (UNGA, A/59/565)

In linking these two points of emphasis, the High-Level Panel report proved to be a crucial step in advancing R2P as a prescriptive norm, and opening the door for its potential diffusion and implementation. The Panel's strong support for R2P on this front presaged an even more significant development along the norm trajectory: the formal endorsement of R2P by the UN General Assembly in Paragraphs 138 and 139 of the Outcome Document of the 2005

World Summit (officially, the High-Level Plenary Meeting of the 60th Session of the UN General Assembly), convened 14–16 September 2005. The language of paragraphs 138 and 139 of that document underscored the international community's shared collective responsibility to protect civilians from genocide, war crimes, ethnic cleansing, and crimes against humanity and to prevent such crimes using all appropriate means (UNGA, 2005). This undoubtedly represented a major breakthrough for R2P. The fact that each of these crimes has established roots in international humanitarian law reflected the intention of proponents – norm entrepreneurs – to clarify and specify R2P's focus so as to render it "narrow but deep," with an eye toward ease of implementation and translation into behavior (Serrano, 2011; Sharma, 2010).

The degree of support articulated by the UN General Assembly captured in the Summit Outcomes document represented a watershed moment for R2P. This was true symbolically and practically, as that document provided a practical legal and policy blueprint for the international community going forward. This blueprint was itself indicative of R2P's refinement into a prescriptive norm with behavior-inducing aspirations (Serrano, 2011; Bellamy, 2009a; Schulz, 2009). The subsequent unanimous approval of UNSCR 1674 ("Protection of Civilians in Armed Conflict"), which explicitly referenced and reaffirmed the R2P provisions promoted by the World Summit, in April 2006 further attests to the emerging normativity of R2P – and its increasingly intensive focus on reaction – a scant five years after its introduction.

Solving the humanitarian intervention problem(s)

Upon its introduction, R2P was lauded by receptive academic and political audiences for its expressed intention to transcend the prevailing paralysis in the debate over humanitarian intervention and, especially, for its reliance on moral suasion in doing so (Melling, 2018; Albright and Cohen, 2008). Yet the immediate focus on humanitarian intervention dovetailed with another, bigger objective. It afforded the ICISS (via the heavily prioritized reaction dimension) with a proving ground for establishing R2P's normativity – a concrete and highly contested behavioral realm for the direction and application of said moral suasion. In this way, the "humanitarian intervention deficit" represented an opportunity for instigating new (or transformed) thinking and practice regarding R2P's "logic of appropriateness" and transforming the prevailing social context around the provision and very nature of security more generally (Thakur and Maley, 2015).

The effort to fashion a new international norm involved far more than a generalized moral appeal for the provision of humanitarian intervention. As will be discussed below, R2P was calibrated with an eye to "solving" the specific problem(s) that impeded the provision of humanitarian intervention. Yet it was the core principle at the heart of those solutions – the effort to redefine the duties and responsibilities of states to their citizens and of the international community to states – that was (and remains) R2P's truly noteworthy aspect.

Overcoming the chief obstacles to humanitarian intervention provision would satisfy the immediate goal of R2P's architects and proponents (greater responsiveness and effectiveness in the face of humanitarian crisis and mass atrocity events) while simultaneously paving the way for a fundamental transformation of the norms of international society. The challenges inherent in pursuing both objectives simultaneously required a "balancing act" of sorts, one infused with a non-trivial degree of pragmatism and compromise (Badescu, 2011).

R2P and legal authorization

As discussed in the preceding chapter, one primary challenge at the heart of the "humanitarian intervention deficit" was its ambiguous and contested legal basis. R2P's response to this challenge relied heavily on moral argumentation steeped in cosmopolitan thought. Specifically, this argument called for an expanded conception of the humanitarian exception – but one tethered to a reaffirmation of the status quo in the form of renewed support for the UN Security Council as the sole competent authority with respect to humanitarian intervention. This attempt at a pragmatic synthesis was prompted by the lessons learned from the backlash to the controversial "managed consent" approach articulated by Boutros-Ghali in the *Agenda for Peace* a decade earlier. Cognizant of the legal issues surrounding intervention without sovereign consent, the ICISS sought to remedy the problem by redefining sovereignty itself. R2P aimed to circumvent the consent issue by replacing arguments over a "right" to intervene on humanitarian grounds with appeals to a collectivized responsibility to act in such cases, one allocated to the international community. In this way, R2P and the "three pillars" on which it rests can be seen as an "outside-in" approach to legal authorization for humanitarian intervention, in contrast to the "inside-out" approach reflected in the concept of managed consent.

The effort by the ICISS to foster a stronger legal basis for humanitarian intervention was undoubtedly indicative of a spirit of liberal internationalism. Transforming the legal foundation underpinning humanitarian intervention necessitated reckoning with prevailing conceptions of state sovereignty in their strictest and most delimiting forms. This particular challenge explains a key secondary feature of the ICISS approach to the legality problem, one which persists in form and function to the present-day: retaining the primacy of the Security Council as the competent authority. This key point of emphasis at the heart of R2P both explains, and is explained by, its eventual codification in UNSCR 1674 in 2006. Whereas R2P was designed in part to surmount the legal obstacles to humanitarian provision by redefining the notion of rights and responsibilities in international society, in seeking greater political support for this venture it retained (and continued to adhere to) the prevailing institutional architecture of collective security provision (Badescu, 2011).

This pragmatic synthesis in response to humanitarian intervention's legal authority problem undoubtedly explains R2P's early traction and prominence.

Though a counterfactual, it seems self-evident that R2P's dual endorsement by the UN General Assembly (in the 2005 World Summit Outcomes Document) and the UN Security Council (via UNSCR 1674) would have been unlikely, if not impossible, without it. In turn, without those endorsements, R2P might very well have wound up being one more addition to the scrapheap of failed idea(l)s in international society. At the same time, this compromise approach can be (and has been; see Hehir, 2010a) seen as reifying one problem (Security Council authorization) in service of attempting to solve another (expanding the legal basis for humanitarian action). Indeed, without meaningful UNSC reform – which as of the date of this writing remains illusory – the tethering of R2P to the UNSC in the legal domain renders it illegitimate by association. This is a position advanced not by R2P's harshest critics, but rather some of its more ardent supporters. For example, in the aftermath of the World Summit and as a consequence of UNSCR 1674, Chesterman (2009) went as far as to argue that R2P was deficient in legal force and weight, representing nothing more than a rhetorical expression of political intent.

Perhaps the riskiest aspect of utilizing R2P in an attempt to provide legal authorization for humanitarian intervention in the longer term is the shaky legal ground on which R2P itself resides. R2P's ambiguous relationship to the most central and enduring concept in international law – state sovereignty, and the related principle of non-interference – puts it in a disadvantageous position, legally speaking. The rootedness of sovereignty and non-interference in international treaty law (the closest thing there is to "hard law" in international law) stands in stark contrast to the lack of any similar legal grounding for R2P in international treaties and conventions. Perhaps the strongest argument for any such grounding with respect to R2P points to its endorsement through UNSCR 1674, although UNSC resolutions represent quasi-legal instruments at best (Scott, 2017).[6]

One common and compelling counterargument advanced by R2P's proponents is that R2P represents an emerging norm of customary law (Payandeh, 2009). As is true of customary law in general, such an argument rests on the presumption that an evidentiary pattern of compliance on the part of recognized and accepted legal personalities (primarily, but not solely, states in international law) on the basis of *opinio juris* is present. In the case of R2P, this argument runs into trouble. The first and most direct issue is that R2P was only formally established in 2001, and only officially recognized as a practice by relevant international legal institutions in 2005 and 2006. Such a short window of time necessarily works against even the (relatively weak) contention of R2P as an ***emerging*** legal custom, in that it is unlikely to have faced (and overcome) a sufficient number and diversity of test cases necessary to justify the claim of customary status.

This temporal problem fuels a second, related one. The short time period of R2P's formal existence in turn raises the bar for compliance, maximizing the discrete importance of the relatively few test cases to which it has been applied. This is not a problem unique to R2P, underscoring the deliberate pace of change evident in most established legal systems (Scott, 2017). As a result R2P tends to be represented (explicitly or implicitly) by its proponents as *de lege ferenda* ("with a view to future law"). This representation is problematic, however, in that a close appraisal of the deeper conceptual and even philosophical underpinnings of R2P works against characterizations of it as emergent. As noted above, R2P's architects did explicitly affix it to existing (and in some cases long-standing) international legal conventions as a means to the end of underscoring a set of preexisting collective responsibilities which R2P sought to uphold and fulfill (Welsh and Banda, 2010). Such a foundation, drawing from established instruments such the UN Charter, the Genocide Convention, the Geneva Conventions and the Rome Statute, proves to be a double-edged sword; while it situates R2P in close proximity to existing domains of international jurisprudence, it also undercuts arguments that its legal weight and force lies in its emergent quality.

Despite representing an ambitious attempt at resolving the ongoing problem of legal authorization for humanitarian intervention, R2P has certainly come up short. R2P remains largely in alignment with the prevailing legal framework that has long shaped international jurisprudence concerning human rights violations and the alleviation of human suffering. As such, and while it may be a point of fine distinction, critiques of R2P's weak legal footing such as those levied above are actually misplaced. Rather than any new or inherent deficiencies, the major shortcoming of R2P in the legal arena was (and is) its perpetuation of existing deficiencies in international law. In this (legal) domain, at least, the attempt to "solve" the humanitarian intervention problem as a proximate achievement on the road to norm diffusion and implementation has yet to bear fruit on either front.

R2P and (in)capacity

Whereas pragmatic concerns with implementation can and do take on various guises, the most significant with respect to humanitarian intervention provision has been and remains a generalized lack of capacity for mounting such operations (Bellamy, 2013; Buchanan and Keohane, 2011). As with the problem of (the lack of) legal authority, the attempt by the ICISS and subsequent norm entrepreneurs to redefine humanitarian intervention as a shared collective responsibility via R2P can also be understood as an attempt at addressing the long vexing problem of (in)capacity and, by extension, as an attempt at establishing a new norm of collective responsibility. In the view of Edward Luck, former Special Adviser to the Secretary-General on R2P, the two objectives were essentially indistinguishable; advancing R2P necessarily involved extending the argument for R2P from what *should* be done to what *can* be done (Glanville, 2016).

To this end, the ICISS sought to galvanize the international community around R2P in order to foster the institutional capacity necessary to deliver on the UN's existing peace and security mandate, as extended to humanitarian crises and complex political emergencies. This intention was clearly articulated in paragraph 139 of the World Summit Outcomes document, in which assembled Heads of State and Governments, via the UN General Assembly, pledged:

> … to commit ourselves, as necessary and appropriate, to helping States build capacity to protect their populations from genocide, war crimes, ethnic cleansing and crimes against humanity and to assisting those which are under stress before crises and conflicts break out.
>
> (UNGA, A/60/L.1, 2005)

As Bellamy (2009b) notes, R2P's proponents intended to shift global attention toward the "practical questions" of how the UN and others might use military personnel to realize R2P. There was, again, a dual purpose inherent in this strategy. With respect to the "humanitarian intervention deficit," doing so would encourage member-states to engage in developing more effective measures for protecting individuals from mass atrocities and threats to human security and well-being. Relative to the wider aim of norm generation and perpetration, the resulting enhancement of capacity building would provide the impetus for behavioral manifestation and reinforcement of the new norm of R2P via tangible and material policy commitments to that end.

Indeed, during the early days of R2P's emerging normativity, R2P's leading entrepreneurs in and around the UN were seized with the question of capacity building. In 2002, the UNSC developed an Aide Memoire, later updated by the Office for the Coordination of Humanitarian Affairs (OCHA), detailing civilian protection measures and used to guide subsequent missions. In 2005, following on the heels of an extensive series of workshops on capacity building relative to the civilian protection mandates convened by the Stimson Center, the UN further intensified efforts toward implementation of R2P (Holt and Berkman, 2006). Indeed, nearly all major multinational organizations and states capable of supplying humanitarian intervention (including not only the UN but also the European Union, the African Union, ECOWAS, and the United States, the United Kingdom, and France, among others) were successfully mobilized by the UN's subsequent endorsement(s) of R2P to carry out full examinations of their capabilities to undertake such operations (Holt, 2005). This emphasis on institutional capacity persisted over time, as reflected in Secretary-General Ban Ki-Moon's (2012) reference to R2P in justifying renewed efforts toward enhancing the UN's capacity for rapid deployment of military personnel for humanitarian purposes.

The attempt to galvanize the international community to remedy the capacity shortfalls long plaguing humanitarian intervention provision was two-pronged. As with respect to the legal authority problem, it drew both from the use of moral appeals to the collective conscience of states and their leaders and citizens as well as through legal and political arguments (re)affirming the primacy of UN Security Council authority. In a recurring theme, proponents of R2P again sought to strike a delicate compromise – in this case, between the opposite extremes of delegating the undertaking of humanitarian intervention entirely to states, and attempting to fashion a cosmopolitan standing force entirely insulated from member-state authority (Pattison, 2007; O'Hanlon, 2004). Seeking a path forward in the face of this stultifying debate, R2P effectively flipped the script entirely – relying on cosmopolitan impulses to structure the argument for action, and member-state participation and engagement under conventional UNSC auspices to advance the action itself.

In light of the provision problems that had previously dogged UN peace operations, and given (ultimately correct) anticipations of resistance on the grounds of state sovereignty and the principle of non-interference, R2P's early norm entrepreneurs calculated that improvements in capacity could only be realized through appeals to member-states. By extension, these appeals would be most effective if couched to provide assurances that existing authority and implementation structures would remain in place. The introduction of the "three pillars" is especially telling in this regard. By introducing a logical progression whereby the potential for external intervention in the affairs of a sovereign state would entail if (and only if) that state fails to carry forth on its responsibilities even with the "encouragement" and "assistance" of the international community, the three pillars proved to be a major concession to proponents of state sovereignty, one borne of a desire to render R2P more admissible from an implementation standpoint.

As ambitious as R2P was in defining and allocating rights and duties on the basis of a cosmopolitan morality, relative to the politics of implementing those rights and duties R2P has proven to be wholly conventional. In seeking to resolve the vexing problem of capacity, R2P's proponents took up the yeoman's task of fostering norm change while leaving the existing institutional architecture of humanitarian intervention more or less unchanged. Maintaining adherence to the exclusive authority of the Security Council over intervention decisions while also avoiding clear-cut decision rules that would automatically invoke R2P's reaction component may very well have been necessary. Indeed, in seeking the buy-in of member-states critical to the actual provision of humanitarian intervention, there may have been no other viable alternative besides splitting the difference between excessive state involvement and none at all. Still, the result to date has been beyond problematic, as the international community's capacity to carry out humanitarian intervention remains woefully inadequate.

R2P and political will

In one leading scholar's estimation, another critical explanation for the "humanitarian intervention deficit" was "the basic political fact that no state wanted to pay the price associated with saving strangers" (Bellamy, 2011: 4). This problem became more visible and more acute in the post–Cold War period, as humanitarian crises proliferated and the possibility for responding to them seemed within reach. Abject failures on the part of the international community such as non-intervention in the Rwandan genocide were, in Ramesh Thakur's estimation, a direct by-product of the lack of "civic courage" and a "collective conscience" (Thakur, 2018). The ICISS took full aim at the absence of such courage and conscience, citing the "failure of international will" in the face of humanitarian crises, mass atrocity events, and systematic deprivations of human rights as a chief justification for the Responsibility to Protect (ICISS, 2001: 1).

The ICISS understood the failure of international will to be largely a collective action problem which could be rectified through appeals to collective responsibility culminating in the fashioning of a new norm of human security. To this end, R2P's early champions saw an effective remedy to the political will problem in the entrapment power sometimes associated with norms and the discourse enveloping them (Risse and Sikkink, 1999). Building on generalized notions of collective responsibility would be a relatively benign way of introducing and socializing states into accepting R2P as a norm, thereby introducing a mechanism to elicit political will for action on the basis of conformity and a desire for perceived legitimacy. Thus the effort to cultivate a climate in which pressure for pro-social behavior and compliance would override material considerations such as the costs, risks, and elusive benefits associated with engaging in humanitarian intervention would serve a dual purpose of cultivating R2P's normativity as well (Glanville, 2016).[7]

Intentions aside, R2P's ultimate effect following its introduction was an amplification of, rather than solution to, the problem of political will. Indeed, in the view of the skeptical Non-Aligned Movement (NAM) and even (though to a lesser extent) early supporters such as the UK and France, insufficient commitment to act in advancing the UN's peace and security mandate was not a problem that an appeal to collective duty could fix (Hehir, 2010b). Instead, appeals of this type would be more likely to result in one of two circumstances, neither desirable. Given the inability of a normative concept to fully engage with the pragmatic utilitarian considerations of cost and risk that so often inhibited states, the more likely of the two was that R2P would abjectly fail in manifesting political will, instead ending up as yet another in a series of empty hortatory declarations. Chandler (2004) saw such an outcome as more likely than not given R2P's unproblematic acceptance of and reliance on the assumptions and values of the liberal peace, which in his estimation made R2P unlikely to attract broad-based international support. Holt and Berkman (2006) pointed to the watered-down consensus agreement emerging from the Summit as a "canary in the coalmine" concerning R2P's generalized lack of political traction and appeal – a perspective shared by Sarkin (2009) and Byers (2005), among others.

The less likely but no less problematic outcome was that R2P might succeed in conjuring up greater political will for intervention– but in a fashion neither envisioned nor intended by its proponents. In advancing a normative argument based on a sense of shared obligation, the prospect of states seizing upon and distorting moral argumentation regarding those shared obligations into a moralistic rationale for intervention (Cohen, 1984) in the pursuit of self-regarding interests was also a real possibility. The result would in this case be a veritable "intervener's charter" providing political and legal cover for the use of coercive force in the pursuit of national interests, advanced under the guise of R2P (Barnett and Zürcher, 2009).

The many significant practical challenges confronting any actor contemplating humanitarian intervention (including a high degree of risk, the prevalence of other-regarding objective(s), and the low probability of success) continued to underwrite the problem of insufficient political will long after R2P's introduction (Seybolt, 2008). Indeed, this problem was greatly compounded in the aftermath of the 9/11 attacks. With the spectacular nature of those attacks recalibrating the security agenda of the international community toward terrorism and counter-terrorism, humanitarian intervention – a dominant issue on the international security agenda throughout the 1990s – was effectively rendered a "tertiary issue" (Weiss, 2004: 136).[8]

As a consequence, exhortations to act on R2P's mandate advanced largely on moral grounds, no matter how well formulated or articulated, have largely attenuated. This attenuation is largely a result of the interaction between the relative diminution in attention and importance afforded to humanitarian response (especially post-9/11) and the long-standing deficit of political will chronicled above. This attenuation is also attributable to the failure of R2P to be widely internalized as a norm, which has mitigated against domestic-level "habitualization" – partly due, again, to the heightened securitization of terrorism (Risse and Sikkink, 1999). Albeit with some exceptions (such as with the Darfur pressure campaign in the United States in the mid-2000s), domestic political pressure in support of humanitarian intervention in those states best poised to act has been fleeting and irregular, and thus not sufficient to override or reconstitute the interest-based calculations of statespersons (Davies and Johns, 2016). Consequently, the attempt to solve the problem of political will and by extension the problem of insufficient humanitarian intervention has led states to adopt an a la carte approach; accepting those aspects of the R2P doctrine they find appealing or non-threatening and ignoring or quietly resisting those they find challenging (Capie, 2012). As a result, it remains possible for long-standing proponents of R2P to lament a lukewarm reception from powerful and influential states and a resulting "R2P-lite" (Weiss, 2012; Macfarlane et al., 2004) at the same time that R2P's loudest critics can point to cooptation by those same actors as a means of justifying unwarranted military intervention (Roberts, 2006; Chandler, 2004).

Blowback: The contentious politics of R2P

One way of assessing norm compliance is through observing demonstrable modification in relevant social behavior (Bicchieri, 2005; Hoffmann, 2002). As was chronicled at length in the introductory chapter, the persistent under-provision of intervention in the face of mounting cases of humanitarian crisis suggests the failure of R2P to attain the status of a norm in international society. This failure is especially acute since, as we have explored at length here, solving that problem was a strategic priority for R2P – an important marker on the road to normativity. In order to better comprehend that failure, the political response of the international community to R2P following its introduction – in the midst of efforts by norm entrepreneurs to promote its implementation – provides useful additional context. On either side of the dual endorsements of R2P by the UN General Assembly and UN Security Council (in 2005 and 2006, respectively), one can observe a high degree of political contestation surrounding R2P – with that contestation directly following from the linkage of R2P to the problem(s) of humanitarian intervention (Zeigler, 2016).

Resistance

R2P as "Trojan horse"

What were the specific parameters of the contentious politics confronting R2P at what was arguably its shining hour? One source of contention was (and remains) the perception that R2P's express linkage to humanitarian intervention makes it a "Trojan horse" for liberal imperialism (Bellamy, 2005). This was a prevalent critique emanating from developing countries, with encouragement and support from countries such as Russia and China (Snetkov and Lanteigne, 2015). Though not without its subsequent particularities, in large part the "Trojan horse" argument traced its origin to the circular and paralyzing debates over intervention and state sovereignty that precipitated the ICISS in the first place. While the mandate presented to the ICISS was to find a path out of this morass, it was clear not long after the R2P's introduction that concerns about infringements upon, and even abrogation of, state sovereignty by Western liberal states remained very real.

The roots of this concern ran deep. Well in advance of its adaptation and incorporation into R2P by the ICISS, the principle of sovereignty as responsibility advanced by Deng and Cohen was publicly characterized by China as a "distortion" and "tarnishing" of the principle of human rights and, more broadly, an attempt to legitimize continuing interference by the West in the affairs of postcolonial states and societies. This point of view was hardly limited to the PRC, and indeed garnered additional support over time (Bellamy, 2009a; UN Commission on Human Rights, 1993). In seeking to forestall this concern, a range of R2P norm entrepreneurs including (but not limited to) ICISS representatives, various civil society groups, and UN Secretary-General Annan undertook extensive efforts to assure crucial states including (but not limited to) the United States, China, Russia, and India of R2P's high threshold for armed intervention. A critical point of emphasis was the commitment to forego humanitarian action if it were "undertaken at the cost of undermining the stability of the state-based international order" (Government of Canada, n.d.).[9]

UNSC authority

A second area of contestation as R2P gained steam in the mid-2000s concerned the role of the UN Security Council and its decision-making authority. This challenge stemmed largely from objections to the assertions by R2P's proponents (such as Annan, and later his successor, Ban Ki-Moon) that as an emergent norm, R2P would galvanize the international community to act more frequently and effectively in responding to humanitarian crises, allowing the UN to more fully and effectively deliver on its peace and security mandate (Bellamy, 2015). The line of argumentation rested on a pair of related and under-examined assumptions. The first was that the UN not only could but in fact ***should*** act more frequently to respond with coercive force to address and alleviate humanitarian crises. The second was that the UN itself was a ready vehicle for humanitarian intervention, with institutional (in)capacity the chief, if not sole, impediment to acting more frequently and decisively.

These assumptions reflected a particular (activist) perspective concerning humanitarian intervention that was ascendant at the time of R2P's genesis. This prevailing mood in large part explains the risky strategy of tying R2P's fate and fortunes to humanitarian intervention. This activist positionality and its underlying liberal internationalist assumptions were reflected not only in the conclusions of the ICISS, but prior to that, in documents such as the Brahimi Report. If they were largely unstated, they were not unrecognized – especially by critics. Indeed, this interventionist spirit at the heart of R2P spawned challenges from states such as China and India (and even to an extent by the Schröder government in Germany) on the grounds that the UN Security Council was a vital political forum not just for dispatching the UN's custodial obligation, but for pragmatically and systematically determining when it entails (Claude, 1963).

Concerns that R2P might serve as an ad hoc mechanism facilitating an interventionist agenda were underscored by claims advanced by Russia (among others) that R2P lacked the formal status and universal authority of the UN Security Council. Pointing to the Security Council's situation in the UN Charter, this line of argument contended that the UNSC possessed singular authority over humanitarian intervention decisions (Rotmann et al., 2014). NATO's circumvention of the UNSC when intervening in Kosovo in 1999, followed by the Machiavellian manipulations of the UN by the US in the run-up to its invasion of Iraq in 2003, served as powerful reinforcements of the view. Taken together, the emergence of R2P as well as the recent track record of Western liberal states *viz.* intervention gave rise to the view (expressed by Hu Jintao at the 2005 World Summit) that R2P posed a direct challenge to the authority of the UNSC, and was an "encroachment" on the UN Charter (Bellamy, 2009b). The subsequent effort to tether R2P to Security Council authority via UNSCR 1674 was a partial concession to this challenge, serving as a measure of damage control in response to portrayals of R2P as outside the bounds of international law.

Rules of engagement

An additional resistance point confronting R2P upon its introduction pertained to how specific (or not) the criteria should be for implementing it – particularly on the reaction dimension. Whereas other major challenges to R2P following its emergence emanated from the BRICS (largely revolving around legal authority) and the Global South (chiefly with respect to the potential for selective misuse), this objection largely sprang forth from the United States (Western, 2009). Particularly objectionable to the United States were any and all proposals intended to foster and facilitate intervention on humanitarian grounds through the introduction of clear-cut decision rules or criteria –criteria that had in fact been included in the High-Level Panel report (Macfarlane et al., 2004; Welsh, 2004). Indeed, the refusal of the United States to allow itself (or by extension the Security Council) to be hemmed in by either restriction on the use of the Security Council veto or the use of military force by any concrete criteria led the Bush Administration to flatly reject the notion of either formal rules or guiding criteria for humanitarian military intervention in May 2002.

In a quest to soften the US position on the ICISS report and R2P, prevalent ideas including French Foreign Minister Hubert Védrine's proposed "code of conduct" for the UNSC (designed to eliminate obstructionist uses of the veto on matters not vital to the security of the P-5 member-states) as well as the ICISS articulation of a set of principles for military intervention largely modeled on just war theory were de-emphasized.[10] Especially crucial in moving R2P over the rules of engagement "hurdle" were Canadian-led efforts to broker consensus at the 2005 World Summit, which ultimately led to an official abandonment of a "code of conduct" in service of attracting greater support from the United States and other states on implementation (Wheeler, 2005). These assurances involved not only reiteration of the UN Security Council's preeminence in the decision-making arena, but also of a guarantee of flexibility in implementation.

The prospect of hard-and-fast decision criteria dictating intervention on R2P grounds has receded into the background as a consequence of the generalized failure of R2P to marshal such behavior. Still, continued reliance on just war theory as a source of inspiration for decision rules for R2P remained in place long after this mid-2000s showdown with the US. (Carati, 2016). No longer a flash point for opposition to R2P, in more recent years the prospect for developing and implementing decision rules, has instead become something of a cause célèbre for R2P's remaining proponents. A chief example is the Accountability, Coherence, and Transparency (ACT) Group's proposed Code of Conduct, which prevails on all members of the UNSC (permanent or rotating) to not obstruct (vote against) any credible draft resolution intended to prevent or arrest mass atrocity events (GCR2P, 2022). While R2P's generalized stagnation means that the rules of engagement question no longer poses a major obstacle to R2P's implementation, its continued resonance is a reflection of the salience it once enjoyed.

Compromise

Confronted by a multi-faceted and variable set of politically charged arguments against it, R2P's norm entrepreneurs adhered to a mixed strategy of moral appeals tied to a politics of conciliation. This strategy represented an attempt to mollify R2P's most strident critics while gradually attracting additional support for the concept, and the normative project undergirding it. Perhaps the primary example of this Janus-faced strategy, as discussed above, was the tripartite logic of the three pillars. The very introduction of the three pillars was undoubtedly politically motivated, and perhaps excessively so in the view of some of R2P's strongest supporters who saw it as undercutting the original intention and vision of the ICISS in favor of an "R2P-Lite" (Weiss, 2006). Similar charges were levied at the 2005 World Summit endorsement, and in the Security Council deliberations leading to the passage of UNSCR 1674 (Garwood-Gowers, 2015). To this point, Porter (2008) has contended that such compromises rendered R2P impotent – reducing it to little more than an inadequate rhetorical instrument, devoid of substance.

While such a critique may be excessive, it is hard to deny that the conciliatory tack pursued by R2P's proponents in the face of early opposition (as chronicled above) had the unintended consequence of emboldening R2P's challengers rather than eliminating its challenges. Even the most steadfast supporters of R2P conceded the strength of R2P's opponents and the mounting strength of their challenges. For example, Gareth Evans acknowledged that the decision to pursue UN endorsement of R2P fomented rather than forestalled political contestation (Evans, 2006). Edward Luck recognized the unresolved tension between R2P and a stricter, "Westphalian sovereignty," leading him to concede that the concern that R2P ideas "might be used by powerful states … to justify coercive interventions undertaken for other reasons is eminently understandable" (Luck, 2009: 17).

As an effort to craft a new security norm – one that would transform the prevailing understanding of moral responsibility, and in the process transfer political authority and decision-making over security provision from the domain of sovereign states to that of the international community – the stakes surrounding R2P were high, and the resistance to it understandably formidable. In retrospect, the biggest misstep on the part of R2P's early norm entrepreneurs in responding to the challenging political landscape they confronted at this critical juncture of norm emergence was not the effort to secure endorsement of R2P by the UNGA and UNSC in 2005 and 2006, or the inevitable diplomatic concessions required by those efforts. Nor was it the introduction and codification of the three pillars framework formalizing and institutionalizing those concessions. Whatever the diluting impact of those concessions, in the end the more significant problem was the flimsy logic on which the argument for the three pillars approach rested; a logic which, in seeking to circumvent the limiting factor of state sovereignty, unintentionally and paradoxically reified it.

In seeking to resolve the fundamental problem of the Westphalian paradigm and the contentious politics it engendered, R2P's early entrepreneurs balanced the three pillars on a dubious fulcrum. That precarious foundation was the argument that external intervention in the internal affairs of a sovereign state and the preservation of state sovereignty are not inconsistent but in fact entirely compatible and complementary (Badescu, 2016). The contention that R2P was in fact a bulwark rather than a challenge to state sovereignty was gamely and repeatedly advanced by the UN Secretariat and some key members of the ICISS. However, it proved to be a bridge too far, especially when it came to attracting support for R2P from key states (Rotmann et al., 2014). Even as R2P came under increasing scrutiny and faced mounting opposition, its early entrepreneurs effectively "doubled down" on the compatibility argument. This was reflected clearly in the Secretary-General's 2009 report: "...the responsibility to protect seeks to strengthen sovereignty, not weaken it. It seeks to help States to succeed, not just to react when they fail" (UNGA A/63/677: 7). Not only was this argument considered duplicitous and implausible by R2P's critics, it ultimately steered the ship of R2P back into the rocky waters of the paralytic humanitarian intervention debate of the 1990s.

This logical sleight of hand, supported most notably by the UN Secretariat, emerged out of a desire to circumnavigate the "intervention debate" of the 1990s (Henderson, 2020). The unintended outcome of this gambit, however, was the consignment of R2P to entanglement within that very same suffocating and circular debate. Having expressly linked R2P to humanitarian intervention – envisioning the latter as an important test case to generate normative traction for the former – it is not altogether surprising that R2P's proponents found themselves trying to thread the sovereignty needle. While perhaps to be expected, such an outcome was nonetheless significant, to the extent that it distanced R2P from the aspirations of the ICISS to resolve rather than revisit the impasse between intervention and state sovereignty. Though these concessions did not sound the death knell for R2P per se, it certainly left it in a state of limbo.

Notes

1 The 2004 UN High-Level Panel laid bare its support for R2P on those very grounds, and subsequent endorsements in the 2005 World Summit Outcomes document and in UNSCR 1674 (2006) only lend further credence to this assessment.

2 Some scholars, such as Glanville (2014), make a persuasive case for this as a return to an earlier conceptualization of sovereignty rather than a contemporary refashioning.

3 The initial stirrings of the ICISS date to early 2000, when Canadian governmental officials Don Hubert, Heidi Hulan, and Jill Sinclair proposed establishing an "International Commission on Humanitarian Intervention." Canada's Foreign Minister Lloyd Axworthy persuaded Annan to endorse the Commission after reworking its title (dropping "humanitarian") to avoid controversy (Bellamy, 2015).

4 As Finnemore and Sikkink (1998) note, norm building typically draws on a combination of inputs, including human agency, indeterminacy, chance, and favorable events.

5 Though the ICISS described the responsibility to prevent as the "single most important dimension" (ICISS, 2001: xi) of R2P, as Bellamy (2009b) notes, the Report dedicated twice as many pages to intervention as to prevention and rebuilding combined.

6 Indeed, as a concept note developed by the President of the UN General Assembly in 2009 recognized, none of the five main documents articulating, developing, endorsing, and outlining implementation plans for R2P – in turn, the High-Level Panel's "Report on Threats, Challenges and Change," the Secretary-General's Report "In Larger Freedom," the Outcome Document of the World Summit 2005, UN Security Council Resolution 1674, and the Secretary-General's Report on "Implementing the Responsibility to Protect" – can be considered a source of binding international law in accordance with those listed in Article 38 of the Statue of the International Court of Justice.

7 Glanville (2016) contends that this is the generally prevailing trajectory of international society concerning issues of human protection since the end of the Cold War, despite some notable and tragic failures.

8 Indeed, in an earlier iteration of this research, throughout 2014 and 2015 I conducted several interviews with mid-level policymakers working for various security institutions (NATO, OSCE) or international and regional organizations with security responsibilities (UN, EU) at various locales in Europe and North America. The constant refrain, or perhaps lament, was some version of this same story; namely, that terrorism had "crowded out" humanitarian crisis and intervention from the policy agenda with, at that time, the rise of Islamic State substituting for al-Qaeda as the primary object of fixation. While these preliminary interviews did not yield useful "data" in the strictest sense of the term, they did help this researcher recalibrate the focus of this project toward investigating the possible causes for the declining salience of humanitarian intervention.

9 This conciliatory tack relative to the relationship between R2P and state sovereignty favored by some of the doctrine's proponents remains very much alive and well. For instance, Serrano (2011) has characterized R2P as an "ally" of sovereignty and a bolsterer of state capacity, interpreting the chief outcomes of the 2009 General Assembly debate and resolution as well as the 2010 "interactive dialogue" as underscoring that complementarity.

10 Here I stress "de-emphasized," particularly with Védrine's proposed "code of conduct" to overrule the UNSC veto. This notion returned to the fore with his successor Laurent Fabius' *New York Times* op-ed in October 2013, and essentially served as the blueprint for France's 2015 Political Declaration calling for suspension of the veto power for the P-5 in cases of mass atrocities (a Declaration currently endorsed by over 100 UN member-states).

Bibliography

Albright, Madeleine K., and William S. Cohen. 2008. "Preventing Genocide: A Blueprint for U.S. Policymakers," *Genocide Prevention Task Force 2008: Addressing Genocide and Mass Atrocities* (8 December 2008). Available online: https://www.ushmm.org/m/pdfs/20081124-genocide-prevention-report.pdf. Last accessed 2 February 2022.

Annan, Kofi. 2002. "The Responsibility to Protect," address to the International Peace Academy, 15 February 2002, UN press release SG/ SM/8125.

Annan, Kofi. 1999. "Annual Report to the UN General Assembly" (20 September). Press release SG/SM/7136. Available online: https://press.un.org/en/1999/19990920.sgsm7136.html. Last accessed 12 July 2022.

Badescu, Cristina Gabriela. 2016. "The Responsibility to Protect: Embracing Sovereignty and Human Rights," in *Negotiating Sovereignty and Human Rights* (pp. 93–110). London/New York: Routledge.

Badescu, Christina Gabriela. 2011. *Humanitarian Intervention and the Responsibility to Protect: Security and Human Rights*. London/New York: Routledge.

Bailey, Jennifer L. 2008. "Arrested Development: The Fight to End Commercial Whaling as a Case of Failed Norm Change," *European Journal of International Relations* 14(2): 289–318.

Bain, William. 2006. "In Praise of Folly: International Administration and the Corruption of Humanity," *International Affairs* 82(3): 525–538.

Barnett, Michael, and Christoph Zürcher. 2009. "The Peacebuilder's Contract: How External Statebuilding Reinforces Weak Statehood," in Roland Paris, Timothy D. Sisk (eds.), *The Dilemmas of Statebuilding* (pp. 37–66). London/New York: Routledge.

Bellamy, Alex J. 2015. "The Three Pillars of the Responsibility to Protect," *Pensamiento propio* 41(20): 35–64.

Bellamy, Alex J. 2013. "Mainstreaming the Responsibility to Protect in the United Nations System: Dilemmas, Challenges, and Opportunities," *Global Responsibility to Protect* 5(2): 154–191.

Bellamy, Alex J. 2011. *Global Politics and the Responsibility to Protect: From Words to Deeds*. New York: Routledge.

Bellamy, Alex J. 2009a. *Responsibility to Protect: The Global Effort to End Mass Atrocities*. Cambridge: Polity Press.

Bellamy, Alex J. 2009b. "Realizing the Responsibility to Protect," *International Studies Perspectives* 10(2): 111–128.

Bellamy, Alex J. 2005. "Responsibility to Protect or Trojan Horse? The Crisis in Darfur and Humanitarian Intervention after Iraq," *Ethics & International Affairs* 19(2): 31–54.

Bellamy, Alex J., and Paul D. Williams. 2011. "The New Politics of Protection? Cote d'Ivoire, Libya, and the Responsibility to Protect," *International Affairs* 87: 825–850.

Bellamy, Alex J., Paul D. Williams, and Stuart Griffin. 2010. *Understanding Peacekeeping*. London: Polity.

Bicchieri, Cristina. 2005. *The Grammar of Society: The Nature and Dynamics of Social Norms*. Cambridge: Cambridge University Press.

Blätter, Ariela, and Paul D. Williams. 2011. "The Responsibility Not To Veto," *Global Responsibility to Protect* 3(3): 301–322.

Booth, Ken. 1991. "Security and Emancipation," *Review of International Studies* 17(4): 313–326.

Buchanan, Allen, and Robert O. Keohane. 2011. "Precommitment Regimes for Intervention: Supplementing the Security Council," *Ethics and International Affairs* 25(1): 41–63.

Byers, Michael. 2005. "High Ground Lost on UN's Responsibility to Protect," *Winnipeg Free Press* (18 September 2005).

Canadian Centre for Foreign Policy Development (CCFPD). 2001. Report from the Ottawa Roundtable for the International Commission on Intervention and State Sovereignty (ICISS). 15 January 2001.Ottawa: DFAIT.

Capie, David. 2012. "The Responsibility to Protect Norm in Southeast Asia: Framing, Resistance, and the Localization Myth," *The Pacific Review* 25(1): 75–93.

Carati, Andrea. 2016. "Mimicking Just War? How the R2P Uses and Misuses the Just War Tradition." Paper presented at *ECPR Annual Conference*, Prague 2016.

Chandler, David. 2004. "The Responsibility to Protect? Imposing the 'Liberal Peace'," *International Peacekeeping* 11(1): 59–81.
Chesterman, Simon. 2009. "Book Review: The Responsibility to Protect: Ending Mass Atrocity Crimes Once and for All, by Gareth Evans," *Cambridge Review of International Affairs* 29: 541–543.
Claude, Inis L. 1963. *Swords into Ploughshares: The Problems and Progress of International Organization*. New York: McGraw Hill.
Cohen, Marshall. 1984. "Moral Skepticism and International Relations," *Philosophy & Public Affairs* 13(4): 299–346.
Cohen, Roberta, and Francis M. Deng. 2016. "Sovereignty as Responsibility," in *The Oxford Handbook of the Responsibility to Protect* (pp. 74–93). Oxford: Oxford University Press.
Cohen, Roberta, and Francis M. Deng. 1998. *Masses in Flight: The Global Crisis of Internal Displacement*. Washington, DC: Brookings Institution Press.
Davies, Graeme A.M., and Robert Johns. 2016. "R2P from Below: Does the British Public View Humanitarian Interventions as Ethical and Effective?" *International Politics* 53(1): 118–137.
Deng, F.M., S. Kimaro, T. Lyons, D. Rothchild, and I.W. Zartman (eds.). 1996. *Sovereignty as Responsibility: Conflict Management in Africa*. Washington, DC: The Brookings Institution.
Epstein, Seymour. 2000. "The Rationality Debate from the Perspective of Cognitive-Experiential Self-Theory," *Behavioral and Brain Sciences* 23(5): 671.
Evans, Gareth. 2006. "Crimes against Humanity: Overcoming Global Indifference," *Journal of Genocide Research* 8: 325–339.
Fearon, James D., and David D. Laitin. 2004. "Neotrusteeship and the Problem of Weak States," *International Security* 28(4): 5–43.
Finnemore, Martha, and Kathryn Sikkink. 1998. "International Norm Dynamics and Political Change," *International Organization* 52(4): 887–917.
Garwood-Gowers, Andrew. 2015. "R2P Ten Years after the World Summit: Explaining Ongoing Contestation over Pillar III," *Global Responsibility to Protect* 7(3–4): 300–324.
Gelpi, Christopher. 1997. "Crime and Punishment: The Role of Norms in Crisis Bargaining," *American Political Science Review* 91(2): 339–360.
Glanville, Luke. 2016. "Does R2P Matter? Interpreting the Impact of a Norm," *Cooperation and Conflict* 51(2): 184–199.
Glanville, Luke. 2014. "Armed Humanitarian Intervention and the Problem of Abuse after Libya," in D.E. Scheid (ed.), *The Ethics of Armed Humanitarian Intervention* (pp. 148–165). Cambridge: Cambridge University Press.
Global Centre for the Responsibility to Protect. 2022. "UN Security Council and the Responsibility to Protect." Available online: https://www.globalr2p.org/calling-for-a-unsc-code-of-conduct/. Last accessed 12 January 2022.
Government of Canada. n.d. "Non-Paper on The Responsibility to Protect and the Evolution of the United Nations Peace and Security Mandate: Submission to the UN High-Level Panel on Threats, Challenges and Change."
Guzzini, Stefano. 2000. "A Reconstruction of Constructivism in International Relations," *European Journal of International Relations* 6(2): 147–182.
Hampson, Fen Osler. 2002. *Madness in the Multitude: Human Security and World Disorder*. Oxford University Press.
Hehir, Aidan. 2012. *The Responsibility to Protect: Rhetoric, Reality and the Future of Humanitarian Intervention*. Basingstoke: Palgrave Macmillan.
Hehir, Aidan. 2010a. *Humanitarian Intervention: An Introduction*. Basingstoke: Palgrave Macmillan.

Hehir, Aidan. 2010b. "The Responsibility to Protect: Sound and Fury Signifying Nothing?" *International Relations* 24(2): 218–239.
Henderson, Stacey. 2020. "Humanitarian intervention and R2P," *Journal of International Peacekeeping* 22(1–4): 325–343.
Hoffmann, Matthew J. 2002. "Entrepreneurs and the Emergence and Evolution of Social Norms," in C. Urban (ed.). *Proceedings of Agent-Based Simulation 3 Conference* (pp. 32–37). Ghent, Belgium: SCS-Europe.
Holt, Victoria K. 2005. *The Responsibility to Protect: Considering the Operational Capacity for Civilian Protection*. Washington, DC: Henry L. Stimson Center.
Holt, Victoria K., and Tobias C. Berkman. 2006. *The Impossible Mandate? Military Preparedness, the Responsibility to Protect and Modern Peace Operations*. Washington, DC: Henry L. Stimson Center.
International Commission on Intervention and State Sovereignty (ICISS). 2001. *The Responsibility to Protect*. Ottawa: International Development Research Centre.
Katzenstein, Peter J. (ed.). 1996. *The Culture of National Security: Norms and Identity in World Politics*. New York: Columbia University Press.
Ki-Moon, Ban. 2012. Responsibility to Protect: Timely and Decisive Response, Report of the Secretary-General, A/66/874-S/2012/578, 25 July 2012.
Kratochwil, Friedrich. 1989. "The Challenge of Security in a Changing World," *Journal of International Affairs* 43: 119–141.
Luck, Edward C. 2010. "The Responsibility to Protect: Growing Pains or Early Promise?" *Ethics & International Affairs* 24(4): 349–365.
Luck, Edward C. 2009. "Sovereignty, Choice, and the Responsibility to Protect," *Global Responsibility to Protect* 1(1): 10–21.
Luck, Edward C. 2008. "Introduction: The Responsible Sovereign and the Responsibility to Protect," in *Annual Review of United Nations Affairs 2006/2007*, vol. 1 (pp. xxxiii–xliv). New York: Oxford University Press.
Macfarlane, S. Neil, Carolin J. Thielking, and Thomas G. Weiss. 2004. "The Responsibility to Protect: Is Anyone Interested in Humanitarian Intervention?" *Third World Quarterly* 25(5): 977–992.
March, James G., and Johan P. Olsen. 1998. "The Institutional Dynamics of International Political Orders," *International Organization* 52(4): 943–969.
Melling, Graham. 2018. "Beyond Rhetoric? Evaluating the Responsibility to Protect as a Norm of Humanitarian Intervention," *Journal on the Use of Force and International Law* 5(1): 78–96.
O'Bannon, Brett R. 2016. *Reassessing the Responsibility to Protect*. London/New York: Routledge.
O'Hanlon, Michael E. 2004. *Expanding Global Military Capacity for Humanitarian Intervention*. Washington, DC: Brookings Institution Press.
Pace, William, and Nicole Deller. 2005. "Preventing Future Genocides: An International Responsibility to Protect," *World Order* 36(4): 15–32.
Pattison, James. 2007. "Humanitarian Intervention and International Law: The Moral Importance of an Intervener's Legal Status," *Critical Review of International Social and Political Philosophy* 10(3): 301–319.
Payandeh, Mehrdad. 2009. "With Great Powers Comes Great Responsibility? The Concept of the Responsibility to Protect Within the Process of International Lawmaking," *Yale Journal of International Law* 35(2): 471.
Porter, Jessica. 2008. "The Responsibility to Protect: A Normative Analysis." Masters diss., University of Western Australia, Department of Political Science and International Relations.
Risse, Thomas, and Kathryn Sikkink. 1999. "The Socialization of International Human Rights Norms into Domestic Practices: Introduction," *Cambridge Studies in International Relations* 66: 1–38.

Roberts, Adam. 2006. "The United Nations and Humanitarian Intervention," in J. Welsh (ed.), *Humanitarian Intervention and International Relations*. Oxford: Oxford University Press.

Rotmann, Philipp, Gerrit Kurtz, and Sarah Brockmeier. 2014. "Major Powers and the Contested Evolution of a Responsibility to Protect," *Conflict, Security & Development* 14(4): 355–377.

Sarkin, Jeremy. 2009. "The Role of the United Nations, the African Union and Africa's Sub-regional Organizations in Dealing with Africa's Human Rights Problems: Connecting Humanitarian Intervention and the Responsibility to Protect," *Journal of African Law* 53(1): 1–33.

Schulz, William. 2009. "Spread Wide the Word: Organizing the Grassroots to End Atrocity Crimes," in R.H. Cooper and J.V. Kohler (eds.), *Responsibility to Protect: The Global Moral Compact for the 21st Century* (pp. 145–160). Basingstoke/New York: Palgrave Macmillan.

Scott, Shirley V. 2017. *International Law in World Politics: An Introduction* (3rd ed.). Boulder, CO: Lynne Rienner.

Serrano, Mónica. 2011. "The Responsibility to Protect and its Critics: Explaining the Consensus," *Global Responsibility to Protect* 3: 425–437.

Seybolt, Taylor B. 2008. *Humanitarian Military Intervention: The Conditions for Success and Failure*. Oxford: Oxford University Press.

Sharma, Serena K. 2010. "Toward a Global Responsibility to Protect: Setbacks on the Path to Implementation," *Global Governance* 16(1): 121–138.

Slaughter, Anne-Marie. 2005. *A New World Order*. Princeton, NJ: Princeton University Press.

Snetkov, Aglaya, and Marc Lanteigne. 2015. "'The Loud Dissenter and its Cautious Partner'–Russia, China, Global governance and Humanitarian Intervention," *International Relations of the Asia-Pacific* 15(1): 113–146.

Teson, Fernando R. 1997. *Humanitarian Intervention: An Inquiry into Law and Morality*. Irvington, NY: Transnational Publishers.

Thakur, Ramesh. 2018. *Reviewing the Responsibility to Protect: Origins, Implementation, and Controversies*. London/New York: Routledge.

Thakur, Ramesh. 2016. *The United Nations, Peace and Security: From Collective security to the Responsibility to Protect*. Cambridge: Cambridge University Press.

Thakur, Ramesh, and William Maley. 2015. "Theorising Global Responsibilities," in R. Thakur and W. Maley (eds.), *Theorising the Responsibility to Protect*, pp. 3–15. Cambridge: Cambridge University Press.

Ullmann-Margalit, Edna. 2015. *The Emergence of Norms*. New York: Oxford University Press.

United Nations Commission on Human Rights. 1993. "Responses of Governments and Agencies to the Report of the UN Special Representative for Internally Displaced Persons." E/CN.4/1993/SR40.

United Nations Development Programme. 1994. *Human Development Report 1994: New Dimensions of Human Security*. New York: Oxford University Press.

United Nations General Assembly. 2005. "2005 World Summit Outcome," UNGA Res. 60/1 (16 September 2005). Available online: https://www.refworld.org/docid/44168a910.html. Last accessed 31 January 2024.

Weiss, Thomas G. 2012. *Humanitarian Intervention: Ideas in Action* (2nd ed.). London: Polity.

Weiss, Thomas G. 2006. "R2P after 9/11 and the World Summit," *Wisconsin International Law Journal* 24: 741.

Weiss, Thomas G. 2004. "The Sunset of Humanitarian Intervention? The Responsibility to Protect in a Unipolar Era," *Security Dialogue* 35(2): 135–153.

Welsh, Jennifer M. (ed.). 2004. *Humanitarian Intervention and International Relations*. Oxford: Oxford University Press.
Welsh, Jennifer M., and Maria Banda. 2010. "International Law and the Responsibility to Protect: Clarifying or Expanding States' Responsibilities?" *Global Responsibility to Protect* 2(3): 213–231.
Wendt, Alexander. 1999. *Social Theory of International Politics*. Cambridge: Cambridge University Press.
Wendt, Alexander. 1992. "Anarchy is What States Make of It: The Social Construction of Power Politics," *International Organization* 46(2): 391–425.
Western, Jon. 2009. "Humanitarian Intervention, American Public Opinion, and the Future of R2P," *Global Responsibility to Protect* 1(3): 324–345.
Wheeler, Nicholas J. 2005. "A Victory for Common Humanity? The Responsibility to Protect after the 2005 World Summit." Paper presented to *The UN at Sixty: Celebration or Wake?* University of Toronto, 6–7 October 2005.
Ziegler, Charles E. 2016. "Critical perspectives on the Responsibility to Protect: BRICS and beyond," *International Relations* 30(3): 262–277.

3 Failure to launch

The political contestation enveloping and entrapping R2P since its introduction has proven a formidable obstacle to transforming the practice(s) of security provision. As we have seen, the common denominator at the heart of the contested politics of R2P was its overt and direct linkage to the problem(s) of humanitarian intervention. The efforts of R2P's chief proponents to strategically navigate that contested terrain only further contributed to the dilution of R2P's impact on intervention behavior and policy.

However, the well-chronicled failure of R2P to enhance the capacity and political will needed to effectively respond to humanitarian crises is merely a symptom (albeit an ethically significant one) of a larger problem. That larger problem is the failure of R2P to launch as a new global norm of and for security provision. The underlying causes of this more fundamental failure of R2P to attain normative status have largely been overlooked even by scholars who acknowledge and accept its broader normative aspirations (Labonte, 2016; Paris, 2014). As a continued consequence of its sustained and close association with humanitarian intervention, much of the discourse surrounding R2P and its success or failure continues to turn on its ability (or inability) to meaningfully alter the dynamic of reaction and response to humanitarian crisis events. Yet, as was discussed previously, R2P was not solely or primarily intended to serve as a solution to the problem(s) of humanitarian intervention. Rather, solving that problem was envisioned as a positive externality that would follow from satisfying the larger objective of introducing a new norm of and for security provision, one steeped in the concept of human security.

The prevailing tendency to assess R2P on the limited basis of its influence (or lack thereof) on the provision of humanitarian intervention makes sense on one level, given the close association forged between the two by many of R2P's proponents. Yet assessing R2P solely on these more limited grounds is problematic for two main reasons. Firstly, this approach to assessment has spawned a series of grossly distorted representations of R2P's relationship with humanitarian intervention – called out here as false narratives attempting to explain away the negative consequences of linking (equating?) R2P and humanitarian intervention. Secondly, assessing R2P on this limited basis perpetuates the notion that R2P was and is entirely consumed with facilitating humanitarian

DOI: 10.4324/9781315105628-4

intervention, thereby impeding an honest appraisal of R2P's failure to achieve its larger aim: launching a new global norm for security provision.

In service of just such an appraisal, this chapter adopts a sociological perspective that takes into account the ideational parameters of R2P as well as the social context in which it was launched. Specifically, I employ a modified version of Finnemore and Sikkink's (1998) norm life-cycle model to critically examine the attempt to advance R2P as a new security norm. This heuristic device provides unique insight into the failure of R2P as a normative project. It reveals the fundamental cause of that failure in the form of a dynamic characterized here as "norm stagnation" – a dynamic that was in turn driven chiefly by R2P's narrow behavioral scope and cultural bias. This dynamic of norm stagnation stands in stark contrast to prevailing theoretical assumptions about the progressive development of new norms, and provides significant explanatory power with respect to the inability of R2P to diffuse within international society following its introduction.

False narratives

As the attempt at promoting R2P as a corrective to the problem(s) of humanitarian intervention unraveled, two distinct – and distinctly false – explanatory narratives for that unraveling have emerged. Both are grounded in reasonable interpretations of R2P's inability to refashion thinking and practice concerning humanitarian intervention and security provision more generally. However, their treatment of the role that the R2P/humanitarian intervention nexus played in stunting R2P's growth is both misleading with respect to that nexus, and problematic with respect to the more fundamental failure of R2P to attain normative status.

The non-interference negation

The first of these narratives is advanced by those prone to characterize R2P's failure as proof that its reaction component was a "bridge too far." From the outset R2P's opponents were quick to deride it as a breach to the long-standing norm of non-interference and an unacceptable usurpation of sovereignty by the international community. Framing the intersection of reaction and the third pillar as a gateway to rampant liberal interventionism, R2P has subsequently been portrayed as a consequential threat to the organizing principle of state sovereignty. Curiously, this retrospective representation of R2P has emanated both from those clinging to the legacy of Westphalia and a desire to maintain the state-centric status quo (Luttwak, 1999) as well as those concerned with the neo-colonial impulses that could be unleashed by looser rules concerning humanitarian intervention (Ayoob, 2002). Either way, according to this narrative, R2P's link to humanitarian intervention rendered it a dangerous overreach, such that its failure was inevitable.

I lend this narrative a convenient shorthand: the *non-interference negation*. Although it has variable permutations and translations, in general this account turns on the purported threat that a looser approach to humanitarian intervention under the guise of R2P represents to the international normative and legal principle of non-interference. This logic is best reflected in the persistence of the "trojan horse" argument referenced previously. Channeling the ghost of E.H. Carr (1939), the non-interference negation frames R2P as a dangerous contemporary manifestation of utopian idealism, marked by a fundamental incompatibility with prevailing social mores as well as a colossal hubris. Similar to Carr's critique of the League of Nations, this representation of R2P characterizes it as an exercise in liberal triumphalism that has created more problems in its aftermath than existed prior to its introduction – with rampant interventionism the tip of the proverbial spear.

Specific to its ties to humanitarian intervention, the non-interference negation contends that R2P has failed to transform security provision because it heightens the prospect for widespread interference in the affairs of sovereign states by opaque, non-democratic international institutions. Such institutions, overtly influenced by Western liberal states, act in the security arena to serve the interests of a small subset of powerful states and elites, relying heavily on moralizing language and rationales in the process. At the very heart of this rebuke of R2P is the conviction that externally generated claims on the authority to intervene forcibly to address humanitarian crisis are excessive, likely to generate negative externalities that undermine the intention to alleviate the crisis, and – most fundamentally – are ethically and legally dubious (Busser, 2019). From this vantage point, as a corrective to the problem(s) of humanitarian intervention, R2P's chief problem is one of excess – that is, too much, too soon.

There is more than a kernel of truth in the criticism inherent in the "non-interference negation" narrative. Certainly R2P's chief entrepreneurs sought to circumvent the stalemated politics of humanitarian crisis defining the international political landscape. However, a retrospective rendering of R2P's failure based on the claim that it was (and is) a dangerous overreach and a means to the end of the total demise of the principle of non-interference is baseless even in light of R2P's original scope, and certainly given its recalibration back toward the Westphalian status quo shortly after its introduction. If anything, with respect to the competing principles of intervention and state sovereignty R2P has over time tacked toward the latter. In this way, the major negative consequence for R2P resulting from its close association with humanitarian intervention is that it has respected the dictates of state sovereignty too much rather than too little (Weiss, 2004).

The revisionist reclamation

The second prevailing narrative regarding the consequences of the close association of R2P with humanitarian intervention emanates not from R2P's critics, but rather its proponents. This narrative is centered around the assertion that R2P is not and never was solely or even primarily concerned with enhancing the international community's capacity and willingness to intervene in order to arrest or alleviate humanitarian crisis. Characterized here as the *revisionist reclamation*, this narrative posits that since R2P was never intended to serve as a means of facilitating humanitarian intervention, its impact cannot and should not be assessed on the basis of whether or not it has.

Prompted by a continuing incapacity and unwillingness on the part of the international community writ large to intervene in humanitarian crisis, this revisionist narrative seeks to salvage R2P by retroactively decoupling it from humanitarian intervention altogether (Chandler, 2015). Advanced by some of R2P's most ardent supporters, this effort largely hinges on de-emphasizing the third pillar responsibilities of the international community, an effort led by Ban Ki-Moon during his tenure as UN Secretary-General (Hehir, 2019; Weiss, 2016). While this revisionist narrative has many and varied translations, all draw from the same wellspring of denial. They cohere around the contention that R2P's overall impact has been significant, and is independent of the under-provision of humanitarian intervention or Security Council disaffection (Welsh, 2015, 2016). From this perspective, seemingly any development related to R2P can be interpreted in a positive light. For example, the absence of an effort by states that have consistently been critical of R2P (including those in the Global South) to fundamentally renegotiate the terms of R2P reflects acceptance of the concept rather than pervasive indifference (Bellamy, 2015).

The revisionist reclamation contends that R2P has had such a demonstrable impact on security thinking and practice that we might even contemplate the prospect of an "R2P regime" (Orchard, 2020). However, this narrative representation also hinges on the premise that R2P be assessed on the basis of its preventative emphasis, concern with shoring up state capacity and effective governance, and/or its attendant notions of collective responsibility. In turn, we are asked to dispense with considerations of R2P's reaction dimension and, by extension, its woefully inadequate impact on humanitarian intervention. Doing so allows us to better appreciate what is alleged to be R2P's indirect yet profound impact. In this way, the revisionist treatment effectively recasts R2P as a "ghost in the machine" (Ryle, 1949).

Some versions of this narrative have proven to be notably unsubtle, selectively framing instances where R2P has manifestly failed to elicit a response from the international community to humanitarian crises as success stories. One such *apologia in extremis* is the contention that R2P's influence is positively reflected in the international community's failure to discharge its responsibility to protect in Syria (Glanville, 2016). According to this argument, while "deeply regrettable," this abject failure still allegedly reaffirms R2P via the excuses provided by states for their refusal to act, the condemnations of Chinese and Russian opposition to UN intervention on the Security Council, and in the overstatement of the impact of the minimal humanitarian efforts they have undertaken (Glanville, 2016). These behaviors allegedly demonstrate that "states thus recognize that the R2P norm matters, and that they need to justify, excuse, or shift blame for its violation" (Glanville, 2016: 185).[1]

Apart from the logical jujitsu involved, the fact that this revisionist reclamation tilts toward apologia such as these have emerged reveals just how vital and relevant the link between R2P and humanitarian intervention remains. Nearly two decades after R2P's endorsement by the UN, the fact that many of its leading supporters remain concerned with humanitarian intervention (even if only to deny its importance) ironically supports the claim that the close association of the two has had a significant, and significantly negative, impact on R2P's normative trajectory. Even if, as former Special Representative Jennifer Welsh (2010) presciently noted well over a decade ago, the principle of sovereign equality is "enjoying a comeback" (Welsh, 2010) this hardly justifies a revisionist decoupling of R2P and humanitarian intervention. Indeed, such revisionism blinds us from an honest appraisal of the roots of R2P's larger failure as a normative enterprise.

Though emanating from different ontological starting points, these retrospective narratives concerning the failure of R2P to elicit more and better responses to humanitarian crisis are essentially two sides of the same coin. Each misrepresents the profound (negative) implications of linking R2P to the persistent problem(s) of humanitarian intervention. These misrepresentations are grounded in each narrative's ideological positionality relative to global governance and intervention. Neither allows for sober and systematic appraisal of the prevailing societal context in which R2P was launched, and the ways in which mounting resistance to the prospect of third-party intervention also derailed the larger aim for R2P: advancing a new global security norm.

Revisiting the norm life cycle

To this point the problems associated with the decision to explicitly tie R2P to humanitarian intervention as a means of launching it have been considered from a political-legal standpoint. In light of the fact that R2P was, at base, an attempt at fashioning a new norm of responsibility in international society we would also be well-served to consider it from a broader sociological perspective as well. The process by which R2P was conceived as well as the approach employed in promoting it, documented in the preceding chapters, are revealing. Together they suggest that the social environment into which R2P was introduced resembled something much closer to a "thin" pluralist-positivist international society of states rather than a solidarist or cosmopolitan social order (Kaldor, 2003; Falk, 1995; Bull, 1977). Accordingly, the success of R2P as a norm-building enterprise hinged on the degree to which prominent states embraced the concept and its underlying norms. In light of all this, a closer investigation of the contested normative space surrounding R2P and the factor(s) that explain its failure to progress along the norm life cycle (Finnemore and Sikkink, 1998) and diffuse through the international society of states is essential.

The norm life cycle

The norm life-cycle model outlines an evolutionary journey of norm development characterized by three sequential and linked stages: emergence, cascade, and internalization (Finnemore and Sikkink, 1998). The emergent stage is one in which norm entrepreneurs actively supply and promote new or different ideas about appropriate behavior. Norm entrepreneurs often utilize an existing organizational or institutional platform in this process, as a way of conferring greater perceived legitimacy on their ideas (Finnemore and Sikkink, 1998). The ultimate aim is to persuade other agents to accept the idea in question and to adjust their understanding and behavior accordingly (Hoffmann, 2002). When that critical mass of receptive agents is reached, and the "logic of appropriateness" (March and Olsen, 1998) has shifted accordingly, a new norm can be said to have emerged.

According to the model, this emergence seamlessly triggers the second stage of the norm life cycle: the cascade. As the acceptance of a new norm increases, and that acceptance extends beyond the critical mass of initial proponents and adherents, the norm "cascades" throughout society – diffusing widely and rapidly on the order of a contagion (Finnemore and Sikkink, 1998: 902). From here, the momentum carries the norm through the third and final stage of the life cycle: internalization, wherein the norm becomes deeply ingrained within society at-large and among its constituent members, such that it is reflexively accepted, and behavioral conformity with its prescriptions (or proscriptions) is rarely questioned. Acceptance of the norm as well as its influence on behavior become in some sense unconscious, as an externally generated idea becomes embedded within domestic society(-ies).

Given its internal logic, the norm life-cycle model itself is also in some sense unconscious. As Hoffmann (2002) points out, the norm life cycle is fundamentally evolutionary in nature, if implicitly so. Consider, for example, the presumption in the model that upon reaching a "tipping point," an emergent norm will necessarily cascade through the international society of states and become internalized within domestic societies (Harrison, 2004). As defined by Finnemore and Sikkink (1998), the tipping point is a crucial threshold, serving as the gateway for a new norm to redefine social behavior. For a new norm to pass this threshold requires it to satisfy two conditions: one, that it attract a "critical mass" of support from a sufficient number of states in the system (they posit one-third); and two, that it be embraced by an issue-specific subset of "critical states," or those states without whom achievement of the substantive goals attendant in the norm-shift would be compromised (Finnemore and Sikkink, 1998). As they envision it:

> what happens at the tipping point is that enough states and enough critical states endorse the new norm to redefine appropriate behavior for the identity called 'state' or some relevant subset of states
>
> (Finnemore and Sikkink, 1998: 902)

Norm stagnation

Although the norm life-cycle model serves as a cornerstone in the conceptual bedrock of constructivist IR, relatively few scholars have critically investigated interruptions or disruptions to it, or their causes. This is problematic, since as the originators of the norm life-cycle model themselves contend, "new norms never enter a normative vacuum but instead emerge in a highly contested normative space where they must compete with other norms and perceptions of interest" (Finnemore and Sikkink, 1998: 897). While the burgeoning constructivist literature in IR has been populated by explanations for norm creation and diffusion (for early and more recent examples, see Bettiza and Dionigi, 2015; Payne, 2001), there remains a "profound theoretical and empirical gap concerning the dynamics of and conditions for the degeneration of international norms" (Panke and Petersohn, 2012). While the progenitors of the norm life-cycle model themselves acknowledged the possibility of emergent norms falling short of "maturity"; that is, failing to cascade and become internalized (Finnemore and Sikkink, 1998: 895), relatively little attention has been paid to the potential factors causing this to occur. This is, itself, a reflection of a troubling degree of non-reflexivity.

The under-specification of the norm life-cycle model in this regard has helped reinforce the belief that norm diffusion is a commonplace and unproblematic process, one that necessarily unfolds along a progressive trajectory (Krook and True, 2012; McKeown, 2009; Harrison, 2004). This line of critique identified an unconscious trend within the constructivist literature to treat norms as *extant* phenomena and their development as linear. Uncritically accepting this assumption is perilous, both from the standpoint of assessing the status of R2P as a normative enterprise as well as for appraisal of the logic and utility of the norm life-cycle model more generally.

The clear inability of R2P to attain normative status in international society begs critical reconsideration of the norm life-cycle model, its internal logic, and the implications of that logic across its three component stages. To that end, I propose a corrective in the form of the concept of norm stagnation. As a theoretical notion, norm stagnation not only helps us to better understand the failure of R2P as a norm, but also suggests a corrective to the non-reflexive positivist ontology underpinning the norm life-cycle model and constructivist IR more generally (Sterling-Folker, 2000). As noted above, the norm life-cycle model implicitly presumes the progression of an emergent norm through the second (cascade) and third (internalization) phases of the model once it has crossed the requisite threshold or "tipping point." And, as was also noted above, the bulk of the heavy lifting in terms of the genesis and perpetuation of a nascent norm is done by norm entrepreneurs at the emergent stage. The concept of norm stagnation acknowledges the prospect of some degree of friction borne of social and political resistance to a nascent norm. Importantly, this friction can and does occur even after a sufficient number of suitably influential agents in society have accepted and embraced it – but, crucially, before that emergent norm becomes ubiquitous and unconsciously accepted.

In that way, the theoretical notion of norm stagnation is of a piece with other, similar process-oriented critiques of the norm life-cycle model grounded in adjacent concepts such as "norm regress" (McKeown, 2009), "norm degeneration" (Panke and Petersohn, 2012), and "norm circulation" (Acharya, 2015). These concepts share the present assumption that procession of an idea along the norm life-cycle model's trajectory is hardly automatic (Bloomfield and Scott, 2016; Krook and True, 2012). These critiques similarly challenge the self-perpetuating character of the model and consider the importance of the "tipping point" to be overdetermined. To that end, the theoretical notion of norm stagnation rests on the presumption that, in fact, the normative space surrounding norm diffusion and internalization is every bit as contested as the space in which new norms are first introduced.

Nascent norms – even those that have reached the tipping point – can and do encounter continued and stiff resistance from various actors opposed to the emergent norm and/or its associated logic of appropriateness (Wunderlich, 2013). This opposition stems from agents opposed to the ideational essence of the norm on its merits, those blindly wedded to the existing societal status quo, or those with a particular grievance with the new norm's entrepreneurs (or any combination of the three). Opposition emanating from any of these three sources is not only likely to be undaunted by the emergent norm's transversal of the "tipping point," but in fact to be magnified and intensified by it. The prospect of diffusion and internalization – that is, of profound social change – portended by satisfaction of the "tipping point" is a lightning rod for those agents who stand in opposition to the advancing norm and/or to its proponents. These agents too are engaged in the mutually constitutive practice of intersubjectivity, working actively to obstruct acceptance and transmittal of the new norm through various attempts at persuasion and meaning-making designed to foment opposition and rejection; that is, a two-way process of "norm circulation" (Acharya, 2015) which generates friction and potential societal resistance. These can produce what Hehir (2019) refers to as "hollow norms."

If, as Finnemore and Sikkink define it, persuasion is best understood as an attempt to "change the utility functions of other players" (1998: 914), it stands to reason that this attempt can be advanced in service of resisting as well as embracing a new norm. As a dynamic and all-encompassing process of socialization, intersubjectivity can and does involve the exchange of ideas of all types, not just those that are progressive or ostensibly virtuous. Critically, this is one side of the coin of intersubjectivity that is not only absent in the norm life-cycle model as currently constituted, but also one that is often overlooked or ignored by norm entrepreneurs themselves. Flush with the seeming success of reaching and surpassing the "tipping point," the presumption among the proponents of an emergent norms – as was the case with R2P – is that norm transmission proceeds along a problem-free and unidirectional path rather than on a conveyor belt continually subject to potential disruption in the form of alternative or counter-ideas.

Here, we see the perils inherent in the blind adherence of some scholars to the false dichotomy of subject/object. At the same time that proponents of the norm life cycle and/or R2P as a nascent norm (see Finnemore, 2003) clung to the fiction that they were objectively describing an emergent process and reality (respectively), they were in fact falling into a cycle of self-perpetuating self-delusion rendering them incapable of recognizing the generalized obstacles to R2P's diffusion as well as the specific obstacles arising from its initial formulation as a "solution" to the "problem" of humanitarian intervention. To this point, an essential component of norm stagnation is its tendency to emerge within societal contexts in which this phenomenon of self-congratulatory laxity on the part of a norm's proponents prevails. Such self-satisfaction in fact is a catalyst for opposition to that self-same (presumably) emergent norm to intensify and become entrenched. Whatever the source(s) of the opposition to the nascent norm, this dynamic of thesis/antithesis – marked by growing obstruction of norm diffusion – is central to the concept of norm stagnation. And it is this dynamic which, in turn, requires, if not demands, a doubling down of support for the norm on the order of that which was originally provided by norm entrepreneurs at the emergence stage (Hoffmann, 2002). The inability of this support to materialize, in concert with the mobilization of opposition, is the push-pull that produces norm stagnation – putting the new norm in a liminal space, suspended between the tipping point and a full cascade (diffusion) and internalization (see Figure 3.1).

The chief theoretical proposition advanced here is that, upon reaching the "tipping point" in the model, norms can and do stagnate rather than diffuse. The abject failure of R2P to attain the status of a norm within international society, in part due to its express linkage to the paralyzing non-starter that was the problem of humanitarian intervention, serves as a powerful illustration of this outcome. As chronicled in the preceding chapter, we can trace R2P's emergence not only to the intellectual labors of the ICISS, but at the ideational level even further back to antecedent concepts such as "sovereignty as responsibility." After taking concrete form in the ICISS report, R2P's endorsement by the UN General Assembly (2005) – indicative of broad support – as well as the UN Security Council (2006) – indicative of pivotal support – seem to more than clear the bar of a "tipping point" as defined by Finnemore and Sikkink (1998).

This poses a quandary relative to the norm life-cycle model: having transcended the tipping point, we should expect to see an extensive diffusion and

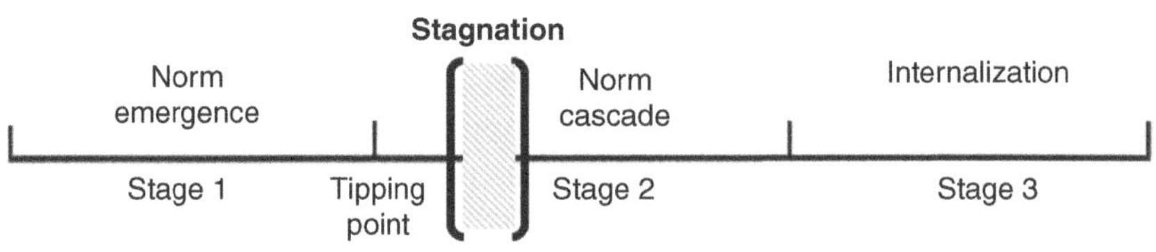

Figure 3.1 Norm Life-Cycle Model [Adapted from Finnemore & Sikkink, 1998].

internalization of R2P. That maturation would manifest itself in an evident and widespread transformation of behaviors of concern (first and foremost humanitarian intervention) in accordance with the logic of this prescriptive norm. Yet this has clearly not occurred. Indeed, a more accurate characterization is that, upon its endorsement by the UN, R2P entered a prolonged period of stasis. As Evans (2008: 288) noted, states that had seemingly committed to R2P through the World Summit Outcomes document in 2005 soon thereafter displayed an "evident willingness...to deflate or undermine the new norm before it is fully consolidated and operational." In light of the pervasive revisionism and resistance R2P encountered after crossing that threshold (Reinold, 2011; Evans, 2008), its failure to proceed through successive stages in the life cycle and consolidate as a norm is self-evident, even if the precise causes for that stagnation are not.

Sources of stagnation

As outlined above, R2P remains trapped in a state of dynamic equilibrium (e.g., a "steady state") in which proponents and opponents of the norm and the behavioral prescriptions associated with it are in rough parity. While R2P has failed to attain the status of an international norm, it does retain evident credibility and support. Having reached the tipping point, it remains in limbo. This is a telling contradiction to the assumed evolutionary trajectory typically associated with the norm life cycle. Indeed, the current state of play with respect to R2P's fortunes as a normative project requires us to reject the fantastical perpetual motion machine-style account of an unbroken linear process of successful communication, transference, and socialization. Instead, the theoretical notion of norm stagnation allows for an alternative outcome in which revisionist agents can and do seek to challenge and recast any desired normative commitment that could meaningfully alter the prevailing status quo (Payne and Samhat, 2004). In light of the interruption in R2P's evolution as an emergent norm, the obvious follow-on question is ***why***. Revisiting the express linkage of R2P to its purported ability to "solve" the humanitarian intervention problem(s) casts an illuminating light on that question.

A successful normative project requires a strong legal and political foundation. As the norm life-cycle model itself indicates, the process by which new norms are fashioned and diffused necessarily unfolds within the bounds of the prevailing social context that it seeks to transform (Finnemore and Sikkink, 1998). As was previously acknowledged, the political and legal challenges confronting the provision of humanitarian intervention – and, by association, the propagation of R2P – were (and are) many and legion. As the chief obstacles to the provision of humanitarian intervention they were concrete problems that R2P was designed ***in part*** to solve – along the path to, and as a consequence of, R2P's transformation of the concept and practice of collective responsibility in international society. Individually and collectively, these obstacles proved too formidable to overcome, continuing to impede and thwart the very behavior (humanitarian intervention) that proponents of R2P intentionally established as a litmus test for the new norm.

The dubious legal basis for humanitarian intervention, as well as the (related) problems of incapacity and lack of political will, pulls double duty here. The specific legal and political challenges enveloping humanitarian intervention provide only a partial causal explanation for R2P's failure to diffuse widely and become internalized throughout the international society of states. While R2P's close association with humanitarian intervention ultimately proved to be its undoing, the problems of legality, institutional capacity, and political will all long predate the introduction of R2P. They are, in fact (as previously discussed) distinct aspects of the persistent problem of humanitarian intervention, a problem with an extensive history and legacy. As such it would be a logical fallacy to attribute them too much explanatory power for R2P's stagnation since they were (and are) problems that predate R2P – problems which in fact R2P was designed to solve. In point of fact, such deep-seated and persistent legal and political challenges are themselves indicative of a broader misalignment between R2P as a normative project and the social environment in which that enterprise has unfolded. In this we are well-advised to remember that translating attaining normativity requires a necessary degree of convergence and conversance (a "goodness of fit") with prevailing social structures and values (Bernstein, 2000).

The chief claim under investigation here is not that R2P has failed to elicit a greater provision of humanitarian intervention, but rather that to date it has failed to attain the status of a behavioral norm in international society. Nowhere here does it say that R2P was or is a hopeless overreach or, even worse, destined to fail. Such a claim is erroneous in light of the degree of political and institutional support R2P received upon its introduction, leading up to and culminating in its endorsement by the UN Security Council. It would also be presumptuous in overlooking the support elements of R2P still receive today from policymakers and academics alike, particularly with regard to the ethic of responsibility for security provision attendant to the state (Paris, 2014). Rather, the "puzzle" is that R2P as a normative venture has stagnated; it is stuck along the trajectory of the norm life cycle, and has not widely diffused or become internalized. Though the association of R2P with humanitarian intervention affords us the reason for R2P's stagnation, there is, undoubtedly, more to the story. To that end, there are two distinct features of R2P's ideational constitution and internal logic that follow from, and reinforce, the doctrine's equivalence with the problem(s) of humanitarian intervention. These elements – a fixed and limited domain for action, and an embedded (Eurocentric) cultural bias – provide additional explanatory power relative to why and how exactly R2P's stagnation has entailed after reaching its tipping point.

Limited scope of action

Two fundamental aspects of R2P's ideational constitution help explain its failure to attain normativity. The first is R2P's narrow domain of possible action relative to behavioral adjustment or alteration. This delimited scope follows, but is also distinct, from R2P's close association with humanitarian intervention. From a sociological perspective, one distinct (and distinctly negative) implication of that association was that it limited R2P's potential to modify social behavior only to the narrow and discrete domain of humanitarian crisis. From the standpoint of launching a new norm, narrowing the scope of relevant behavior in this way is sub-optimal. Fundamentally, norms derive their social power from their ability to govern and shape (or re-shape) the behaviors and practices of constituent members of society (Schultz et al., 2007). If and when an idea advances to the status of a norm, it is generally understood that its behavioral implications and translations will be reflected broadly and in a sustained fashion within the society in question. Conversely, an idea that manifests in and informs one particular form of behavior on an occasional and discrete rather than constant and ubiquitous basis can hardly be said to be a norm at all.

It is essential to recognize here that R2P's chief architects never intended for R2P to only exert influence over decisions and behaviors stemming from the incidence of humanitarian crisis (Paris, 2014). R2P was introduced with the broader purpose of transforming the international order by redefining notions of responsibility, sovereignty, and security – representing, in the words of then Secretary-General Annan, a "…new equation, with human life, human dignity, and human rights raised above the entrenched concept of state sovereignty" (Annan, quoted in Luck, 2008: 7). As such the fundamental objective of R2P was to remake international social norms and behavior concerning human security and human rights more generally. While inflection points of humanitarian crisis certainly provide one opportunity for the pursuit of said objective, they are hardly the only occasions in which human suffering and the violation of basic human rights are experienced or deserving of redress. Nor are they the only (or best) opportunities for advancing moral-ethical appeals to collective responsibility or fundamentally transforming the Westphalian order.

Delimiting the field of action in this way was (and is) antithetical to the spirit and larger objective of R2P. Indeed, the perils associated with distinguishing and delineating between acute and chronic instances of human suffering and rights violations are well chronicled, and would have been well known to the architects and early proponents of R2P. Donnelly (1993) tilled this conceptual ground well over a generation ago, distinguishing between systematic human rights violations (defined as an enduring condition associated with the actions of the state relative to its citizens) and humanitarian crisis (defined as an acute break from prevailing patterns in the actions of the state relative to its citizens triggered by some idiosyncratic causal factor). From this perspective, human rights violations involve the concerted actions of a state to deprive its own nationals of their basic human rights, whereas humanitarian crises are defined by a "greater number" of individuals experiencing suffering typically as a result of "extraordinary circumstances" that are "not the result of more or less direct actions of the government" (Donnelly, 1993: 612–613).

Donnelly pointed to humanitarian crises caused by or associated with intra-state conflict as a means of illustrating the implications of the difference for potential response and redress. As the conditions of humanitarian crisis amid a civil war or other intra-state conflict often (but need not necessarily) arise as an indirect and unplanned by-product of political violence, Donnelly argued that an effective response to such events is less likely to require or rest on coercion and thus less likely to confront objections predicated on strict adherence to state sovereignty and non-interference (Donnelly, 1993: 613). A similarly structural depiction can be found in Roberts (1993: 436), who notes that human rights violations in intra-state conflicts "...take place against a background in which state structures have broken down in some parts of the world, giving way to anarchy and violence."

If we accept these characterizations, then the need for a new norm eliciting a behavioral transformation along the lines of that portended by R2P is actually greater in situations of chronic and enduring human rights violations than in situations of acute humanitarian crisis (Karp, 2015). This claim can be substantiated on a number of fronts: the greater complicity, involvement, and/or intentionality involved in the infliction of harm upon people by the state itself; the potential for greater or broader harm to be inflicted over a prolonged period of time as a result of a seemingly "non-extraordinary" circumstance; associated power dynamics working against efforts to reduce or eliminate such harm, including (but not limited to) a magnified role for appeals to state sovereignty and non-interference as barriers to harm reduction or elimination.

Other prominent scholars working in the domain of humanitarian action reject the utility of distinguishing human rights violations on the basis of whether they result from an enduring misuse or abuse of state power or as the by-product of an acute crisis (Karp, 2015). In this view the two scenarios are typically interrelated, with humanitarian crises a sporadic and spasmodic upwelling produced by and indicative of enduring structural violence latent within society. To this end, Hoffman and Weiss (2006) argue that interpretations of armed violence and humanitarianism (and the various networks, actors, and processes associated with each) as discrete systems mistakenly overlooks the reality that they are intimately linked in both historical and contemporary practice.

This perspective reaffirms the perils of drawing stark distinctions between acute crisis events and chronic and enduring scenarios of suffering and rights violations, but for a very different reason. Unlike Donnelly's contention that the latter is actually more salient and problematic than the former, scholars such as Hoffman and Weiss assert that the importance of the distinction itself is overdetermined, particularly where political violence is involved. They contend that widespread human suffering rests on the overlap and intersection between conflict dynamics and human rights abuses – an overlap and intersection that is introduced and perpetuated by parties to the conflict (Kaldor, 2007; Duffield and Waddell, 2006). Illustrative examples of the interactive and reciprocal relationship between armed conflict and humanitarian crisis are legion.

They include the purposeful subjecting of non-combatants to systematic and strategically motivated campaigns of human rights abuses (including forced displacement, rape, arbitrary detention, and so forth), the tragic specter of mass killings, and the extensive involvement of humanitarian agencies within the conflict zone for the purposes of "triage" (Weiss, 1994).

Out of these insights comes an increasing recognition that the extensive and egregious human rights violations that lie at the heart of humanitarian crisis are in fact a natural and inevitable outgrowth of the purposive and enduring actions of non-state actors and remnants of and claimants to state authority. The breaches of human rights and crimes against humanity that too often typify them are carried out in conjunction with and in service of the strategic, political, economic, and/or ideational objectives and programs of these political actors, diminishing human life and dignity in the process (Robertson, 2006). Accordingly, the imperative of civilian protection entails in either scenario, chronic or acute (Bellamy and Williams, 2009; Holt and Berkman, 2006).

As demonstrated here, linking R2P to humanitarian crisis via intervention runs counter to the objectives and intentions of R2P's architects to craft a new security norm, since crisis scenarios are hardly the only occasions in which widespread human suffering is experienced. Apart from restricting R2P's field of action and thereby undercutting the effort to foster a new norm, this undue emphasis on discrete humanitarian crisis events subsequent to the launch of R2P's normative agenda also explains the disproportionate emphasis that has been paid to building out R2P's reaction component, largely at the expense of codifying the rebuilding and prevention components. From its very inception, rebuilding and prevention were understood as vital not only from the standpoint of building institutional and policy capacities but also – and perhaps more importantly – as critical dimensions of R2P as a norm (Bellamy, 2015). For example, the "immensely important" second pillar task of identifying and extending critical resources to states to assist them in the task of prevention and rebuilding – an endeavor that would have the positive externality of shoring up ideational support for R2P more generally – has largely been sacrificed on the altar of reaction and the third pillar (Bellamy, 2015).

Embedded cultural bias

A second ideational element of R2P that helps account for its stagnation as a norm is the reflexive and culturally specific definition and translation of "humanitarian action" embedded within it (Acharya, 2015). At the center of this prevailing understanding of humanitarian action lies a quasi-religious belief both in the universal appeal of humanitarianism itself and in a particular conception of rights and values oriented around the primacy of the individual – with those rights and values presumed to be best translated and served through liberal political and economic arrangements (Donini et al., 2006). To that end, proponents of and actors within the contemporary "humanitarian world" (Maxwell and Gelsdorf, 2019) strongly emphasize liberal state-building as a salve for a wounded world wracked by crisis and disorder (Smith, 2020; Sabaratnam, 2017). The re-imagination of, and recommitment to, a particular "humanitarianism" that emerged from the ashes of the Cold War to be reified in R2P is a decidedly Western and Eurocentric one, with roots in colonial ontologies and practices (Cunliffe, 2016).

Given the assumed universal appeal and applicability of liberal rights and values (and attendant institutional arrangements), threats to them have come to be conflated with threats to humanity itself (Menon, 2016). Thus humanitarian action in general, and intervention in particular, has expanded beyond the traditional bounds of alleviating direct physical suffering experienced by human bodies, defined by Maxwell and Gelsdorf (2019) as the "humanitarian imperative." Instead, contemporaneous with the development of R2P, the range and scope of humanitarian action has expanded dramatically. Beyond a redress for human suffering, the humanitarian agenda assumed political, ethical, and moral dimensions – overlapping and intersecting with the promotion of civil and political rights, neo-liberal economic development, and liberal political institutions, all seen as crucial requisites and reinforcements for a humane existence (Maxwell and Gelsdorf, 2019).

Accordingly, when not only bodies but also the rights and values associated with and ascribed to those bodies become acutely threatened – especially by political actors – it is no longer only bodies but also the rights and values affixed to them that were (and are) deemed worthy and deserving of protection and promotion through targeted and forcible action (Perugini and Gordon, 2015). As we have seen, in contemporary humanitarian thought and within the parameters of R2P this action can and should include coercive force when deemed necessary for the realization of the "liberal peace" which – by extension – is presumed to positively contribute to the alleviation of human suffering (Pugh, 2016).

This line of reasoning and series of purportedly causal connections have profoundly shaped the predominant (liberal) modality of thinking about intervention since the Cold War (Bellamy and Wheeler 2008; Weiss 2004; Teson 2001). As Davidson (2012) notes, humanitarian intervention can be seen as akin to a form of international policing, whereby powerful liberal states ostensibly act in the name of reducing harm and upholding justice while their underlying goal is the coercive management of at-risk and risky populations. In this way the practice of intervention can be seen as a practice employed by a unified core to coercively reorder the periphery (Turner and Kühn, 2016), with R2P a contemporary response to IR's original quandary: how to effectively "administer" an unruly (read: non-white) world (Vale and Thakur, 2020; Vitalis, 2015).

Accordingly, what followed in the wake of R2P's introduction and codification (via UNSCR 1674) has been a prevailing approach to humanitarian action recognizing and prioritizing a (moral) responsibility to protect not only in situations where a threat to human bodies from direct physical violence is evident, but in situations where a threat to a desired set and conceptualization of rights and values is identified (Welsh, 2004).[2] It is crucial to acknowledge that such "threats" and "duties" are always associated with and oriented toward the distant "other," as are the corrective practices following from them (Jabri, 2007). That diagnosis then paves the way for the prescription of targeted external intervention, to "fix" some latent deficiency (Xypolia, 2022). Among numerous examples, perhaps the starkest remains the "humanitarian intervention" directed at Qaddafi's regime in Libya in 2011–2012, authorized under UNSCR 1973 in part via invocation of R2P and civilian protection. Here, the systematic infliction of harm against civilians was treated as a direct consequence of the pathologies of the regime, such that the singular focus on the regime resulted in a lack of attentiveness to similar harms perpetrated by rebel factions as well as a lack of a sustained and effective response to persistent humanitarian challenges (including violence against civilians) after Qaddafi was deposed (Graubart, 2015). In this way the Libya intervention, advanced under R2P auspices by the UN Security Council, was the crowning manifestation in a series of top-down, externally imposed interventions in places such as Bosnia, Kosovo, Timor-Leste, and Côte d'Ivoire – all of which undermined domestic capacity and produced dynamics of dependency, a perspective espoused not only by postcolonial scholars but even by mainstream institutions such as the Council of Europe (Keranen, 2016).

From a critical vantage point, the particular diagnostic and prescriptive aspects of humanitarian intervention realized in and through R2P are best understood as a contemporary manifestation of the structured relations of colonial difference (Sabaratnam, 2017). Underwritten by a sense-making binary of order/disorder closely tied to the domestic/international binary (Niang, 2020), the practice of humanitarian intervention as well as the doctrinal endorsement of that practice via R2P both reflects and reaffirms a global power hierarchy and subjectivities which are legacies of colonialism (Xypolia, 2022). By extending the domain of humanitarian action from a concern with the physical realm of bodies to the metaphysical realm of rights and values – always "there," and never "here" (Jabri, 2007), R2P could be seen as providing political and even quasi-legal cover for continued Western interference, expansion, and "ordering" in the political, social, economic, and cultural domains of ostensibly sovereign (but strictly delimited) postcolonial societies (Niang, 2020). It is also a practice which teeters precariously on the brink of the "savage-victim-savior" complex (Mutua, 2001).

In light of the preceding discussion, it is perhaps unsurprising that the cultural bias embedded within the post–Cold War humanitarian agenda in general and R2P in particular has privileged a neo-liberal interventionist agenda while also neglecting more practical and pragmatic considerations (Kashyap, 2023). Some vital questions – including, but not limited to, what constitutes an acute threat to humanity, what a suitable response to that threat looks like, and who decides – have long been lodged deeply within the blind spot of liberal thought (Davidson, 2012). As a result, even after the introduction of R2P they have been left unresolved and therefore effectively subject to the discretion of the intervener on an ad-hoc basis, a problem identified early on in R2P's lifespan by former UN Human Rights Commissioner Louise Arbour (Gallagher, 2013). This scenario – dubbed by Roland Paris (2014) as R2P's "structural problem" – has continually recurred in debates over invoking R2P both in the abstract and in specific cases. And, to the extent any attempt has been made to answer these questions, those answers have often fallen back upon long-standing liberal assumptions about the danger posed to individuals, society, and the international order by illiberal regimes and even more fundamentally the inherent disorder that exists in the realm of the "international" (Niang, 2020; Doyle, 1986).

Within this realm, prevailing liberal prohibitions against intervention may be (and often are) relaxed when liberal states encounter "non-civilized" or non-well-ordered societies, especially weak ones (Rawls, 1993; Doyle, 1983; Mill, 1859). And, when societies that are not well-ordered are gripped by widespread human suffering – and especially when that suffering is attributable (either through neglect or intent) to the governing regime – the rule of non-intervention can be (should be?) rendered null and void (Xypolia, 2022). As Reid (2006) notes, the pathway to perpetual peace is paved by the establishment of an international society of liberal democracies, maintained through the technologies of global governance (Duffield 2010; Dillon and Reid 2009; De Larrinaga and Doucet 2008). As such, it is not difficult to envision how and why humanitarian intervention and R2P could be conceived of both as a response to threats to liberal norms and institutions (and the values underlying them) as well as a technique to advance them (Kashyap, 2023).

Two especially abhorrent features of the landscape of "new wars" – the systematic targeting of civilian populations, and the decreased capacity and in some cases willingness of states to protect those populations and their rights – provided significant impetus for the renewed emphasis on morality and the quest for a more robust ethic and practice of humanitarianism among liberal thinkers and policymakers alike (Weiss, 2006; Axworthy, 2001; Brahimi, 2000). However, the particular shape and tenor of the new humanitarian agenda – including its hubristic presumption of universality – goes a long way toward explaining why that quest was not a widely shared one. While the eventual rejection of R2P by powerful states like Russia and China has been well chronicled, and attributed to hegemonic aspirations and/or rejection of Western norms (Gegout and Suzuki, 2020; Averre and Davies, 2015), opposition to R2P and the "new" humanitarian agenda underlying it has in fact been widespread among prominent non-aligned countries including Brazil, Egypt, and India as well as numerous developing countries (Keranen, 2016).

That strand of opposition to R2P has much more to do with suspicion of the motives of liberal states and their track record of utilizing humanitarian justifications instrumentally in order to override and supersede state sovereignty, both past and present. That opposition, in turn, draws its strength not only from past practice but from the embedded liberal bias woven throughout the doctrine of R2P. Likely as a function of the monolithic canonical narrative concerning the purportedly universal humanitarian "turn" in the 1990s, in point of fact skepticism regarding R2P had its own roots and expressions dating to that time. That "turn" should not be understood as a single, unproblematic fact but very much as the playground for renewed debates over, and concern about, liberal imperialism (Davidson, 2012). Those debates continued apace, and even intensified, with the introduction of what was perceived both by proponents and detractors as a more formalized and formidable doctrine of humanitarian intervention in the guise of R2P.

Disjuncture and its consequences

The evident preoccupation with tying R2P to a narrow behavioral domain of crisis response by its proponents as well as the culturally biased conception of humanitarian action residing at the center of R2P's intellectual universe each served as significant causes of the societal disconnect which confronted R2P following its introduction and ascendance to the "tipping point" in 2005/2006. Each helps explain R2P's misalignment with and alienation from prevailing dynamics and constituencies *extant* within international society. As a result, each had the effect of alienating a specific constituency that was important for the perpetuation and diffusion of R2P as a new norm.

Alienated constituencies

As Bellamy (2009) concedes, wrapping R2P around the humanitarian intervention axle undermined the entire enterprise by reducing R2P's scope to the reaction domain. From the standpoint of some of R2P's earliest and most committed advocates, this reductionism directly contradicted the larger objective of norm transformation in the security realm (Schnabel, 2012). In fact it was antithetical to that aim, since the promotion of a prescriptive norm aimed at transforming social behavior writ large – here concerning security practice in the realm of civilian protection – is not well served by linkage to a narrow and particular realm of behavior (Engel and Porto, 2010).[3]

Designating R2P as first and foremost a solution to the problem(s) of humanitarian intervention proved a chief source of that societal disconnect. Doing so had the unintended effect of alienating some of the doctrine's natural allies in the form of individuals, non-governmental organizations, and states that were otherwise favorably disposed toward the goal of transforming existing security norms and practices. Whereas positioning R2P as a corrective to the problem(s) of humanitarian intervention made concessions to the Westphalian conception of state sovereignty and reaffirmation of the non-interference clause necessary from a strategic standpoint, to some of R2P's most ardent supporters they were a bridge too far (Bellamy and Williams, 2011). This was evident in expressed frustrations over R2P's limited impact and mounting resistance emanating from policymakers and policy analysts in supportive states such as Canada, Sweden, and Norway as well as from individual norm entrepreneurs including Kofi Annan, Lloyd Axworthy, Lakhdar Brahimi, Gareth Evans, Edward Luck, and others (Mennecke and Stensrud, 2021; Kersten, 2015).[4]

The second source of societal disconnect confronting R2P emerged from the alienation of another distinct and perhaps even more important constituency: the array of non-Western states who were agnostic (and thus open to persuasion) regarding R2P as a new security norm. Not unlike other post–Cold War forays in the promotion of regime governance (e.g., the process leading up to the Kyoto accord, and the negotiations that culminated in the Rome Statute), clear blocs emerged upon the introduction of R2P. As with those initiatives, upon R2P's codification in the mid-2000s most states in the Global South including influential actors such as India, Pakistan, and Iran expressed general support in theory for the genesis of a new security norm while reserving judgment on the merits of R2P as a specific foray in that direction – precisely because of its close association with humanitarian intervention (Rahman, 2005).

Initial equivocation among non-Western states did not stem from lack of concern or interest; in fact, many such states were highly engaged with R2P upon its emergence given its direct pertinence to, and potential ramifications for, them (Smith, 2022). For one thing, many developing countries then (as now) disproportionately faced security challenges including, but not limited to, humanitarian crisis (natural or human-induced) and a lack of sufficient capacity to address them. Likewise, many had previously been targets of and for third-party intervention under UN auspices or otherwise. It was in fact this historical legacy of sovereignty violations that proved to be a crucial factor explaining the skeptical and non-committal position of many developing countries toward R2P after its introduction (Thakur, 2019). That legacy, and the very real concerns spawned by it, was greatly magnified by the particularistic (Western) conception of humanitarianism residing at the center of R2P's universe. This cultural baggage, compounded by the fraught legacy of intervention in non-Western states and societies, inhibited the process of intersubjective persuasion necessary to promote and diffuse R2P as a new norm, ultimately convincing many developing countries that R2P would be counter-productive to their security interests and needs (O'Hagan, 2015).

Reversion to the mean

There is some degree of irony revealed in these two sources of societal disconnect, both with a common taproot in the close association of R2P with humanitarian intervention. By virtue of being evidently out of step with prevailing trends in international society upon the time of R2P's introduction, this association came to blunt what was intended to be a progressive and ambitious attempt at transforming the norms of that society. What ultimately resulted over the ensuing two decades has been a gradual morphing of R2P into a conservative, status quo-oriented anachronism as the doctrine itself was reduced to a tool for perpetuating past practice and reproducing the problems inherent in it.

The culture of possibility oriented around a potential transformation of international law and a new "internationalist spirit" (Orford, 2013) was dashed as R2P reverted to the mean. The result was a neglect, if not outright abandonment, of R2P's prevention and rebuilding dimensions. Instead, discourse and practice concerning R2P fell back into a timeworn and outdated approach to security provision predicated on coercive, Western-led discretionary adventures in triage and crisis management (Gholiagha, 2015). Any prospect for a "new moral order" (Douzinas, 2003) in which state sovereignty was "defined down" (Etzioni, 2016) in favor of a heightened emphasis on the security of the individual and security as emancipation (Booth, 1991) was lost in foregrounding the quest to solve the problem(s) of humanitarian intervention.

Much of the reasoning that gave rise to R2P in the first place was that the Westphalian arrangement and the strict statist paradigm on which it was predicated were themselves anachronistic. The original impetus for R2P held that the problem(s) of humanitarian intervention were distinct and discrete manifestations of this more fundamental problem. In light of this, returning to the quaint logic and limiting trap of "saving strangers" proved not only to be empirically unsound but conceptually unworkable (Hehir, 2012). The irony of R2P's long slide into norm stasis is that the dynamics in the security arena that elicited the original effort to devise a new norm of security thinking and practice have only intensified in the ensuing two decades. As transnational challenges and threats to the well-being and existence of humans (individually and collectively) mount and themselves grow more salient, the spatial and temporal distinctions rampant within a humanitarian agenda tied to discrete responses to acute crises and wedded to the promotion of (liberal) rights and values have essentially collapsed into meaninglessness.

By extension this collapse has rendered an R2P tethered to those distinctions effectively and essentially irrelevant. That irrelevance is borne out in the degree to which contestation over R2P has gradually been replaced by radio silence, with the concept itself devolving over the past decade from lightning rod to dead letter. This is hardly the anticipated or desired outcome of those proponents of R2P who launched it with normative aspirations over two decades ago. At the same time, it bears remembering that the shaky foundation of humanitarian intervention on which the normative project of R2P came to rest – and which paved the way to irrelevance – was the product of discrete choices by norm entrepreneurs. Those choices came to dominate the discourse and policies surrounding R2P, and were strategically deployed out of a desire to enhance its appeal (Paris, 2014). Ultimately, as we have seen, they have proven to be miscalculations that explain R2P's stagnation as a norm. They were also deviations from a much stronger original ideational foundation for advancing R2P as a norm, one which retains the potential for resuscitating it today: the concept of human security.

A way forward?

The preceding presents a critical diagnosis of the fundamental causes of R2P's stagnation and, ultimately, its failure to date as a normative project. That diagnosis explicitly transcends the superficial and epiphenomenal (if not inevitable) political contestation and backlash that confronted R2P upon its introduction, largely due to its close association with humanitarian intervention and its attendant problems. While R2P did indeed face consequential opposition from consequential opponents as its life cycle unfolded, as Finnemore and Sikkink (1998) remind us, this is a typical feature of any norm's emergence into a contested political and ideational space. In point of fact, the failure of R2P to diffuse throughout international society and become internalized and consolidated as a norm is better understood as a function of the basic elements of its construction selected upon by R2P's advocates and leading entrepreneurs.

Two central tenets or building blocks of the normative project at the heart of R2P proved to be perilous foundations that crumbled under the weight of application. A strictly delimited scope and focus on discrete crisis events, as well as non-reflexive neo-liberal tendencies toward "saving strangers" have individually and jointly led to the stagnation of what was advanced as a revolutionary post-Westphalian global norm concerning sovereignty and security. Yet while R2P has undoubtedly failed to launch as a new norm of (and for) security provision R2P, it is not dead, but rather trapped in ideational purgatory. And perhaps paradoxically, inherent in the foundational causes of R2P's stasis lies the potential for salvaging it as a new norm.

Notes

1 A similar, perhaps stronger, version of this comes to us from Bellamy and Dunne (2016: 12): "the fact that relevant international actors do not always directly invoke R2P is not evidence of its absence."

2 To this point, Jennifer Welsh – who later (in 2013) succeeded Edward Luck as Special Representative to the Secretary-General for R2P – defined humanitarian intervention as "coercive interference in the internal affairs of the state, involving the use of armed force, with the purposes of ***addressing massive human rights violations*** or preventing widespread human suffering" (2004: 3; emphasis added).

3 Here a distinction must be drawn between R2P's narrow scope with respect to its tripwires for invocation and its broader remit regarding the transformation of security practices (Genser, 2022). Inarguably, R2P has been expressly designed for application to specific scenarios (consistent with the Rome Statute) in which human rights violations are acute and especially egregious (i.e., mass atrocity crimes arising from imminent or ongoing acts of genocide, war crimes, crimes against humanity, and ethnic cleansing) rather than those defined by generalized and chronic human rights violations. However, when said "tripwires" are triggered, R2P's scope of and for action with regard to civilian protection is anything but circumscribed – as reflected in its aim to transform security norms and practices across the trajectory of reaction, rebuilding, and prevention.

4 A series of preliminary interviews with NATO, EU, and OSCE officials in fall 2014 bore all the hallmarks of this tension between R2P in concept and in practice. Clear illustration of this can be found in Evans' "The Dream and the Reality" speech (Evans, 2020).

Bibliography

Acharya, Amitav. 2015. "The Responsibility to Protect and a Theory of Norm Circulation," in R. Thakur and W. Maley (eds.), *Theorising the Responsibility to Protect* (pp. 59–78). Cambridge: Cambridge University Press.

Averre, Derek, and Lance Davies. 2015. "Russia, Humanitarian Intervention and the Responsibility to Protect: The Case of Syria," *International Affairs* 91(4): 813–834.
Axworthy, Lloyd. 2001. "Human Security and Global Governance: Putting People First," *Global Governance* 7(1): 19–23.
Ayoob, Mohammed. 2002. "Humanitarian Intervention and State Sovereignty," *International Journal of Human Rights* 6(1): 81–102.
Bellamy, Alex J. 2015. "The Three Pillars of the Responsibility to Protect," *Pensamiento propio* 41(20): 35–64.
Bellamy, Alex J. 2009. "Realizing the Responsibility to Protect," *International Studies Perspectives* 10(2): 111–128.
Bellamy, Alex J., and Tim Dunne. 2016. "R2P in Theory and Practice," in *Oxford Handbook of the Responsibility to Protect* (pp. 3–17). Oxford: Oxford University Press.
Bellamy, Alex J., and Nicholas J. Wheeler. 2008. "Humanitarian Intervention in World Politics," *The Globalization of World Politics* 5: 479–496.
Bellamy, Alex J., and Paul D. Williams. 2011. "The New Politics of Protection? Cote d'Ivoire, Libya, and the Responsibility to Protect," *International Affairs* 87: 825–850.
Bellamy, Alex J., and Paul D. Williams. 2009. "The West and Contemporary Peace Operations," *Journal of Peace Research* 46(1): 39–57.
Bernstein, Steven. 2000. "Ideas, Social Structure and the Compromise of Liberal Environmentalism," *European Journal of International Relations* 6(4): 464–512.
Bettiza, Gregorio, and Filippo Dionigi. 2015. "How Do Religious Norms Diffuse? Institutional Translation and International Change in a Post-Secular World Society," *European Journal of International Relations* 21(3): 621–646.
Bloomfield, Alan, and Shirley V. Scott. 2016. *Norm Entrepreneurs and the Politics of Resistance to Global Normative Change*. London/New York: Taylor & Francis.
Booth, Ken. 1991. "Security and Emancipation," *Review of International Studies* 17(4): 313–326.
Brahimi, Lakdar. 2000. "Report of the Panel on United Nations Peace Operations," A/55/305-S/2000/809 (21 August 2000). Available online: http://www.un.org/peace/reports/peace_operations/docs/a_55_305.pdf. Last accessed 24 July 2020.
Bull, Hedley. 1977. *The Anarchical Society: A Study of Order in World Politics*. London: Macmillan.
Busser, Mark. 2019. *Ethics, Obligation, and the Responsibility to Protect: Contesting the Global Power Relations of Accountability*. London/New York: Routledge.
Carr, Edward Hallett. 1939. *The Twenty Years' Crisis, 1919–1939*. London: Palgrave Macmillan.
Chandler, David. 2015. "The R2P is Dead, Long Live the R2P: The Successful Separation of Military Intervention from the Responsibility to Protect," *International Peacekeeping* 22(1): 1–5.
Cunliffe, Philip. 2016. "Still the Spectre at the Feast: Comparisons Between Peacekeeping and Imperialism in Peacekeeping Studies Today," in Mandy Turner and Florian P. Kühn (eds.), *The Politics of International Intervention: The Tyranny of Peace* (pp. 59–76). London/New York: Routledge.
Davidson, Joanna. 2012. "Humanitarian Intervention as Liberal Imperialism: A Force for Good," *Polis Journal* 7(1): 2–37.
De Larrinaga, Miguel, and Marc G. Doucet. 2008. "Sovereign Power and the Biopolitics of Human Security," *Security Dialogue* 39(5): 517–537.
Dillon, Michael, and Julian Reid. 2009. *The Liberal Way of War: Killing to Make Life Live*. New York/London: Routledge.
Donini, Antonio, Larry Minear, Sippi Azarbaijani-Moghaddam, Greg Hansen, Tasneem Mowjee, Karina Purushotma, Ian Smillie, Elizabeth Stites, and Xavier Zeebroek. 2006. "Humanitarian Agenda 2015: Principles, Power, and Perceptions,"

Feinstein International Center (September). Available online: https://fic.tufts.edu/publication-item/humanitarian-agenda-2015-principles-power-and-perceptions/. Last accessed 12 August 2022.

Donnelly, Jack. 1993. "Human Rights, Humanitarian Crisis, and Humanitarian Intervention," *International Journal* 48(4): 607–640.

Douzinas, Costas. 2003. "Humanity, Military Humanism and the New Moral Order," *Economy and Society* 32(2): 159–183.

Doyle, Michael W. 1986. "Liberalism and World Politics," *American Political Science Review* 80(4): 1151–1169.

Doyle, Michael W. 1983. "Kant, Liberal Legacies, and Foreign Affairs, Part 2," *Philosophy and Public Affairs* 12(4): 323–353.

Duffield, Mark. 2010. "The Liberal Way of Development and the Development—Security Impasse: Exploring the Global Life-Chance Divide," *Security Dialogue* 41(1): 53–76.

Duffield, Mark, and Nicholas Waddell. 2006. "Securing Humans in a Dangerous World," *International Politics* 43(1): 1–23.

Engel, Ulf, and João Gomes Porto. 2010. *Africa's New Peace and Security Architecture: Promoting Norms, Institutionalizing Solutions*. London/New York: Routledge.

Etzioni, Amitai. 2016. "Defining Down Sovereignty: The Rights and Responsibilities of Nations," *Ethics & International Affairs* 30(1): 5–20.

Evans, Gareth. 2020. "R2P: The Dream and the Reality." Speech delivered at the European Centre for the Responsibility to Protect Annual Lecture. Leeds University (26 November 2020).

Evans, Gareth. 2008. "The Responsibility to Protect: An Idea Whose Time Has Come… and Gone?" *International Relations* 22(3): 283–298.

Falk, Richard. 1995. *On Humane Governance: Toward a New Global Politics*. Cambridge: Polity.

Finnemore, Martha. 2003. *The Purpose of Intervention: Changing Beliefs about the Use of Force*. Ithaca: Cornell University Press.

Finnemore, Martha, and Kathryn Sikkink. 1998. "International Norm Dynamics and Political Change," *International Organization* 52(4): 887–917.

Gallagher, Adrian. 2013. *Genocide and its Threat to Contemporary International Order*. Basingstoke: Palgrave Macmillan.

Gegout, Catherine, and Shogo Suzuki. 2020. "China, Responsibility to Protect, and the Case of Syria," *Global Governance: A Review of Multilateralism and International Organizations 26*(3): 379–402.

Genser, Jared. 2022. "The Responsibility to Protect and the Organization of American States: A Path Forward for Atrocity Prevention and Response in the Americas." *Report of the General Secretariat of the Organization of American States* (15 September 2022). Washington, DC.

Gholiagha, Sassan. 2015. "To Prevent Future Kosovos and Future Rwandas: A Critical Constructivist View of the Responsibility to Protect," *The International Journal of Human Rights* 19(8): 1074–1097.

Glanville, Luke. 2016. "Does R2P Matter? Interpreting the Impact of a Norm," *Cooperation and Conflict* 51(2): 184–199.

Graubart, Jonathan. 2015. "War is Not the Answer: The Responsibility to Protect and Military Intervention," in R. Thakur and W. Maley (eds.), *Theorising the Responsibility to Protect* (pp. 200–220). Cambridge: Cambridge University Press.

Harrison, Ewan. 2004. "State Socialization, International Norm Dynamics, and the Liberal Peace," *International Politics* 41: 521–542.

Hehir, Aidan. 2019. *Hollow Norms and the Responsibility to Protect*. Basingstoke: Palgrave MacMillan.

Hehir, Aidan. 2012. *The Responsibility to Protect: Rhetoric, Reality and the Future of Humanitarian Intervention*. Basingstoke: Palgrave Macmillan.

Hoffman, Peter J., and Thomas G. Weiss. 2006. *Sword & Salve: Confronting New Wars and Humanitarian Crises*. Lanham, MD: Rowman & Littlefield.

Hoffmann, Matthew J. 2002. "Entrepreneurs and the Emergence and Evolution of Social Norms," in C. Urban (ed.), *Proceedings of Agent-Based Simulation 3 Conference* (pp. 32–37). Ghent, Belgium: SCS-Europe.

Holt, Victoria K., and Tobias C. Berkman. 2006. *The Impossible Mandate? Military Preparedness, the Responsibility to Protect and Modern Peace Operations*. Washington, DC: Henry L. Stimson Center.

Jabri, Vivienne. 2007. "Solidarity and Spheres of Culture: The Cosmopolitan and the Postcolonial," *Review of International Studies* 33(4): 715–728.

Kaldor, Mary. 2007. *Human Security*. Cambridge: Polity.

Kaldor, Mary. 2003. *Global Civil Society: An Answer to War*. Cambridge: Polity.

Karp, David Jason. 2015. "The Responsibility to Protect Human Rights and the RtoP: Prospective and Retrospective Responsibility," *Global Responsibility to Protect* 7(2): 142–166.

Kashyap, Rina. 2023. *The Political Economy of Security/Development in the Neoliberal Age: R2P and the UN*. Springer Nature.

Keranen, Outi. 2016. "What Happened to the Responsibility to Rebuild?" *Global Governance* 22(3): 331–348.

Kersten, Mark. 2015. "The Responsibility to Protect doctrine is faltering. Here's why." *Washington Post* (Monkey Cage), 8 December 2015. Available online: https://www.washingtonpost.com/news/monkey-cage/wp/2015/12/08/the-responsibility-to-protect-doctrine-is-failing-heres-why/. Last accessed 12 December 2022.

Krook, Mona L., and Jacqui True. 2012. "Rethinking the Life Cycles of International Norms: The United Nations and the Global Promotion of Gender Equality," *European Journal of International Relations* 18(1): 103–127.

Labonte, Melissa. 2016. "R2P's Status as a Norm," in *The Oxford Handbook of the Responsibility to Protect* (pp. 133–150). New York: Oxford University Press.

Luck, Edward C. 2008. "Introduction: The Responsible Sovereign and the Responsibility to Protect," in *Annual Review of United Nations Affairs 2006/2007*, vol. 1 (pp. xxxiii–xliv). New York: Oxford University Press.

Luttwak, Edward. 1999. "Kofi's Rule: Humanitarian Intervention and Neocolonialism," *The National Interest* 58: 57–62.

March, James G., and Johan P. Olsen. 1998. "The Institutional Dynamics of International Political Orders," *International Organization* 52(4): 943–969.

Maxwell, Daniel, and Kirsten Heidi Gelsdorf. 2019. *Understanding the Humanitarian World*. London/New York: Routledge.

McKeown, Ryder. 2009. "Norm Regress: US Revisionism and the Slow Death of the Torture Norm," *International Relations* 23(1): 5–25.

Mennecke, Martin, and Ellen E. Stensrud. 2021. "The Failure of the International Community to Apply R2P and Atrocity Prevention in Myanmar," *Global Responsibility to Protect* 13(2–3): 111–130.

Menon, Rajan. 2016. *The Conceit of Humanitarian Intervention*. New York: Oxford University Press.

Mill, John Stuart. 1859 (1873). "A Few Words on Non-Intervention," in *Dissertations and Discussions*. New York: Holt & Company.

Mutua, Makau. 2001. "Savages, Victims, and Saviors: The Metaphor of Human Rights," *Harvard International Law Journal* 42(1): 201–245.

Niang, Amy. 2020. "The International," in Ann B. Tickner and Karen Smith (eds.), *International Relations from the Global South* (pp. 97–114). London/New York: Routledge.

O'Hagan, Jacinta. 2015. "The Responsibility to Protect: A Western Idea?" in R. Thakur and W. Maley (eds.), *Theorising the Responsibility to Protect* (pp. 285–304). Cambridge: Cambridge University Press.

Orchard, Phil. 2020. "Contestation, Norms, and the Responsibility to Protect as a Regime," in Charles T. Hunt and Phil Orchard (eds.), *Constructing the Responsibility to Protect: Contestation and Consolidation* (pp. 28–49). London/New York: Routledge.

Orford, Anne. 2013. "Moral Internationalism and the Responsibility to Protect," *European Journal of International Law* 24(1): 83–108.

Panke, Diana, and Ulrich Petersohn. 2012. "Why International Norms Disappear Sometimes," *European Journal of International Relations* 18(4): 719–742.

Paris, Roland. 2014. "The 'Responsibility to Protect' and the Structural Problems of Preventive Humanitarian Intervention," *International Peacekeeping* 21(5): 569–603.

Payne, Rodger A. 2001. "Persuasion, Frames and Norm Construction," *European Journal of International Relations* 7(1): 37–61.

Payne, Rodger A., and Nayef H. Samhat. 2004. *Democratizing Global Politics: Discourse Norms, International Regimes, and Political Community*. Albany, NY: SUNY Press.

Perugini, Nicola, and Neve Gordon. 2015. *The Human Right to Dominate*. New York: Oxford University Press.

Pugh, Michael. 2016. "Lineages of Aggressive Peace," in Mandy Turner and Florian P. Kühn (eds.), *The Politics of International Intervention: The Tyranny of Peace* (pp. 77–93). London/New York: Routledge.

Rahman, Radzi. 2005. *Statement by the Chairman of the Coordinating Bureau [Malaysia] of the Non-Aligned Movement on Behalf of the Non-Aligned Movement. Delivered at the Informal Meeting of the Plenary of the General Assembly Concerning the Draft Outcome Document of the High- Level Plenary Meeting of the General Assembly (21 June 2005)*. New York: United Nations.

Rawls, John. 1993. "The Law of Peoples," *Critical Inquiry* 20(1): 36–68.

Reid, Timothy B. 2006. "Killing them Softly: Has foreign aid to Rwanda and Uganda Contributed to the Humanitarian Tragedy in the DRC," *Africa Policy Journal* 1: 74–81.

Reinold, Theresa. 2011. "The United States and the Responsibility to Protect: Impediment, Bystander, or Norm Leader?" *Global Responsibility to Protect* 3(1): 61–87.

Roberts, Adam. 1993. "Humanitarian War: Military Intervention and Human Rights," *International Affairs* 69(3): 429–449.

Robertson, Geoffrey. 2006. *Crimes Against Humanity: The Struggle for Global Justice*. Penguin UK.

Ryle, Gilbert. 1949. "Descartes' Myth," in *The Concept of Mind*. London: Hutchinson.

Sabaratnam, Meera. 2017. *Decolonising Intervention: International Statebuilding in Mozambique*. London/New York: Rowman & Littlefield.

Schnabel, Albrecht. 2012. "The Responsibility to Rebuild," in W. Andy Knight and Frazer Egerton (eds.), *Routledge Handbook on the Responsibility to Protect* (pp. 50–63). London/New York: Routledge.

Schultz, P. Wesley, Jessica M. Nolan, Robert B. Cialdini, Noah J. Goldstein, and Vladas Griskevicius. 2007. "The Constructive, Destructive, and Reconstructive Power of Social Norms," *Psychological Science* 18(5): 429–434.

Smith, Karen. 2022. "R2P at the UN: The Problem of Selective History and Incomplete Narratives," *Global Responsibility to Protect 14*(3): 273–276.

Smith, Karen. 2020. "Order, Ordering, and Disorder," in Arlene B. Tickner and Karen Smith (eds.), *International Relations from the Global South: Worlds of Difference* (pp. 77–96). London/New York: Routledge.

Sterling-Folker, Jennifer. 2000. "Competing Paradigms or Birds of a Feather? Constructivism and Neoliberal Institutionalism Compared," *International Studies Quarterly* 44(1): 97–119.

Teson, Fernando R. 2001. "The Liberal Case for Humanitarian Intervention," Available online: https://ssrn.com/abstract=291661 or http://dx.doi.org/10.2139/ssrn.291661

Thakur, Ramesh. 2019. "Global Justice and National Interests: How R2P Reconciles the Two Agendas on Atrocity Crimes," *Global Responsibility to Protect* 11(4): 411–434.

Turner, Mandy, and Florian P. Kühn. 2016. "The Tyrannies of Peace and the Politics of International Intervention," in Mandy Turner and Florian P. Kühn (eds.), *The Politics of International Intervention: The Tyranny of Peace* (pp. 1–18). London/New York: Routledge.

Vale, Peter, and Vineet Thakur. 2020. "IR and the Making of the White Man's World," in Arlene B. Tickner and Karen Smith (eds.), *International Relations from the Global South: Worlds of Difference* (pp. 56–74). London/New York: Routledge.

Vitalis, Robert. 2015. *White World Order, Black Power Politics: The Birth of American International Relations*. Ithaca: Cornell University Press.

Weiss, Thomas G. 2016. *Humanitarian Intervention* (3rd ed.). Cambridge: Polity.

Weiss, Thomas G. 2006. "R2P after 9/11 and the World Summit," *Wisconsin International Law Journal* 24: 741.

Weiss, Thomas G. 2004. "The Sunset of Humanitarian Intervention? The Responsibility to Protect in a Unipolar Era," *Security Dialogue* 35(2): 135–153.

Welsh, Jennifer M. 2016. "From Commitment to Implementation: Ten Years of the Responsibility to Protect," Statement by Jennifer Welsh, Special Adviser to the UN Secretary General on the Responsibility to Protect Thematic Panel Convened by the President of the General Assembly: Trusteeship Council Chamber, United Nations (26 February 2016). Available online: https://www.un.org/en/genocideprevention/documents/responsibility-to-protect/Doc.6_2016-02-26-PGA%20Event%20RtoP%20at%20Ten%20Welsh.pdf. Last accessed 25 October 2020.

Weiss, Thomas G. 1994. "Triage: Humanitarian Interventions in a New Era." *World Policy Journal* 11(1): 59–68.

Welsh, Jennifer M. 2015. "Mediation and Sanctions: Applying Conflict Prevention Tools in Atrocity Crime Settings," in Serena K. Sharma and Jennifer M. Welsh (eds.), *The Responsibility to Prevent: Overcoming the Challenges to Atrocity Prevention* (pp. 103–118). Oxford: Oxford University Press.

Welsh, Jennifer M. 2010. "Implementing the Responsibility to Protect: Where Expectations Meet Reality," *Ethics & International Affairs* 24(4): 415–430.

Welsh, Jennifer M. (ed.). 2004. *Humanitarian Intervention and International Relations*. Oxford: Oxford University Press.

Wunderlich, Carmen. 2013. "Theoretical Approaches in Norm Dynamics," in Harald Muller and Carmen Wunderlich (eds.), *Norm Dynamics in Multilateral Arms Control: Interests, Conflicts, and Justice*, pp. 20–47. Athens, GA: University of Georgia Press.

Xypolia, Ilia. 2022. "From the White Man's Burden to the Responsible Saviour: Justifying Humanitarian Intervention in Libya," *Middle East Critique* 31(1): 1–19.

4 Responsibility revisited

Moving beyond a superficial assessment of R2P as a (failed) instrument for the provision of humanitarian intervention allows for diagnostic evaluation of R2P not only as a concept but also as a normative project. With respect to the latter, the disjuncture between R2P's ideational underpinnings and the social context in which the doctrine was launched proved to be the chief source of R2P's stagnation as a norm. Tellingly, this disconnect between the theoretical notion of R2P and the prevailing mores of the "international society of states" (Bull, 1977) in the early 21st century was completely illegible to proponents of R2P at the time. Compelling proof of this critical blind spot is the fact that the linkage of R2P to the problem(s) of humanitarian intervention was a conscious strategic move by norm entrepreneurs – one that, as we have seen, backfired in ways that continue to reverberate within international society. Whereas that association generated obstacles from a policy implementation standpoint, it also paved the way for a high degree of "friction" within international society which has proven to be the chief impediment to R2P's evolution and diffusion as a norm.

At the same time, when appraising R2P more broadly as a normative project it is also important to recognize the potential inherent in the dynamic process of intersubjectivity that is essential to meaning making and norm generation. That dynamism suggests that salvaging R2P's normativity is theoretically possible (Wendt, 1999). As Paris (2014) reminds us, R2P has always featured elements beyond coercion and reaction, and at its core promotes ethical ideas about proactively safeguarding humans from extreme harm that retain traction in international society. If we reject the absurd premise that international relations are governed by "iron laws," then the type of ferment and contestation that has marked R2P since its arrival and marred its intended path to normativity could be, in Radice's (2016: 20) turn of phrase, "a harbinger of modest progress rather than a certain marker of hollow failure." Viewed in this way, R2P was not and is not destined to fail as a normative enterprise – provided that its ideational essence can be translated in a way that is more palatable than the well-worn and highly problematic "saving strangers" modality that has prevailed to date.

DOI: 10.4324/9781315105628-5

Indeed, if R2P is to be resuscitated as a norm, that project must be predicated on something more than the credentials of its proponents or its internal logic (Thakur and Maley, 2015). In order to attain normativity R2P (like any idea) requires a foundational "logic of appropriateness" derived from alignment with other prevailing or emergent societal norms (Wunderlich, 2013; Bernstein, 2000). To this end, this chapter lays out the first part of a two-part blueprint for the reconstruction of R2P as a norm. This blueprint focuses on reimagining R2P's core elements of responsibility and protection. Reconstructing R2P in this fashion requires tearing it down to the studs; or, less colloquially, revisiting its ideational origins and revealing their fundamental overlap with the human security agenda.

The R2P – human security nexus

The reduction of R2P to little more than a doctrine of and for humanitarian intervention was more than a strategic misstep. The greater significance and implications of this syncretism stems from the fact that it was a de facto abandonment of the fundamental aims of the ICISS and of R2P's very ideational basis. While the ICISS was inarguably concerned with "solving" the problem(s) of humanitarian intervention, that problem was never the sole or even primary concern of R2P's architects. Indeed, the ICISS itself stressed that interventions to halt atrocities alone are insufficient in fulfilling the responsibility to protect (Keranen, 2016). Reducing R2P to a doctrine for the promotion of humanitarian intervention, rather than treating humanitarian intervention as a litmus test for the doctrine of R2P, proved a major departure from R2P's initial intent and structure, one that betrayed the concept's larger significance (MacArthur, 2008).

Building on the theoretical notion of "sovereignty as responsibility," the ICISS' efforts were rooted in the twin objectives of transforming international security norms to embrace a prevailing ethic of moral responsibility, and transferring political authority and decision-making regarding security provision from sovereign states to the international community. These objectives in turn featured two requisite criteria. First, R2P required that the presumptive "international community" supplant states as the primary source of, and authority for, security action (transference). Second, R2P required that individuals supplant states as the primary referent in security norms (transcendence). These lofty aims were infused throughout the work of the ICISS and its recommendations – but were not unique to them. In their commitment to a redefinition, if not rejection, of state sovereignty and the doctrine of non-interference, the efforts of the ICISS in formulating were unmistakably influenced by the human security agenda.

The human security agenda

The initial stirrings of human security– first defined by the UN Development Programme (1994) to refer to the condition of safety from chronic threats (such as hunger, disease, and political repression) as well as protection from sudden and harmful disruptions in everyday life – can be found in the gradual decline of the military and ideological confrontation animating Cold War geopolitics in the 1980s. The looming demise of this structuring device, magnified by very real changes on the ground in terms of security threats and challenges, reaffirmed ongoing efforts by more critically inclined scholars to propel thought and practice away from the reified concepts of anarchy and state sovereignty (Ullman, 1983). Tellingly, those changes on the ground were the very same events and developments that had also reanimated debates over humanitarian intervention (see Chapter 1). A proliferation of ethnic conflict, humanitarian disaster, and general social disorder emerging from the ashes of the Cold War in places such as Somalia, Rwanda, the former Yugoslavia, Liberia/Sierra Leone, and beyond magnified the inadequacy of the traditional approach for security thought and practice.

A central theme prevalent in efforts to address the inadequacy of conventional wisdom regarding security at the dawn of the post–Cold War era was a desire to "broaden" and "deepen" security as an analytical domain; that is, to expand the range of phenomena considered within the realm of "security," and to incorporate a fundamental concern with the effects of these phenomena on referents other than the state, and in particular individuals (Buzan et al., 1998; Baldwin, 1997; Krause and Williams, 1996). These distinct yet mutually reinforcing impulses, advanced by the Copenhagen and Aberystwyth Schools in particular, were at their intellectual core responses to the ontological and epistemological question of why some issues and actors receive priority treatment, while others with crucial security implications do not (Huysmans, 1998). These focal points of the broadening and deepening agenda(s) necessarily revealed the need for a new approach to security provision and a new way of thinking about responsibility in the security realm.

The intellectual contributions of the Paris, Copenhagen and Aberystwyth Schools dovetailed neatly into (and fueled) the emergent concept of human security (Paris, 2001). This approach, which rose to prominence in the mid-1990s, was itself borne of a concern with a fuller and more adequate accounting for human well-being, opportunity, and economic development concerns under the heading of security studies (Hettne and Söderbaum, 2005; Duffield, 1999). As Kerr (2009) notes, the end of the Cold War suggested to some the possibility of the related shift away from a state-centric view of security and toward a global development agenda, with the latter resulting as a "peace dividend" of the former. This was given voice in the United Nations Development Programme's (UNDP) 1994 Human Development Report, which explicitly called for transition "...from an exclusive stress on territorial security to a much greater stress on peoples security" (UNDP, 1994: 22).

As the first official articulation of the concept, the HDR also notably stressed that human security turns first and foremost on safety from chronic threats (e.g., hunger, disease, political repression) and only secondarily on protection from sudden injurious disruptions to daily life (UNDP, 1994, p. 23). Picking up on the 1994 HDR, advocates of a human security approach – a network encompassing numerous INGOs as well as states such as Canada, Japan, and Norway – adopted and promoted a sectoral positionality akin to that developed by Buzan, Wæver, and deWilde (1998). Consequently, economic well-being and inequality, public health, nutrition, environmental quality, educational access and attainment, rights provision, and political empowerment were explicitly designated as security concerns (Sheehan, 2005; Paris, 2001).

The importance of these conditions and the attainment of them are especially relevant due to their impact on, and interaction with, what Amartya Sen refers to as the "capabilities" and "functionings" (Sen, 2004) and Booth (1991) the "emancipation" of the individual. To this point, as the Report itself notes, the human security agenda represented a radical departure from prevailing approaches to security which privileged sovereign states and overlooked "…the legitimate concerns of ordinary people who sought security in their daily lives." (UNDP, 1994: 22). This reconceptualization of security as a right to which citizens within a "well-ordered society" (liberal or hierarchical) are entitled (Rawls, 1993) is expressed in the UN definition of human security itself (Commission on Human Security, 2003).

Hailed upon its introduction as a new paradigm for scholars and practitioners alike, one persistent criticism that has continually dogged human security is whether it can be effectively translated into meaningful policy gains. Given the scope of possible issues and concerns that can and do reside under the human security banner, it has been deemed by some as lacking in precision and consequently limited in utility (Paris, 2001). The expansiveness of the concept of human security creates practical obstacles with respect to establishing priorities for action, allocating resources, and navigating potential trade-offs between competing aims. These problems in turn expose human security to the accusation that it lacks substance. The fact that human security has retained this open-endedness even as it has evolved and matured as a concept lends credence to the assertion that its proponents have a vested interest in keeping the concept vague and its associated agenda broad. As this line of reasoning goes, this "big tent" approach to human security incorporates and sustains buy-in from a plethora of actors (pivotal states, NGOs, development and humanitarian agencies) with a wide range of issues and priorities (Tadjbakhsh, 2013). This big tent in turn confers additional benefits via the securitization process; keeping human security broad in concept allows for transformation of more (and different) policy issues into security "threats," thereby (theoretically) attracting more attention and interests to them (Sjostedt, 2019).

Inflection points

Though not without merit, debates over its supposed conceptual imprecision overlook the fact that the human security agenda has direct and critical implications for the structuring devices of international politics. Whatever the difficulties extant in translating it into policy, human security as a concept fundamentally challenges status quo values and institutions and their postures toward human welfare and the collective interest (Newman, 2013). In this way human security is closely aligned, if not essentially intertwined, with the ideas that reside at the heart of R2P as well as R2P's broader normative agenda (Kerr, 2009).

Like the ICISS and other early proponents of R2P, advocates of human security were motivated from the start by an overarching desire to transform both thinking and practice relative to security provision (Hehir, 2014). The impulses that gave rise to this particular redefinition of security shared R2P's fundamental interest in de-centering the state as the primary referent for security concern, as the arbiter of what constitutes a security threat, and as the main actor responsible for responding to said threats. Consequently, societies, groups, and individuals became relevant answers to the question "security for whom?" while the source of security threats included anything that could conceivably inflict harm on those actors (Paris, 2001).

Yet in the view of at least one leading scholar, the fundamental linkages between R2P and human security were systematically undercut by intentional efforts to disentangle the two concepts over time (Newman, 2013). One commonplace tactic in this vein has been the framing of R2P as little more than a pragmatic version of human security, distinguished chiefly by its discipline and definition, in contrast to the supposedly sprawling and amorphous concept of human security (MacArthur, 2008). This framing was employed by some of R2P's staunchest supporters, including Edward Luck (the first Special Adviser to the Secretary-General on R2P) who sought to engender support for R2P in its emergent phase by juxtaposing its (alleged) specificity and precision with the breadth and vagueness of human security (Luck, 2008).

One prominent critic of R2P, privileging the "revolutionary potential" of human security viz. the allegedly status quo orientation of R2P, characterized R2P as merely an instrument used to "sanitize" human security (Hehir, 2014). This position is very much of a piece with parallel debates over the appropriate focus of human security, while also uncritically accepting Western over non-Western translations of both human security and R2P alike (Howe, 2018). These debates are centered on whether human security is better served by pursuing the broad goal of "freedom to," which would confront the root causes of human insecurity, or the narrow objective of "freedom from," which limits the focus largely to discrete responses to insecurity stemming from political causes (Kerr, 2009; Krause, 2007).

Assuming this posture necessarily discounts the "revolutionary potential" of R2P itself, particularly if we rightly recall the (stalled) normative aspirations of its architects. As Hehir (2014) contends, early proponents of R2P did in fact employ a strategic calculus focused on altering the behavior of states – a calculus at odds with his view of human security as a fundamental and direct challenge to the state-based order itself. Yet, as was discussed at length previously, that strategic calculus was introduced gradually, as a strategic move designed to curry favor for R2P in the face of opposition. In its original iteration and intent,

R2P – like human security – sought to empower individuals at the expense of states, full stop (Hehir, 2014).

Efforts at introducing distance between R2P and human security – whether motivated by support or opposition to the former – ultimately betray the reality that R2P and human security are wholly complementary not only intellectually but also in their broader and shared normative aspirations (MacArthur, 2008). Consequently, like R2P, human security has also withered as a consequence of being "watered down" for presumably strategic reasons by those seeking to elicit wider acceptance (Newman, 2013). The result in both cases has been a tacit reaffirmation of existing political, legal, and normative constraints in the form of "R2P-lite" (Weiss, 2006). This is a move that works at cross-purposes with the grander normative ambitions at the heart of both concepts.

This diminished version of human security (as well as R2P) is embodied through institutional expressions within the UN system. The 2003 UN High-Level Panel on Threats, Challenges, and Change, the 2005 World Summit Outcomes document, and the creation of Special Representative/Special Adviser positions for the Responsibility to Protect, for the Prevention of Genocide and Mass Atrocities, Children and Armed Conflict, and the like were all individually and collectively indicative of a strictly delimited "take" on human security and protection within the UN Secretariat. The particular distillations of the ideas underlying the human security agenda and R2P alike are far more indicative of a pluralist/positivist international order predicated on thin cooperation between and among sovereign states than the solidarist vision and transnational scope of R2P and human security (Dunne, 2015; Newman, 2013).

The hollowing out of both the concept of human security and the doctrine of R2P betrays the moral and ethical claims embedded within, and the deeper normative shift implied by, them (MacArthur, 2008). The irony of the mainstream (and delimited) institutional expressions of both R2P and human security is that these efforts to capture and bind the two concepts in service of status quo maintenance have instead revealed and reaffirmed the clear "fit" between them. This "fit" entails both ideationally and in an applied, policy sense. They are essentially two sides of the same coin, with human security representing a new vision and R2P a new way of – and rationale for – acting on that vision. This nexus is particularly evident in their shared understanding and operationalization of responsibility.

Responsibility as sovereignty

Despite the best efforts of some analysts and political officials to disentangle R2P and human security, an emphasis on the collective responsibility for the alleviation of human suffering has always been, and remains, integral to each (Newman, 2013). In returning to the central problem of this research, it is this complementary and mutually reinforcing dynamic between R2P and human security that provides the impetus for reanimating R2P as a normative project.

The undercurrents that gave rise to the concept of human security were of a piece with the ICISS' agenda: to transfer responsibility in the security arena from states to the international community writ-large, and to transcend state-centric security norms and redefine security threats and responses (i.e., notions of protection) around a new referent – humans, individually and collectively.

Revisiting R2P's origins and overlap with human security uncovers and underscores its fundamental emphasis on inverting the relationship between the state and the individual and redefining their associated and attendant ethical and moral duties within the security arena. While both R2P and human security have been thwarted in their normative aspirations, at base each seeks to advance a solidarist vision of international society. Within such a world, free and secure individuals are an essential element of and for peace and security between, among, and within states (Newman, 2013). It is this solidarist vision at the heart of both R2P and human security that in turn invokes the prospect of a shared moral commitment to maintaining human well-being across borders, proactively and without partiality. Such an arrangement goes beyond sovereignty as contingent on delivery of the responsibility to protect; rather, the responsibility to protect is the very source of sovereignty itself.

Questions of responsibility

Reducing R2P to a mere rationale for humanitarian intervention requires a parallel downsizing of the conception of responsibility at the heart of the Responsibility to Protect. Indeed, a key facet of the "saving strangers" problem is its narrowing of the scope of responsibility to little more than a question of who is responsible for authorizing and engaging in interventions. It is unsurprising that a circumscribed approach to R2P privileging reaction over prevention and rebuilding has produced a similarly circumscribed treatment of responsibility. Yet the result has been beyond problematic for R2P's normative evolution, sidelining fundamental questions about what responsibility actually entails in international society as well as who exercises it. Short circuiting the critical and philosophical debates elicited by the ICISS' more robust engagement with notions of collective responsibility has delimited intersubjective exchanges around R2P, reducing them to the well-worn topic of reaction via humanitarian intervention. Consequently, for much of R2P's lifespan debates over responsibility have been limited to practical matters; that is, developing specific criteria for when and where a responsibility to protect entails, and fleshing out the decision-making process surrounding it – thereby stunting the potential growth and evolution of R2P as a norm.

To the extent that R2P represents an ambitious project to advance prescriptive norms concerning security practice(s), it must directly engage with and furnish an answer to the question of how a responsibility to protect should be conceived and to whom that responsibility, so defined, entails. What does "responsibility" mean within the context of international society? Who is "responsible" to act in the protection of civilians from harm? A failure to directly and effectively contend with these questions following R2P's introduction to international society has almost certainly contributed to its stagnation as a norm. However, if we return to the ideational and conceptual origins of R2P, it is possible to locate meaningful engagement with and responses to both questions – engagements which provide the catalyst for resuscitating R2P.

What is responsibility?

The effort to advance a new ethic of responsibility of and for human security corresponded with other contemporaneous developments, including the presumptive emergence of a new humanitarian ethos (Finnemore, 2003; Wheeler, 2000). Individually and collectively, these developments were thought to typify the zeitgeist within international society at the dawn of a new millennium (Iancu, 2014). In turn, they generated and necessitated renewed efforts to define the nature and essence of responsibility within a solidarist international society of states (Bull, 1977). This was an intellectual enterprise with longer and deeper antecedents, including and perhaps especially in the renaissance of moral theory emerging in the wake of the Vietnam War, as prominently reflected in Michael Walzer's seminal *Just and Unjust Wars* (1977).

Among Walzer's many contributions to applied morality in international relations was his reaffirmation of distinct specifications of responsibility relative to war residing within the *ad bellum, in bello*, and (eventually) *post bellum* domains. Of particular relevance to critical re-evaluation of R2P was Walzer's consideration of how and in what ways these distinctions and specifications might apply to humanitarian crises and the limitation of harm. Not unlike R2P and the "three pillars" approach it engendered, just war theory allocates primary moral (and, by extension, legal and political) responsibility for the limitation, if not avoidance, of harm and suffering according to domain of action. States and their leaders bear the brunt of the responsibility to limit harm when it comes to the war-decision, whereas the burden on the individual increases in the conduct of war.[1] These distinctions were sharpened by the highly specified criteria subsumed within each domain, criteria that have long typified just war theory and have subsequently influenced attempts at translating R2P principles in the policy arena (Butler, 2012).

Inspired by Walzer, a cohort of just war theorists following in his wake have subsequently grappled with questions of application and implementation concerning contemporary moral, ethical, and legal dilemmas such as humanitarian intervention, post-conflict reconstruction, terrorism and insurgency, and the like (Rochester, 2016). This thrust of contemporary just war theory explains, at least in part, the theory's influence on the formulation of R2P (Carati, 2016). As with just war theory's clear delineation of responsibility by behavioral domain, its specification of concrete limits and workable constraints on and for action has also proven useful to efforts to those seeking to maximize R2P's impact on policy and practice, including and especially with regard to intervention (Bellamy, 2008).

However, just war theory's influence on R2P is evident not only in the applied but also in the ideational realm. As Orford (2013) notes, for all of its flaws just war theory represents at base a centuries-old attempt at infusing a moral conscience and a clearly specified regard for the rights of the individual person into the prevailing system of temporal (worldly) authority. As a timeless and timely instrument for informing moral deliberation over the responsibility for limiting and avoiding the infliction of harm upon innocent persons in "real-world" scenarios, the synergies and overlap between R2P and just war theory are profound. By challenging enduring principles such as sovereignty and non-interference on moral grounds, just war thinking represents an important antecedent to R2P both as a concept and as an emergent norm (Orford, 2013). Just war theory's profound influence on the development of R2P is directly attributable to the theory's natural law underpinnings and presumption of the existence of a universal moral standard that supports the protection of humans as a normative commitment. This universal moral standard invokes the potential for reasonable and justifiable exceptions to the state-centric legalist paradigm outlined by Walzer (1977) – exceptions which have subsequently made their way into the doctrine of R2P (Bellamy, 2008).

Ultimately, just war theory's most compelling and fundamental influence on the ideational constitution of R2P stems from a shared (re)affirmation of the existence of a universal, inviolable, and collective moral duty to protect civilians from harm. With respect to R2P as well as just war theory, this duty is understood to represent a central responsibility of, and for, international society. Indeed, for good or ill one can draw a straight line intellectually and conceptually from the extensive and elaborate precepts of just war theory to the civilian protection mandate of R2P. Whereas the scope of consideration and deliberation has been significantly narrowed in the latter case, R2P ascribes the same moral primacy and weight to reducing and preventing harm to civilians that just war theorists do to non-combatants (Koontz, 1997). And in light of the natural law underpinnings it shares with just war theory, R2P treats this responsibility as a universal as well as primary concern, specifying it as a duty that is attendant to all members of the international community. In an additional parallel to just war theory, R2P aims to normalize and institutionalize this prevailing ethic of moral responsibility to alleviate or prevent harm. Although, as was discussed extensively, R2P has failed to attain the status of a behavior-conditioning or inducing norm, its inhibition of direct appeals to moral relativism and sovereign prerogative by states and their leaders engaged in the imposition of harm is at least a tepid reflection of this objective (Hehir, 2011).

In light of this influence from just war thinking, the prevailing understanding of responsibility at the (original) heart of the Responsibility to Protect is that of a universal and shared obligation. Further, the dispatch of this duty should be understood by the international community as a prescriptive social norm (Keranen, 2016). This conceptualization of responsibility embedded within R2P by its architects relies heavily on the Principle of Collective Moral Liability (PCML).[2] The premise of the PCML is fairly straightforward; the idea is of the existence of a "responsible collective" of moral agents liable for a given outcome (Copp, 1979). Here, with respect to R2P, that "responsible collective" is the international society of states, and that given outcome the protection of civilians from harm and the provision of and for their well-being and security.

Although not explicitly referencing R2P or the intellectual labors of the ICISS, Corlett's (2001) specification of the terms of the PCML is nonetheless illustrative regarding the conceptualization of responsibility at the heart of the Responsibility to Protect. Like R2P, the PCML makes harm avoidance a moral imperative. The PCML goes as far as to equate negligence in the obligatory pursuit of a given outcome with creating an unreasonable risk of harm to others (2001: 573). Translated to an R2P context, the failure to pursue the collective obligation of human security provision strongly connotes negligence by compounding harm (i.e., adding to the harm that individuals already experience through insecurity by failing to act to alleviate that harm). Relatedly, the logic of the PCML is evident in R2P's understanding of negligence as something that can be (is) reflected in both the action(s) and inaction of the collective and its constituent members. This reasoning tracks closely with R2P's emphasis on sovereignty as responsibility, and its attendant notion that a state may forfeit its sovereignty not only if it is ***unable*** but also if it is ***unwilling*** to provide for the security and safety of its population.

Additionally, as reflected in the establishment as well as the work of the ICISS, the PCML attributes the cause of negligence to the wants and beliefs of the responsible collective. Here the logical synergies with R2P are especially clear and profound. For one, the failure to act on the obligatory pursuit of a given outcome (i.e., of human security provision) is understood as the result of self-interest. As was discussed at length previously, the entire impetus for the Responsibility to Protect came from a desire to undercut continued strict adherence to the statist paradigm and the many and varied ways in which the Westphalian state-system reified the interests of states at the expense of the well-being of individuals and society at-large. With the self-regarding impulses of sovereign states being the root of the problem to which R2P sought remedy, it stands to reason that the understanding of responsibility at the heart of R2P shared the logic of the PCML: namely, that the "wants and beliefs" (i.e., self-regarding interests) of individual members of the collective posed the biggest obstacle to the pursuit of the desired outcome (i.e., human security provision).

It is also the case that the prevailing notion of responsibility at the heart of R2P shared the perspective of the PCML that the failure to realize, or even undertake, the obligatory pursuit of a given desired outcome should be considered a ***collective*** failure. In part this is due to the fact that, in the terminology of the PCML, the responsible collective in the case of R2P – the international society of states – is both an intentional and voluntary agent. Therefore, the commitment of the international community to the principles of R2P was (and remains) reflective of these attributes, particularly in light of R2P's endorsement by the international society of states in the World Summit

Outcomes document in 2005 and in UNSCR 1674 in 2006. As the moral responsibility of security provision is therefore a duty intentionally and voluntarily taken up by the responsible collective, the prospect that any failure to pursue the given outcome (protection) might be directly attributable to a few or even to one individual member of the collective (i.e., state), and attributable to the "wants and beliefs" (i.e., self-interest) of that state is, with regard to the assignation of moral liability, irrelevant.

As a means to the end of promoting R2P as a social norm, its architects realized the necessity of defining security provision as an entirely and even radically collective enterprise (Papamichail and Partis-Jennings, 2016). Doing so would be the best, if not the only, way of breaking the existing stranglehold of states on the domain of international security. This was not primarily or necessarily because that stranglehold was the root cause of security failures, but rather because articulating such a radically collective position regarding rights and responsibilities within the security domain had the potential to cultivate investment in, and ownership of, that domain from non-state actors as fellow members of (international) society at-large. As Papamichail and Partis-Jennings (2016) contend, this framing of R2P offered the greatest potential for enhancing empathy, legitimacy, and efficacy in the security realm. Successfully promoting these qualities would necessarily transform the security arena, in turn making it more amenable to new ways of thinking about security and the norms governing security provision (Papamichail and Partis-Jennings, 2016).

Responding to the need for a corrective to what the Brahimi Report dubbed a "moral failure," the ICISS and other early proponents of what became R2P adopted the logic of the PCML that the imposition of harm in the form of the inability to act to provide human security was both caused by, and the fault of, the responsible collective. In other words, if the responsibility to protect goes unfulfilled, it is the fault of the international community, full stop. The implications of this reasoning are self-evident in the formulation of the three pillars approach. By virtue of defining the Responsibility to Protect as a wholly collective moral responsibility and the failure to act on it as a wholly collective moral liability, an opening for transferring sovereign authority in the security arena from the sovereign state to the international community was realized, both as a backstop (pillar 2) and as a substitute (pillar 3).

Through this prevailing translation of the concept of responsibility in international society, R2P's early entrepreneurs were motivated by an unshakable conviction that appeals to a collective responsibility (read: moral duty) to respond in the face of mass atrocities would ultimately pave the way for a transfer of authority in the provision of security and, more fundamentally, for transcendence of existing norms governing that provision. This is reflected in the contention of proponents such as ICISS member Gareth Evans (2006), who argued that resistance to R2P was attributable more to "global indifference" than principled opposition. Consequently, better efforts to demonstrate the gravity of mass atrocities to all states and to appeal to their moral sensibilities would prove an effective mechanism for promoting greater adoption of, and adherence to, R2P as a norm. By extension, discord over R2P could be expected to naturally recede over time, as the need to implement R2P would gradually be realized as a function of the increasing visibility of, and by extension concern with, mass atrocities among statespersons (Evans, 2011). Still, while defining the Responsibility to Protect as a collective moral obligation might carry some of the proverbial water relative to R2P's normativity, R2P's architects realized that a more focused and better elaborated answer to the question of who specifically constituted the "responsible collective" was needed.

Who is responsible?

The architects of R2P operationalized the concept of responsibility as a collective duty for which the international community was morally liable. This operationalization sought to build on other ethical and normative developments afoot within international society in order to cultivate a norm of civilian protection in line with the human security agenda. In so doing, the importance of formulating an answer to the question of who bears that responsibility as defined, as well as a broadly appealing and persuasive rationale for that answer, was well understood by R2P's early proponents (Illingworth, 2022; Thakur, 2016). So too was the need for that supporting rationale to be ambitious, far-reaching, and conversant with other existing and/or emergent norms if the larger goal of eliciting societal buy-in and transforming security norms were to be achieved (Tadjbakhsh, 2013; Elster, 1985).

To that end, and inspired by a collectivist ethos shared by human security proponents, R2P's architects grounded their recommendations for the reassignment of responsibility for security provision in a fashion that challenged, if not repudiated, continued adherence to the predominance of the Westphalian-Weberian state (Bellamy, 2015; Pace and Deller, 2005). Wresting authority over security matters away from the sovereign state required a radical reconceptualization of the referent for security thinking and practice (as will be discussed in Chapter 5). Yet before a reconceptualization of the ***subject*** of security could entail, a new way of thinking about who is responsible for ***providing*** security in the first place was also necessary. The allocation of the responsibility for security provision on which R2P was initially established – whereby the onus was shifted from the state to the international society of which it was a component – drew its inspiration from the same source as the human security approach; namely, the notion of sovereignty as responsibility.[3]

As reflected in its initial concern with addressing the security needs of internally displaced persons (see Weiss and Korn, 2006), sovereignty as responsibility was highly conversant with the "deepening" impulse at the heart of the human security agenda (Buzan, Wæver, and deWilde, 1998). At its very core, sovereignty as responsibility and later R2P embraced Booth's (1991: 319) emancipatory ontology and in particular the claim that, *contra* prevailing thinking and practice in the security arena, states should be treated as means and people as ends (rather than the other way round). As the forerunner to

R2P, the notion of sovereignty as responsibility was a portent of an ontological shift with profound practical implications. Translated through R2P, it simultaneously bound the state as an entity into a redefined approach to security provision while also conditioning and infringing upon its claim to supreme authority (Boli, 2001).

To assert that responsibility is a prerequisite of sovereignty *ipso facto* brings the two concepts into ethical and logical parity, thereby negating the primacy of the latter and opening the door for a reassignment of that responsibility in the event that prerequisite cannot be or is not being satisfied. As Orford (2011) contends, the vocabulary of responsibility employed in conjunction with R2P is intended to serve as a discursive tool for conferring and allocating authority rather than as a binding and imposing stricture. The logic of responsibility assignation was simple and non-controversial: namely, the moral duty to provide for the security of the population was first ascribed to the sovereign entity responsible for that population. It was also somewhat radical in its implications, since this meant holding the sovereign state accountable for the dispatch of a duty it had long possessed as a function of the social contract, but which it could (and did) act upon intermittently and indiscriminately, and even directly violate (Cunliffe, 2006).

Prior to its entanglement in the humanitarian intervention problem(s), R2P was in fact a bold venture that recognized the need to reallocate the division of labor with regard to security provision in order to arrive at the ultimate destination of human protection and the centering of the human as security referent. To this end, the architects of R2P attempted to reframe what could be (and had been) understood as a political and legal contest over the proper role of the state in the provision of security as, instead, a matter of and for moral concern. Enter the "three pillars."

From a strategic standpoint, the three pillars approach (first introduced in paragraphs 138 and 139 of the 2005 World Summit Outcomes document) reflects a presumption on the part of the proponents of R2P that the answer to the state-centric machinations that dominated not only humanitarian intervention but security provision more broadly required elevating such matters to the level of shared moral obligation (Bellamy and Williams, 2011). In order to unlock the grip of the state on security matters, the ICISS had initially elected to (re)define security provision as a collective enterprise, with duties attendant to all concerned – including and *especially* states. Those duties, understood as fundamental moral obligations, were later specified in graduated form and codified in the World Summit Outcomes document, with the state retaining the "pole position" of primary responsibility in the first pillar (UNGA, 2005, A/RES/60/1, para 138–139).

However, while the state was assigned *primary* responsibility for security provision (including, but not limited to, protecting populations from genocide, war crimes, crimes against humanity, and the like) under R2P, this is a far cry from *sole* or *unquestioned* responsibility. Again in the spirit of conditionality, the key difference lies in the clear and unequivocal allocation of the collective moral responsibility for security provision on a *secondary* basis to the international community. Notwithstanding important but ancillary debates about who or what constitutes the "international community," the World Summit Outcomes document – representing, alongside UNSCR 1674, the apex of R2P's norm evolution to date – offers clear evidence of a contingency plan in the form of a backstop to (pillar 2) as well as a substitute for (pillar 3) states in the dispatch of this collective responsibility for security provision.

The secondary positionality of the international community relative to the duty for and authority over security provision should not be constituted as subordination to the Westphalian-Weberian state, but rather adjacency (Orford, 2013). Indeed, the original understanding of responsibility at the heart of R2P contended that the moral obligation to ensure the well-being of the human person is a shared one between the sovereign state and the international community, with the latter serving as an alternative instrument for carrying forth that obligation (Erskine, 2019). *Ipso facto*, the state's role as a security actor has (and necessarily must) change, from monopolistic to primary under the aegis of what is a collective enterprise.

Defining the responsibility to protect expressly as a moral obligation does the work here. Doing so makes security provision no longer a discretionary matter that can be left (or bound) to the dictates or whims of the state. It is instead transformed into a collective responsibility – universal and indivisible – which states forego at their peril. Doing so may (should?) result in forfeiture of their sovereign authority in the security realm. This is the case whether states lack the capacity or the will to carry out their sovereign responsibility to protect their population.[4] This prevailing conception of responsibility at the heart of R2P in its fullest iteration treats security as a public good; that is, non-rival and non-excludable, making the duty to provide and steward it the responsibility of the international community in the event the sovereign state itself cannot meet that obligation, or refuses to.

As was discussed previously, the three pillars approach could be (and has been) criticized as naïve or short-sighted (Crossley, 2018; Borgia, 2015). Certainly it backfired in practice, as states have proven themselves unyielding with respect to sovereignty over security matters despite (because of?) the advancement of R2P. However, as this research demonstrates, there is copious evidence in support of the claim that this recalcitrance on the part of many states stems from the fateful decision to tether R2P to the contested and problematic issue of humanitarian intervention. It is then at least plausible that the failure of R2P to take hold as a norm of collective moral responsibility for the provision of (human) security is a result of poor execution and strategy rather than an outright rejection of the proposed allocation of responsibility through the three pillars framework.

Understood in this way, the premise of security provision as collective obligation remains viable simply by virtue of the fact that it has never been fully put to the test. The rejection of the notion of collective responsibility deeply embedded within R2P is an artifact of the previously documented syncretism adopted (fatefully) by R2P's proponents following its initial formulation – a problematic syncretism which betrayed the fullness of R2P's normative agenda and ambitions. As such, and by extension, R2P retains at least the theoretical potential to transform the proposition of a responsibility to protect from a zero-sum joust over sovereign authority to a positive-sum recalibration of a shared moral duty. At a minimum this suggests that the opportunity for moral suasion regarding that responsibility still exists.

The preceding discussion lays bare that R2P's original answer to the question of "whose responsibility?" relative to the protection and promotion of human well-being (e.g., human security provision) required a recalibration of the sovereignty quotient. This re-allocation of security responsibilities is clearly indicative of R2P's original and ambitious normative aspirations. Making sovereign authority contingent on the ability and willingness of the state to carry out its fundamental responsibilities to its citizens had the potential to strengthen the legitimacy of the state as an entity in general, reinforcing the relational aspect of (and "thickening") international society in the process. For instance, newly accountable states (or, states newly held to account) could elect to rise to the challenge of delivering on the moral obligation of providing for the security of their populations, which would enhance their social legitimacy. Likewise, framing security provision as a moral duty of states could have the effect of reining in the behaviors of particular states and leaders prone to abuse of their authority under the guise of sovereign immunity.

More to the point, the assertion of sovereignty as responsibility – or, in the guise of R2P, of sovereignty as *moral* responsibility – vitally strengthened the position of the population at-large by asserting the (moral) rights of the individual viz. the state in the security discourse. This was a means to the end of transforming the relationship between the state and the human being in the security arena, and the norms governing that relationship. As such, the prevailing notion of responsibility on which R2P was established had the potential for the type of broad appeal necessary for R2P to gain normative traction. It was then – and, as will be discussed below, remains today – an idea with both traction and salience to those marginalized or rendered insecure by the practices of the state itself, or to those who view the state as fundamentally inadequate as a security actor.

Reconstructing responsibility

The first step in returning R2P to relevance entails if we embrace its original articulation of the nature of responsibility in the security arena. In tethering R2P to humanitarian crisis reaction, debates over responsibility were reduced to debates over who is "responsible" for that reaction or whether the "responsibility" to react does or should trump that of rebuilding and prevention. Revisiting R2P's ideational basis and aims prior to its diversion to the problem(s) of humanitarian intervention reveals a close synergy with the parallel concept and concerns of human security. Doing so also uncovers clear answers to critical questions concerning the nature of responsibility in international society. These answers are steeped in a translation of responsibility which contends that the responsibility for security provision in the international arena is a wholly collective moral obligation shared by individual states and the community in which they are embedded. Revisiting what R2P initially had to say about the nature of responsibility and to whom it entails allows for a return to the long ago expressed and still unfulfilled need for a humanitarian space delinked from the constraints of territory and sovereignty (Weiss and Chopra, 1995). In this formulation, states are "first among equals" when it comes to security provision – bound to act on their moral responsibility to do so, or to cede their authority if they do not.

The potential for R2P's normative renewal stems in no small part from a growing alignment between the doctrine's ideational foundation and the prevailing realities of contemporary international society. To some degree, this alignment can be explained by the changing nature and heightened intensity of transnational and human security threats and challenges. As will be considered at length in the next chapter, such evident and undeniable changes in the international security landscape make an overture toward "protection" in the form of human security provision more broadly appealing and less radical in conception than was the case a quarter-century ago.

However, this apparent synergy between R2P's underlying (if stagnant) normative agenda and the security imperatives of contemporary international society is not solely attributable to the mounting specter of existential threats of a transnational character. As reflected here, R2P's potential for renewed relevance and applicability also stems from its original operationalization of responsibility and the possibilities inherent in it. These possibilities are especially great amid the apparent demise of a rule-based order and the utter absence of any accountability for the systematic assault on, and erosion of, human security (Callamard, 2024).

Revisiting the defining features of R2P's conception of responsibility allows us to see that while a quarter-century ago R2P may have been an idea ahead of its time, it was also timeless. Today, international society has caught up, as the evident need for (human) security provision in the face of growing existential threats mounts, along with the quest for answers to the question of who is responsible for providing it (Panebianco, 2022; Carnegie et al., 2021; Nurhasanah et al., 2020). In the fullness of R2P's ambition to transform the norms of international security by articulating a collective moral obligation to react to threats to human security, rebuild societies in their wake, and even prevent their very occurrence it is possible to discern a pathway for reconstructing R2P and reanimating the norm life cycle in the process. As will we see in the next chapter, that pathway comes into even fuller relief when one takes into account R2P's untapped potential to stimulate and sustain human protection.

Notes

1 While a moral responsibility certainly entails in the aftermath of war, the domain of *jus post bellum* is relatively newer and, as a result, less fully articulated – leaving the assignation of (primary) responsibility for "justice after war" a less settled question (Orend, 2007).

2 See, for example, Corlett (2001).

3 This qualification of state sovereignty first introduced in the 1990s – wherein the state obtains in order to meet the security and survival needs of those individuals within its midst, rather than vice versa – certainly represented an inversion of mainstream IR thinking at the time. It also was very much a product of that time, bubbling to the surface in various forms and guises such as the human security and sustainable development agendas during what Booth (1991) characterized – hopefully – as an "interregnum" on the road to the New Times.

4 What constitutes the population of concern, and accordingly the extent of the state's moral obligation, is also a matter of extensive debate. Narrower formulations limit the state's responsibility to protect to citizens, and wider conceptions including permanent residents, legal immigrants, asylum seekers and refugees, or any person located within the territorial jurisdiction of a state. Though vitally important, this debate is outside the bounds of the current discussion.

Bibliography

Baldwin, David A. 1997. "The Concept of Security," *Review of International Studies* 23(1): 5–26.

Bellamy, Alex J. 2015. "The Three Pillars of the Responsibility to Protect," *Pensamiento propio* 41(20): 35–64.

Bellamy, Alex J. 2008. "The Responsibility to Protect and the Problem of Military Intervention," *International Affairs* 84(4): 615–639.

Bellamy, Alex J., and Paul D. Williams. 2011. "The New Politics of Protection? Cote d'Ivoire, Libya, and the Responsibility to Protect," *International Affairs* 87: 825–850.

Bernstein, Steven. 2000. "Ideas, Social Structure and the Compromise of Liberal Environmentalism," *European Journal of International Relations* 6(4): 464–512.

Boli, John. 2001. "Sovereignty From a World Polity Perspective," in Stephen D. Krasner (ed.), *Problematic Sovereignty: Contested Rules and Political Possibilities* (pp. 53–82). New York: Columbia University Press.

Booth, Ken. 1991. "Security and Emancipation," *Review of International Studies* 17(4): 313–326.

Borgia, Fiammetta. 2015. "The Responsibility to Protect Doctrine: Between Criticisms and Inconsistencies," *Journal on the Use of Force and International Law* 2(2): 223–237.

Bull, Hedley. 1977. *The Anarchical Society: A Study of Order in World Politics*. London: Macmillan.

Butler, Michael J. 2012. *Selling a 'Just' War: Framing, Legitimacy, and U.S. Military Intervention*. Basingstoke: Palgrave Macmillan.

Buzan, Barry, Ole Wæver, and Jaap de Wilde. 1998. *Security: A New Framework for Analysis*. Boulder, CO: Lynne Rienner.

Callamard, Agnès. 2024. "Gaza and the End of the Rules-Based Order," *Foreign Affairs* (15 February). Available online: https://www.foreignaffairs.com/israel/gaza-and-end-rules-based-order. Last accessed 25 February 2024.

Carati, Andrea. 2016. "Mimicking Just War? How the R2P Uses and Misuses the Just War Tradition." Paper presented at *ECPR Annual Conference, Prague (Czech*

Republic). Available online: https://air.unimi.it/bitstream/2434/438510/2/CARATI%20-%20Paper%20ECPR%202016.pdf
Carnegie, Paul, Victor T. King, and Magne Knudsen. 2021. "Human Security, Marginality and Precariousness in Southeast Asia," *International Journal of Asia Pacific Studies* 17(1): 1–28.
Commission on Human Security. 2003. "Human security Now: Protecting and Empowering People." New York: United Nations. Available online: https://digitallibrary.un.org/record/503749?ln=en&v=pdf. Last accessed 12 February 2024.
Copp, David. 1979. "Collective Actions and Secondary Actions," *American Philosophical Quarterly* 16(3): 177–186.
Corlett, J. Angelo. 2001. "Collective Moral Responsibility," *Journal of Social Philosophy* 32(4): 573–584.
Crossley, Noële. 2018. "Is R2P Still Controversial? Continuity and Change in the Debate on 'Humanitarian intervention'," *Cambridge Review of International Affairs* 31(5): 415–436.
Cunliffe, Philip. 2006. "Sovereignty and the Politics of Responsibility," in Christopher J. Bickerton, Philip Cunliffe, and Alexander Gourevitch (eds.), *Politics Without Sovereignty: A Critique of Contemporary International Relations* (pp. 53–71). London/New York: Routledge.
Duffield, Mark. 1999. "Globalization and War Economies: Promoting Order or the Return of History?" *Fletcher Forum of World Affairs* 23(2): 21–38.
Dunne, Tim. 2015. "The Responsibility to Protect and World Order," in Ramesh Thakur and William Maley (eds.), *Theorising the Responsibility to Protect* (pp. 81–100). Cambridge: Cambridge University Press.
Elster, Jon. 1985. "Rationality, Morality, and Collective Action," *Ethics* 96(1): 136–155.
Erskine, Toni. 2019. "Coalitions of the Willing and the Shared Responsibility to Protect," in Richard Beardsworth, Garrett Wallace Brown, and Richard Shapcott (eds.), *The State and Cosmopolitan Responsibilities*. New York: Oxford University Press.
Evans, Gareth. 2011. "Ethnopolitical Conflict: When is it Right to Intervene?" *Ethnopolitics* 10(1): 115–123.
Evans, Gareth. 2006. "Crimes against Humanity: Overcoming Global Indifference," *Journal of Genocide Research* 8: 325–339.
Finnemore, Martha. 2003. *The Purpose of Intervention: Changing Beliefs about the Use of Force*. Ithaca: Cornell University Press.
Hehir, Aidan. 2014. "From Human Security to the Responsibility to Protect: The Co-Option of Dissent," *Michigan State International Law Review* 23: 675.
Hehir, Aidan. 2011. "The Responsibility to Protect and International Law," in Phillip Cunliffe (ed.), *Critical Perspectives on the Responsibility to Protect: Interrogating Theory and Practice* (pp. 84–100). London/New York: Routledge.
Hettne, Björn, and Fredrik Söderbaum. 2005. "Intervening in Complex Humanitarian Emergencies: The Role of Regional Cooperation," *The European Journal of Development Research* 17(3): 449–461.
Howe, Brendan. 2018. "Divergent Interpretations of the R2P and Human Security: Implications for Governance Challenges in Myanmar," *Korean Journal of Security Affairs* 23(1): 80–101.
Huysmans, Jef. 1998. "Security! What Do You Mean? From Concept to Thick Signifier," *European Journal of International Relations* 4(2): 226–255.
Iancu, Andreea. 2014. "The Responsibility to Protect: A Just War Theory Based Analysis," *SEA–Practical Application of Science* 2(5): 341–348.
Illingworth, Richard. 2022. "An R2P Commission: A Proposal for Holding States Accountable to Their Responsibility to Protect," *Global Studies Quarterly* 2(1): 1–12.

Keranen, Outi. 2016. "What Happened to the Responsibility to Rebuild?" *Global Governance* 22(3): 331–348.

Kerr, Pauline. 2009. "Human Security and Diplomacy," in Myriam Dunn Cavelty and Victor Mauer (eds.), *The Routledge Handbook of Security Studies* (pp. 131–142). London/New York: Routledge.

Koontz, Theodore J. 1997. "Noncombatant Immunity in Michael Water's Just and Unjust Wars," *Ethics & International Affairs* 11(1): 55–82.

Krause, Keith. 2007. "Towards a Practical Human Security Agenda." Policy paper, Geneva Centre for the Democratic Control of Armed Forces, no. 26. Geneva: DCAF.

Krause, Keith, and Michael Williams. 1996. "Broadening the Agenda of Security Studies: Politics and Methods," *Mershon International Studies Review* 40(2): 229–254.

Luck, Edward C. 2008. "Introduction: The Responsible Sovereign and the Responsibility to Protect," in *Annual Review of United Nations Affairs 2006/2007*, vol. 1 (pp. xxxiii–xliv). New York: Oxford University Press.

MacArthur, Julie. 2008. "A Responsibility to Rethink? Challenging Paradigms in Human Security," *International Journal* 63(2): 422–443.

Newman, Edward. 2013. "The United Nations and Human Security: Between Solidarism and Pluralism," in Mary Martin and Taylor Owen (eds.), *Routledge Handbook of Human Security* (pp. 245–258). London/New York: Routledge.

Nurhasanah, Siti, Marthen Napang, and Syaiful Rohman. 2020. "Covid-19 as a Non-Traditional Threat to Human Security," *Journal of Strategic and Global Studies* 3(1): 54–68.

Orend, Brian. 2007. "Jus Post Bellum: The Perspective of a Just-War Theorist," *Leiden Journal of International Law* 20(3): 571–591.

Orford, Anne. 2013. "Moral Internationalism and the Responsibility to Protect," *European Journal of International Law* 24(1): 83–108.

Orford, Anne. 2011. *International Authority and the Responsibility to Protect.* Cambridge: Cambridge University Press.

Pace, William, and Nicole Deller. 2005. "Preventing Future Genocides: An International Responsibility to Protect," *World Order* 36(4): 15–32.

Panebianco, Stefania. 2022. "Human Security at the Mediterranean Borders: Humanitarian Discourse in the EU Periphery," *International Politics* 59(3): 428–448.

Papamichail, Andeas, and Hannah Partis-Jennings. 2016. "Why Common Humanity? Framing the Responsibility to Protect as a Common Response," *International Politics* 53(1): 83–100.

Paris, Roland. 2014. "The 'Responsibility to Protect' and the Structural Problems of Preventive Humanitarian Intervention," *International Peacekeeping* 21(5): 569–603.

Paris, Roland. 2001. "Human Security: Paradigm Shift or Hot Air?" *International Security* 26(2): 87–102.

Radice, Henry. 2016. "The Responsibility to Protect as Humanitarian Negotiation: A Space for the 'Politics of Humanity'?" *International Politics* 53(1): 101–117.

Rawls, John. 1993. "The Law of Peoples," *Critical Inquiry* 20(1): 36–68.

Rochester, J. Martin. 2016. *The New Warfare: Rethinking Rules for an Unruly World.* London/New York: Routledge.

Sen, Amartya. 2004. "Capability and well-being," in Martha Nussbaum and Amartya Sen (eds.), *The Quality of Life* (pp. 30–53). New York: Rutledge.

Sheehan, Michael. 2005. *International Security: An Analytical Survey.* Boulder, CO: Lynne Rienner.

Sjostedt, Roxanna. 2019. "Assessing Securitization Theory: Theoretical Discussions and Empirical Developments," in Michael J. Butler (ed.), *Securitization Revisited: Contemporary Applications and Insights* (pp. 28–46). London/New York: Routledge.

Tadjbakhsh, Shahrbanou. 2013. "In Defense of the Broad View of Human Security," in Mary Martin and Taylor Owen (eds.), *Routledge Handbook of Human Security* (pp. 63–77). London/New York: Routledge.
Thakur, Ramesh. 2016. "The Responsibility to Protect at 15," *International Affairs* 92(2): 415–434.
Thakur, Ramesh, and William Maley. 2015. "Theorising Global Responsibilities," in R. Thakur and W. Maley (eds.), *Theorising the Responsibility to Protect* (pp. 3–15). Cambridge: Cambridge University Press.
Ullman, Richard. 1983. "Redefining Security," *International Security* 8(1): 129–153.
United Nations Development Programme. 1994. *Human Development Report 1994: New Dimensions of Human Security*. New York: Oxford University Press.
United Nations General Assembly. 2005. High-level Plenary Meeting of the 60th Session of the UN General Assembly, World Summit Outcome, UNGA Res. 60/1 (16 September 2005). Available online: https://www.refworld.org/docid/44168a910.html. Last accessed 31 January 2024.
Walzer, Michael. 1977. *Just and Unjust Wars: A Moral Argument with Historical Illustrations*. New York: Basic Books.
Weiss, Thomas G. 2006. "R2P after 9/11 and the World Summit," *Wisconsin International Law Journal* 24: 741.
Weiss, Thomas G., and David A. Korn. 2006. *Internal Displacement: Conceptualization and Its Consequences*. London/New York: Routledge.
Weiss, Thomas G., and Jarat Chopra. 1995. "Sovereignty Under Siege: From Intervention to Humanitarian Space," in Gene M. Lyons and Michael Mastanduno (eds.), *Beyond Westphalia? National Sovereignty and International Intervention* (pp. 87–114). Baltimore, MD: Johns Hopkins University Press.
Wendt, Alexander. 1999. *Social Theory of International Politics*. Cambridge: Cambridge University Press.
Wheeler, Nicholas J. 2000. *Saving Strangers: Humanitarian Intervention in International Society*. New York: Oxford University Press.
Wunderlich, Carmen. 2013. "Theoretical Approaches in Norm Dynamics," in Harald Muller and Carmen Wunderlich (eds.), *Norm Dynamics in Multilateral Arms Control: Interests, Conflicts, and Justice* (pp. 20–47). Athens, GA: University of Georgia Press.

5 Rethinking the referent

Like its embedded notion of responsibility, the concept and ethic of protection initially introduced by R2P bears all the hallmarks of normative aspiration. The original emphasis of R2P relative to responsibility was on ***transferring*** the moral duty to protect human beings from states to the international community – and fashioning a new norm of collective responsibility for the provision of human security in the process. As the present chapter reveals, the onus with regard to protection itself was on ***transcending*** prevailing thinking and practice(s) within the realm of international security. Rather than maintaining the privileged position of the state as the central referent in and for security thinking and practice, R2P's architects sought to introduce a new security norm oriented around protecting the well-being of individual persons.

As with its underlying notion of responsibility, R2P's original articulation of protection was informed by the concept of human security. It was also influenced by two distinct and contemporaneous efforts within the field of security studies to "deepen" and "broaden" prevailing understandings of, and approaches to, security (Watson, 2011). R2P's new approach to protection, centered around the security of individuals and situated within an expanded security horizon, was fully conversant with its conceptualization of a "responsibility to protect" as universal moral duty. And, as with the attempt at fashioning a new norm of collective responsibility, the goal of prioritizing human subjectivity within the security realm also fell by the wayside as R2P's normative evolution stagnated.

If R2P's normative aims are to be reanimated, doing so requires a return to and reconsideration of R2P's original position regarding protection. This chapter uncovers the potential inherent in R2P as an instrumental vehicle of and for the protection of human well-being. It does so by engaging with and unpacking R2P's prescient insights relative to three considerations: protection for ***who***, protection from ***what***, and ***how*** to protect. This reconsideration of the concept of human protection infused within the very design of R2P reveals a profound recognition of, and reckoning with, the so-called "insecurity dilemma" (Bilgin, 2020). Identified by scholars well over a generation ago (Glenn, 1997; Jackson, 1990), the insecurity dilemma is fundamentally rooted in the incapacity and/or unwillingness of the state to adequately meet the security imperatives

DOI: 10.4324/9781315105628-6

of those for whom it is allegedly responsible. This dilemma has not only persisted but intensified along with the proliferation of a wide range of chronic, transnational, and even existential security threats which are beyond the capacity of states to address. Inherent in R2P's answers to the questions of protection identified here lies a potential remedy to this dilemma and, by extension, a potential avenue for rebooting R2P's normative agenda.

Protection for who?

R2P's original translation of protection reflected an understanding of security that was radically human-centered, revealing the influence of a critical security studies approach emergent in the 1970s and 1980s (e.g., Ullman, 1983). While the direct impact of this new epistemological direction in security studies on the ICISS is subject to debate, its influence on the intellectual and social context in which R2P was fashioned is undeniable. Specifically, the efforts of the so-called Aberystwyth School and scholars such as Kenneth Booth, Richard Wyn Jones, and others to "deepen" the concept of security as well as that of the so-called Paris School and the intellectual labors of scholars including Didier Bigo and Jef Huysmans (2002) who worked to uncover the coercive underpinnings of security practices and technologies were critical influences on R2P's initial understanding of, and approach to, protection.

"Deepening" security

In the spirit of a prevailing zeitgeist, the conversance between the emphasis of the Aberystwyth School on deepening security as both a concept and practice wholly centered on the well-being of the individual and the normative ambitions of R2P concerning protection is clear. The main point of intersection lies in two structuring and interrelated claims: first, that the only logical and practicable referent for security thought and practice is the human person, and second, that the fetishization of the state as a security actor can not only obstruct but also directly undermine security provision (Jones, 2018). Drawing from the insights of the Frankfurt School and post-positivism, the fundamental proposition of the Aberystwyth School was that security is best understood as a condition of individual emancipation from external constraints (Nunes, 2012). Such constraints include not only physical harm and suffering but also translations of structural violence and oppression that impede human flourishing (Peoples and Vaughn-Williams, 2015; Booth, 1997).[1]

This view of security also necessarily rejects the predominant state-centric approach to security provision. Apart from their status as a means to the end of emancipation and freedom for individuals, states themselves represent little more than abstractions (Booth, 1991).[2] Further to this point, Booth stresses that states are inappropriate vehicles for security provision in that they are both unreliable and illogical (Booth, 1991: 320). To characterize states as unreliable security agents is to recognize that not all states are created equally; some are invested in the business of security provision for those in their charge, while others are decidedly not (consider, for example, Putin's Russia). This characterization of the unreliability of states as the locus of and for security is informed by recognition of their sins of omission (i.e., prolonged equivocation regarding climate change mitigation) and commission (i.e., repeated chemical weapons attacks by the Assad regime against civilian targets in the Syrian civil war). Likewise, and by extension, Booth points to a fundamental illogic in a state-centric orientation to security thinking and practice: namely, that the primary duty of the Weberian-Westphalian state is to afford security to individuals under its jurisdiction, not the other way around.[3]

These two interrelated claims underpin what Booth characterized as "emancipatory realism": a pragmatic recalibration of interests and power as means to the end of advancing the well-being of the human person (Krause and Williams, 1997; Jones, 1996, 2001; Booth, 1991, 2005). In this emancipatory thrust we can also discern the very same basis for a recalibrated relationship between the state and the individual that inspired R2P's (re)conceptualization of responsibility. Indeed, among the other features attendant in the "deepening" impulse at the heart of human security and by extension R2P, one that is particularly suggestive of R2P's normative aspiration was its call for a fuller accounting of, and remedy, for deployment of coercive practices and logics by states against individuals (Jones, 2018). In this way we can see how R2P's attempt to advance a new ethic of protection centered around the individual person (transcending prevailing thinking and practice) complements and reinforces the transference of security responsibilities from the state to the international community.

Problematizing the state

Another epistemological tributary leading to the development of the Responsibility to Protect was the "Paris School" of security studies. Associated with scholars such as Didier Bigo (Bigo and Guild, 2005; Bigo, 2002, 2000, 1996) and Jef Huysmans (Huysmans, 2006, 2002, 2000), this school of thought drew inspiration from Foucault's work on discipline, biopolitics, and technologies of security. The development of the Paris School was also attributable in part to prevailing social dynamics within Europe concerning population movements and the fashioning of a "justice and home affairs" pillar in the Treaty of Maastricht in 1992. The result was a blending of insights from political sociology and critical theory in service of critically interrogating topics and practices such as policing, coercion, and the securitization of migration (Bigo and Guild, 2005; Bonelli, 2005; Huysmans, 2000; Ceyhan and Tsoukala, 1997). As the very center of these interrogations was an explicit recognition and critique of governmentality as a mechanism for imposing and maintaining social order (Rose et al., 2006).

Although the conversance of the Paris School approach with R2P is not immediately obvious, its critical diagnosis and appraisal of the order-inducing function of institutionally endorsed coercion was key. The insights of the Paris School provided an impetus for wider recognition of the crowding out of the individual by the state within the security arena, both ontologically and practically (Browning and McDonald, 2013). It also helped reveal the ways in which the state is complicit in, or even the origin source for, the construction of threats to the security of those individuals to whom they are (allegedly) responsible (Bigo, 2002). This was a feature which not only distinguished the Paris School at the vanguard of critical security studies, but also positioned it in direct opposition to an international societal status quo arrayed around the central role of states as (uncontested) security actors.

Taken together, these insights point to the peril of unconsciously accepting the notion of the state as the appropriate referent for security thinking and practice. Doing so necessarily directs the focus for that thinking and practice to the unique interests and imperatives that determine, and impinge upon, each state's own security and by extension the collective security of the international society of states (Bull, 1977). These interests and imperatives are assumed to be known to states and their leaders, who consequently enjoy a position at the commanding heights of security provision (Katzenstein, 1996). The conceptualization of security that results naturally reifies the centrality of the state as well as the concept of state sovereignty within the security realm, with the security concerns of sub-state constituents, other states, or the international system given short shrift (Masco, 2014). The larger implication here is that the security concerns of human beings are obscured or omitted amid the abstractions of the state and its alleged security imperatives. So long as the state remains the security referent, it has license to act on those alleged imperatives, whether or not doing so contributes to or enhances the security and well-being of those in its charge – or even denudes it, becoming a source of threat to its own people (Commission on Human Security, 2003). Such was the fundamental challenge which the ICISS was tasked to remedy.

While dismissed by some as a matter of arcane theoretical posturing (Walt, 2010; Mutimer, 2009), determining the appropriate referent for security thinking and practice has direct implications for security provision. Who or what one chooses to prioritize within the security arena plays an essential role in establishing how security is defined, what the chief threat(s) to security is (are), and how those threats can be managed (Buzan and Hansen, 2010; Walker, 1997). At a bare minimum, the reification of the state as security actor imposes intellectual and philosophical constraints on human agency with profound implications for security as a practice (Bilgin, 2002). To this point, while never directly repudiating states as security actors, from the outset the ICISS clearly articulated the need for states to forfeit their unquestioned primacy in the security realm. R2P's answer to the state-centric machinations that had previously dominated questions of civilian protection was to elevate such matters to the level of collective obligation of the international community writ large (Bellamy and Williams, 2011).

Codification of this rejection of the monopoly of the state in the security arena can be found in the Three Pillars approach introduced in the 2005 World

Summit Outcomes document (paragraphs 138 and 139). While a key function of the pillars is to specify the role of the international community as a backstop to, or even surrogate for, the state on matters of civilian protection and atrocity prevention, the other side of that coin is equally important. Logically speaking, transferring sovereign authority from the state to the international community (via the second and third pillars) renders the state fundamentally accountable to the international community with respect to the provision of security to those under its jurisdiction. The Three Pillars approach is a seamless extension of the work of the ICISS and a translation of R2P's foundational notion that the well-being of the human person is both a moral obligation and a shared one that *may* involve, but necessarily *does* transcend, the state (Erskine, 2014; emphasis added). As such, the secondary position of the international community relative to the duty for and authority over civilian protection and atrocity prevention as articulated in the Three Pillars framework does not reflect subordination to the Westphalian-Weberian state, but rather adjacency (Orford, 2013).

R2P's acknowledgment of the insufficiency and inadequacy of the state as a security actor is not altogether surprising. Such a posture would be expected given the decline of state capacity and concomitant proliferation of threats to human security that inspired R2P in the first place (Axworthy, 2001). To this point, Orford (2013) emphasizes that R2P's ethic of protection was borne of the recognition that "millions of human beings remain at the mercy of civil wars, insurgencies, state repression, and state collapse" (ICISS, 2001). The conceptualization of protection advanced by the ICISS in response to this recognition in turn reflected the premise that "security must make sense at the basic level of the individual human being for it to make sense at the international level" (McSweeney, 1999: 16). Viewed in this light, R2P can be seen as an extension and reinforcement of the impulse toward deepening *extant* within the security studies field.

Protection from what?

Fully accounting for R2P's positionality *viz*. the state requires recognizing not only the influence of critical security studies on the development of R2P, but also areas of divergence. With respect to R2P's ethic of protection, the key point of departure is the underlying impetus for challenging the state's monopoly over security provision. For CSS thinkers (and in particular the Paris School) that challenge stemmed (and stems) from the state's inadmissibility and even ***illegitimacy*** as a security actor. By contrast, for the ICISS and the generation of R2P advocates that followed, that challenge to the monopoly of the state over security provision was informed by a concern with the state's ***inadequacy*** within the security realm. The emergence (or, perhaps more accurately, expanded recognition) of a plethora of "new" security threats and challenges of broader scope and remit only served to further expose and magnify that inadequacy.

"Broadening" security

Embedded recognition of the limits (conceptual and practical) of the state as a security actor within R2P betrays the imprint of another tributary of the human security agenda: namely the attempt at "broadening" security studies associated with the Copenhagen School. Rising to prominence in the post–Cold War era, the Copenhagen School centered its efforts on expanding the range of recognized phenomena potentially constituting a security "threat" and, by extension, our understanding of security itself. At its very heart was a perceived need for scholars and practitioners to expand their horizons for thinking about security provision and threats beyond the familiar confines of political and military sectors (McSweeney, 1996). These efforts undoubtedly shaped the social and intellectual climate that ultimately promulgated R2P.

In service of this broadening agenda, the Copenhagen School drew on the sectoral approach first outlined by Buzan in *People, States, and Fear* (1983). The sectoral approach situated security concerns across five distinct (but not mutually exclusive) sectors: ***military*** (concerns produced by the reciprocal interaction of the armed offensive and defensive capabilities and/or perceptions of states and their leaders); ***political*** (concerns produced in relation to the organization stability (or instability) of states, governing systems, and ideologies); ***economic*** (concerns generated by limited or unequal access to economic resources needed to sustain an acceptable level of social welfare); ***societal*** (concerns triggered by either excessive adherence *or* real/perceived threats to traditional patterns of language, culture, religious and national identity, or custom); and ***environmental*** (concerns prompted by threats to the local, regional, or global ecosystem and the natural resource base on which human life depends).

The effort to broaden security considerations as reflected in the sectoral approach undoubtedly expanded the analytical purview of security studies as a field of inquiry. It also deeply complicated the policy agendas of numerous states and international institutions (Floyd, 2007). The primary source of this complication was the call for "exploring threats to referent objects, and the securitization of those threats, that are nonmilitary as well as military" (Buzan et al., 1998: 4). Beyond the obvious challenge it posed to the traditional (realist) emphasis on military security, this broadening impulse also helped reinforce the parallel move toward "deepening" and its central assertion that the state was (is) not the sole or primary referent for security studies and/or policy (Buzan, 1997). Instead, the appropriate referent(s) for security thinking and practice can and does vary in conjunction with the sector(s) in which a security concern is situated. In a larger sense, the central concern for security provision varies on a case-by-case basis; whether the international system, the state, or the individual (or some combination of the three) is the appropriate focal point is contingent on the nature of the security concern or "threat" in question (Buzan, 1997).

This aspect of the broadening agenda has two distinct consequences for R2P's ethic of protection. First, it requires those engaged in the study of security and ***especially*** those responsible for security provision to remain flexible in determining the subject of security concern in a given scenario. The process of discerning the security referent is dynamic, context-specific, and decidedly not zero-sum; rather, it turns on the source, nature, and extent of the threat in question. For R2P, this implication is reflected in an approach to protection which centers on affording that protection to individuals explicitly and to a greater degree and extent than at any time in modern history. At the same time, it is also reflected in the fact that R2P necessarily retains a significant place for the state in the process of affording security protection to the individual. In its very design and logic, R2P accepts multiple conditions: (a) that the security of the state(s) and individuals may be (and often is) intertwined; (b) the security of the state(s) and individuals could be jointly compromised and simultaneously in need of "protection"; (c) in some circumstances the security of the individual (and by extension the primary responsibility to "protect" the individual) resides with and is best served by the state in question (i.e., the state with jurisdiction).

The second major consequence of the broadening move as it relates to R2P's ethic of protection stems from its incorporation of non-traditional sectors (societal, economic, environmental) into mainstream security thinking and practice. Expanding the range and scope of what constitutes security considerations is a process that predates the sectoral approach. Indeed, that approach itself was the by-product of an intellectual movement for redefining security dating back to the 1970s – a movement centered on recasting the security referent from national to international (Ullman, 1983; Freedman, 1998). Regardless of its origin story, the broadening of security thinking and practice to include societal, economic, and environmental (alongside political and military) considerations heightened the need for an approach to protection explicitly emphasizing protecting individuals and social groups. In lockstep with the revelation of "new" (or, perhaps, newly recognized) realms of and for security consideration came the revelation of "new" (again, newly recognized) types of security threats.

Protection amid the "coming anarchy"

The convergence of these two revelations in turn produced a third: the uniquely vulnerable position of individuals relative to such threats. Expanding the range and scope of potentially securitized phenomena reveals the distinct vulnerability of human beings in the face of threats of a (global) political, societal, economic, or environmental nature (Buzan and Waever, 2003). Likewise, privileging humanity as the ontological subject of security expands the range of phenomena that could be construed as threatening to humans and by extension might warrant protective measures. These two intellectual propositions are essentially complementary. To this point, while the sectoral schema sketched out above is not all-encompassing, it offers not only a more expansive picture of contemporary security threats but also a basic roadmap for rethinking security provision with the security of human beings at the center. This secondary function of the sectoral approach stems from its revelation of the animating role that globalization plays across a wide range of potential security threats spanning multiple sectors (Buzan et al., 1998).

While the benefits of globalization and complex interdependence are many and oft-celebrated (Friedman, 2007; Keohane and Nye, 2001), the depth and expanse of networked interactions between and among societies and individuals is not unproblematic. Indeed, numerous contemporary threats to human security are wholly or at least in part unintended outcomes or negative externalities produced by the extensive and intensive transformations wrought by globalization. From a security standpoint, the extensity and intensity that has typified globalization in the late 20th and 21st centuries has increased both the sensitivity and vulnerability of an ever-greater number of actors to an increasingly wide range of economic, societal, and environmental security threats (Baldwin, 1980). As Hanlon and Christie (2016) note, threats to human security emanating from these sectors can be grouped into four main categories: ***physical*** (threats eliciting pain, injury, ailment, or death); ***economic*** (threats to property, economic opportunity, or access to material resources); ***political*** (threats arising from denial of basic rights, restrictions on political liberty, limits to political participation); and ***status*** (threats to an individual's place within the social order).

Undoubtedly the transformational impacts of globalization in its various forms (political, social, economic, cultural, technological, and ideational) on international and domestic society pose tangible challenges to human security (Madrueño-Aguilar, 2016; Hampson, 2012). So too does the backlash against globalization and its consequences, particularly in cases when the anger, confusion, and grievance underlying and animating that backlash is radicalized, weaponized, and violently displaced on other individuals and/or social groups (Eichengreen, 2018; Karakaya, 2018). Yet it is not just or even primarily the direct material consequences of globalization nor the turn to political and/or physical violence within, between, or across societies by its "discontents" (Devetak, 2007; Stiglitz and Pike, 2004; Sassen, 1999) that is of concern here. Beyond these two legible threats to human security lies a pervasive and underlying perception of vulnerability and powerlessness relative to the expansive and existential security threats produced and delivered by globalization itself (UNDP, 2022).

Contemporary international society is typified by a chronic condition of human insecurity resulting from the naked exposure of individuals to the dislocating, densely networked, and largely ungoverned processes of globalization (Fukuda-Parr, 2003). These processes have become deeply embedded and institutionalized in the structures of both domestic and international society to a point of unconsciousness, rendering them invisible to some and beyond the reach or control of others (Sassen, 2016; Araghi, 2012). Though the processes of globalization may be distant, abstract, and opaque, the effects of these processes on human security are quite real and profound both in terms of material

(Steger et al., 2023; Kalleberg, 2018; Mittelman, 2010) and psychological (Colantone et al., 2019; Sharma and Sharma, 2010) well-being. Delivered via predatory market activity, transnational crime networks, dynamics of forced migration and displacement, transmission of novel pathogens, climate networks, cyberspace, or various other pathways of transmission these threats, typical of the "new" security environment described above, could aptly be characterized as the "dark side" of complex interdependence (Butler, 2019).

At the heart of the matter is the degree to which the destabilizing, volatile, and seemingly haphazard effects of global economic, social, technological, and ecological processes and dynamics are contributing to and enhancing human insecurity and vulnerability *en masse* (Oliver-Smith, 2013; Brodie, 2003). The degree to which these processes and dynamics are gaining salience not only in the field of security studies but more importantly throughout international society itself is in turn illuminating concerns that were once considered to be associated either with a "security" or "development" agenda, as opposed to the intersection or combination of the two (Collier, 2003). As issues such as climate change, pandemic disease, and forced migration gain greater salience and traction throughout international society, they are also unveiling the heightened vulnerability of the vast majority of the world's population.

Given the objective (material) and, perhaps more importantly, subjective (perceived) importance of inequality, poverty and relative deprivation, resource scarcity and environmental degradation, crime, disease, external and internal migration, and the like within the "new security environment," we stand on the brink of an international social reality in which these abject threats to human security are only nominally related to states and their interests and capabilities. This revelation concerning the nature of the contemporary security landscape and the relationship between globalization and human (in)security in turn highlights the need for new forms of, and ways of thinking about, civilian protection. Given its emphasis on human security as reflected in its fusion of both the deepening and broadening impulses (as outlined here), R2P's ethic of protection has the potential to meet this evident need.

As discussed previously, the influence of the broadening move in security studies on the architects of R2P was chiefly manifested in an "outside-in" approach that read into the emergence of an expansive and diverse range of security concerns an imperative need for an intentional focus on human protection. Lost in translation, however, were the direct implications for human (in)security from threats largely emanating from outside the military and political realms such as pandemic disease or climate change. While these phenomena certainly have military and political implications and translations, unlike civil wars or ethnic cleansing campaigns the bulk of the harm and risk they impose upon humans stems from their economic, social, and/or environmental dimensions.

Yet while the ethic of protection originally articulated by the ICISS was chiefly focused on human (in)security as a by-product of inter-state and intra-state armed conflict and mass atrocity events, the inherent logic of R2P concerning protection grants it distinct applicability for the qualitatively different threats of today. In large part this stems from the fact that the supposition of a "new" security environment rests on the same revelation that produced R2P a generation ago: namely, that the changing structural and societal dynamics of the post–Cold War era were responsible for the heightened insecurity for millions of people around the world (Butler, 2019). In that spirit, we turn to the question of how to protect.

How to protect?

Chronic threats to human security are embedded within the very fabric of contemporary international society. As discussed above, they are produced (and reproduced) by transnational networks and processes of commerce, transportation, migration, information technology, and resource consumption. Further compounding the disruptive and dislocating impacts of these networks and processes is the well-chronicled decline of the state as a security actor relative to non-state actors (Abrahamsen and Williams, 2010; Van Creveld, 1999). Not to be overlooked in the "new security environment" ushered in by the end of the Cold War is a dynamic of displacement, whereby non-state actors including transnational corporations (TNCs), non-governmental organizations (NGOs), networked non-state terrorists and paramilitaries, private military and security contractors (PMSCs), and the like have altered and eroded the authority over security matters and even basic governance traditionally enjoyed by states (Davis, 2009).

The growing influence of NSAs in the security arena not only speaks to the general emergence of non-state actors in international society but, on the other side of that coin, challenges to the monopoly – and by extension basic capacity – of the state as a security actor. The pervasive and enduring condition of human insecurity spawned by global and transnational networks and processes has been compounded by the intentional and protracted effort to dismantle and/or diminish regulatory oversight and governance in general (McGrew and Held, 2002). In the face of increasing downward pressure from global and transnational forces and actors, what has resulted is tantamount to the state's abdication not only of the responsibility to protect its citizens but also of the fundamental responsibility to govern (Kaldor, 2012).

The insecurity dilemma

In the absence of any effective intermediary to provide or advocate for their security and well-being, those without the means or capacities for self-protection are especially vulnerable to the vagaries of capitalist exploitation, weaponized information and data mining, human trafficking, forced displacement, resource extraction, and the like. Scholars have dubbed this scenario, playing out against the backdrop of globalization and state incapacity, the "insecurity dilemma" (Bilgin, 2020).[4] Not unlike R2P, the insecurity dilemma draws its origins from the 1990s, as a phenomenon originally associated with the breakdown in social order caused by ethnic conflict (Glenn, 1997). While the range of potential catalysts for the dilemma have subsequently been expanded, the insecurity dilemma still fundamentally turns on the diminished capacities of states as security actors (Sørensen, 2007). As Weinstein et al. (2004) contend, the insecurity dilemma is the sum outcome of three critical problems confronting the state: its inability and/or unwillingness to maintain basic order and protect civilians in its jurisdiction (the "security gap"), its inability and/or unwillingness to provide other public or social goods such as welfare, liberty, and the rule of law (the "capacity gap"), and its resulting lack of buy-in and support from its citizens (the "legitimacy gap").

Deeply rooted in social structures and spatially and metaphysically distant and seemingly haphazard dynamics, the threats posed by processes of globalization and transnationalism both magnify, and are magnified by, the insecurity dilemma. The resulting incapacity or unwillingness of the state to mitigate the destabilizing and dislocating effects of globalization makes those effects particularly pernicious, since effective amelioration of these threats is beyond the capacity of most of the world's population (Fontana, 2022). In the absence of effective governance of these processes and/or mitigation of their negative externalities, the result is a human (in)security landscape defined by chronic, diffuse, and universal threats to human well-being.

The threats to human security inherent to global and transnational forces and processes are not only an individual-level concern, but a societal one. Designating the individual as the security referent does not divorce the nature and effect(s) of threats and risks confronting the individual from the larger social and natural environment in which they exist; indeed, human security is typically understood as a collective enterprise (Adger et al., 2014).[5] This insight speaks to the need for security provision – i.e., "protection" – at the societal level as efforts to prioritize threats to human security, and to effectively respond to them, are typically beyond the means and capabilities of the individuals or social groups most directly or immediately impacted. Indeed, one is unlikely to be able to investigate, arrest, and prosecute organized crime lords, thwart an ethnic cleansing campaign, prevent or treat a disease, or mitigate the effects of rising global temperatures without external support (Black, 2016).

While R2P is chiefly oriented to the threats posed by states and/or armed combatants to individuals, its embedded ethic of protection makes it both a theoretically relevant and practically useful tool for contending with the insecurity dilemma and the dynamics of globalization and transnationalism that (re)produce it. R2P's relevance and utility in this regard stems from its explicit recognition of the state's inherent limitations *viz.* security provision. In returning to the distinction introduced previously, R2P was designed not only to provide a mechanism for redress of those "sins" of commission by states inflicted on those to whom it ostensibly bears security obligations, but also for "sins" of omission wherein states are unable to carry out those obligations effectively. This animus for R2P helps explain, in part, the formulation of the Three Pillars approach and its layered allocation of responsibility, as well as the continued relevance and utility of that approach as the basis for the provision of human security. The Three Pillars approach was (and is) consistent with and reflective of the ICISS' perspective that in some cases the state's failings in the security arena are borne of incapacity rather than illegitimacy (Chandler, 2010).

This subtle but important distinction in the critical posture of the ICISS toward the state speaks to a valuable degree of nuance inherent to R2P. That posture is grounded not only in recognition of the state's potential or occasional abuse of sovereign authority but also in the practical limits of that sovereign authority-- a recognition that there are security challenges which the state cannot adequately meet. This degree of nuance has exposed R2P to harsh critique from those who consider the state anachronistic or, worse, a tool of and for oppression (Scott, 2020; Lacher, 2003). Yet resident in R2P's moderated critique of the state as a security actor lies evident potential for reanimating its normative aims. From its very inception, R2P was predicated on elevating the protection of individuals to the status of a priority concern for international society at-large. This elevation of the security of individuals (i.e., human security) is especially pertinent in a dynamic security environment defined by chronic, diffuse, and universal threats to human well-being. The reality of these threats playing out against the backdrop of a state-based security apparatus that is severely compromised and ineffectual in the face of said threats is one that requires, if not demands, remedy.

Prevention-as-protection

Absent effective governance of the processes of globalization and/or mitigation of their negative externalities by the state, what has resulted is a security landscape defined by chronic, diffuse, and universal threats to human well-being. R2P's ethic of protection has significant (if untapped) potential as a remedy to this globalized (in)security dilemma. While the original stated focus of the ICISS was the alleviation of widespread insecurity caused by civil wars, insurgencies, state repression, and state collapse (i.e., residing largely in the military and political sectors), as we have seen R2P offers a prescription for protecting individuals from a broad range of complex security threats outstripping the capacity of states as security actors. This prescription is reflected in R2P's central, if oft-overlooked, focus on prevention.

The human-centered approach to protection at the heart of R2P is sufficiently pliable to allow for application to the broad range of complex and multifaceted threats typifying the "new security environment." However, tapping into this pliability requires returning to R2P's roots as a doctrine not only of reaction but also and especially of prevention. Doing so in turn requires confronting and overcoming the single greatest obstacle to the diffusion and internationalization of R2P as a security norm – its long-standing and highly fraught linkage to humanitarian crisis intervention. Here, again, lies another problematic manifestation of the strategic move to reduce R2P to a covering rationale for humanitarian intervention. Entrapping R2P within the interminable debate over humanitarian intervention has severely limited its applicability as a mechanism for promoting human security and, in turn, constrained its normative potential by tying R2P to the anachronistic "saving strangers problem" (Hopgood, 2014).

As discussed at length previously, the focus on R2P as a reactive instrument intended to foster human protection in acute, contained, and discrete cases of humanitarian crisis has held sway over most of the doctrine's lifespan. This has obscured the more expansive aims of R2P's architects and proponents. Yet even within the narrow realm of reaction, R2P featured a somewhat radical reformulation of sovereign authority, proposing a surrogate arrangement for civilian protection when the state proved unable or unwilling to respond to the threat or actual occurrence of large-scale loss of life or widespread forced displacement. Moreover, R2P explicitly treated such occurrences as systematic and egregious violations of human rights, not only (or merely) the "horrors of (new) wars" (Murdie, 2017; Serrano and Weiss, 2014).

Beyond these considerations, the most compelling evidence of the broader ambitions of the ICISS and the doctrine of R2P they devised is its clear emphasis on and articulation of a responsibility not only to respond to atrocities and human rights violations but in fact to prevent harm to individuals in the first place (Rosenberg, 2009). As conceived by the ICISS, prevention was understood not only as a fundamental responsibility but also a means for efficiently and effectively delivering on the mandate of civilian protection. In that way, prevention is fully conversant with R2P's ethic of protection. To this point, R2P expressly operationalizes prevention (and, by extension, protection) in a way that is both ***expansive*** in scope and ***proactive*** in nature.

As a reflection of its expansive scope, prevention-as-protection encompasses a broad remit including

> ...targeting unaccountable governance structures, reforming a security apparatus that supports a repressive regime and acts with impunity, rectifying patterns of discrimination against particular population groups through political and legal reform, and supporting transitional justice mechanisms where there has been a lack of recourse to redress for past injustices, atrocity crimes, and systematic human rights violations.
>
> (Jacob, 2019: 5)

Prevention-as-protection thus concerns deficiencies in political representation, the rule of law, social justice, and human rights accountability, among others (Jacob, 2019). In terms of proactivity, R2P's articulation of prevention extends the scope of protection beyond the amelioration of direct threats to human well-being and security. Rather, protection also calls for action to address underlying structural conditions that "generate the potential and likelihood" that mass atrocities and other forms of harm will occur (Jacob, 2019). Thus, prevention-as-protection is inherently proactive, reflecting the position that early intervention can and does enhance human security by strengthening societal resilience (Reike et al., 2015).

The deficiency and absence of societal resilience and/or state capacity is the underlying condition responsible for the proximate causes of human (in)security around the world – including deficient access to food, water, shelter, and basic health care, lack of economic opportunity, and the suppression or violation of various civil and political liberties. The under-supply or lack of provision of these goods is typically a function of ill-designed, underperforming, and/or repressive social, political, and economic structures and institutions afflicting an increasingly large proportion of the world's population (UNDP, 2022). Moreover, as reflected in their codification in the ICCPR and ICESCR (King and Murray, 2002), these causes of human insecurity are understood as basic human rights which citizens are entitled to and which states are legally responsible to provide (Bellamy, 2011; Deng et al., 1996).

This is a problem which R2P's prevention dimension, as a mechanism of and for human protection, was (and is) specifically designed to address. Given the recognized status of the foundational components of human security (food, shelter, health, free expression, etc.) as basic human rights and legal obligations, it makes little sense to continue to disaggregate instances of acute, contained, and discrete "crises" from chronic, diffuse, and universal conditions of human insecurity and to prioritize the former for (re)action while failing to address the latter. Beyond the prevention of harm associated with the (continued) proliferation and intensification of acute, contained, and discrete cases of humanitarian crisis, in its broader and proactive guise prevention can extend R2P's ethic of protection to the chronic, diffuse, and universal threats that typify the conventional global and human security landscape.

The potential that a return to, and renewed emphasis on, R2P's logic of prevention-as-protection has in terms of providing an answer to the question of ***how*** to protect humanity in the face of mounting existential threats such as global climate change, forced migration, or pandemic disease (among others) provides speaks to this relevance and applicability (Panebianco, 2022; Carnegie et al., 2021; Nurhasanah et al., 2020). In revisiting R2P in full, its evident potential to fill the void at the heart of the insecurity dilemma through its proactive logic of prevention-as-protection is clear. So too is its relevance as an ethic of (and for) human protection in a "new" security environment defined by global disorder and domestic-level anarchy (Vershbow, 2016; Zartman, 2008; Kaplan, 1994).

Reconstructing protection

Though largely overlooked as a result of the prevailing and reductive emphasis on reaction, the expansive scope and proactive nature of R2P's prevention dimension are crucial to its contemporary relevance and applicability.

The need for security protection is especially acute in situations where the well-being (physical and otherwise) of human beings is not only threatened by the actions (or inactions) of the state, but also by forces and factors too big not only for individuals but for the state itself to contend with. The threat posed to human security by pressing threats such as, for example, climate change and pandemic disease require us to reconsider the contemporary salience and utility of the ethic of protection embedded within R2P as well as its underlying logic(s). Prevention thus represents a proactive approach to protection that can reduce threats and vulnerabilities associated with globalization and transnationalism and the underlying structural inequality and violence they sometimes perpetuate.

As sometime critic Roland Paris (2014) pointed out a decade ago, R2P has always featured elements beyond coercion and reaction, and at its core promoted ethical ideas about proactively safeguarding humans from extreme harm that are only gaining further and deeper traction in international society. The heightened vulnerability of the vast majority of the world's population as a consequence of the collision between globalization and transnationalism on the one hand, and the declining capacity of the state as a security actor on the other, has produced an international societal context that is far more receptive to R2P both as a concept and as a potentially new norm of human security today than at any point since (and including) its introduction.

Admittedly, the formula for tapping into that receptivity is not entirely clear. Undoubtedly it would require a basic move toward reconfiguring the political, institutional, and even discursive landscape around R2P in ways that extract it from the clutches of the triage model of reaction. Capitalizing on the emergence of a logic of appropriateness within contemporary society requires R2P's proponents to emphasize and build on its capacity to serve as an ethic of human protection and even global care, via its oft-overlooked prevention dimension (Bohm and Brown, 2020). Certainly well-functioning states (a condition itself subject to debate and interpretation) can and perhaps should retain a role within that reconfigured landscape. At the same time, it is beyond contention that any such reconfiguration must avoid repeating the mistakes of the past – namely, the undeniable, audacious, and self-defeating liberal do-gooderism/imperialism that typified R2P's "failure to launch" as a new norm of human security.

Effectively drawing from the richness of R2P's ethic of protection and reconfiguring it for contemporary international society demands authentic "bottom-up" stakeholder politics in which "internationals" embrace a secondary role as resources (Autesserre, 2014). This is especially true in light of the prevailing shift toward a post-liberal international order (Pattison, 2021). Necessarily such practices in authentic politics must take different forms in different societies, and should reflect the political, social, and cultural context and security/insecurity dynamics of those societies. They also must prioritize transparency and remain steadfastly adaptable to changing circumstances. The devil is decidedly in the details, and such a transformation represents an enormous undertaking. That being said, capitalizing on an apparent logic of appropriateness emerging within contemporary international society cannot be accomplished without a fundamental and unwavering commitment to avoid revisiting the path of R2P's stagnation, and instead pursuing what Gray (2022) refers to as a "relational R2P." This is a concern I will take up in further detail in the subsequent (concluding) chapter.

In returning to the focus of the present chapter, it seems evident that R2P offers a clear blueprint for "rethinking the referent" in security terms – which, by extension, translates into part of the larger blueprint for resuscitating R2P's normative ambitions. As discussed here, rethinking the referent involves three distinct if interrelated components: deepening the focus on the well-being of individuals, broadening the landscape to include the scope of (non-traditional) security concerns actually threatening those individuals, and reconfiguring the dynamic of security provision toward proactive and preventive measures (and away from the paralysis of reaction via humanitarian intervention). As this chapter reveals, a full and close (re)appraisal of R2P's ethic of protection demonstrates its potential utility and applicability in all three areas. Indeed, R2P offers clear answers to the questions of *protection for who?*, *protection from what?*, and *how to protect?* These are perhaps ***the*** seminal questions for security thinking and practice in contemporary international society, and as such they speak to the untapped potential inherent in R2P as both an ethic of protection and a norm of, and for, human security.

Notes

1 As Richard Wyn Jones (1999: 23) emphasizes, "emancipation … is a process rather than an end point; a direction rather than a destination…there is always unfinished business in the task of emancipation."

2 Emancipation as articulated within security studies is itself hardly an unproblematic notion. Following Booth's articulation, one basis for subsequent criticism was the rootedness of emancipation in "Western" liberal values, including an overt and excessive emphasis on the individual (Fierke, 2015: 182; Barkawi and Laffey, 2006: 350; Ayoob, 1997: 127). A related critique points to the concept as a pretext for a "neo-imperialistic" interventionism employed ostensibly to "emancipate" while instead claiming the agency of the "emancipated" and serving as a device for the expansion of liberal values and the states and institutions that benefit from said expansion (Fierke, 2015). While this critique has significant merit, it is not directly relevant to the argument here concerning the place of "emancipation" in security studies and its influence on the formulation of R2P's human-centered logic and ethic of protection.

3 Booth uses the analogy of a homeowner investing a small fortune in structural repairs that undermine rather than enhance the well-being of its inhabitants to illustrate this illogic.

4 A related phenomenon of a more critical bent is the so-called "security trap," which attributes the problem of pervasive human insecurity to the interaction of global and transnational forces with state capture and/or corruption (see Bailey, 2014; C.A.S.E., 2006).

5 Consider, for example, that the factors that impinge upon one individual's security usually impinge upon the security of numerous others as well; an outbreak of

disease, a proliferation of crime in one's neighborhood, or a policy of "ethnic cleansing" declared by a government against an ethnonational group are all effective examples.

Bibliography

Abrahamsen, Rita, and Michael C. Williams. 2010. *Security Beyond the State: Private Security in International Politics*. Cambridge: Cambridge University Press.

Adger, W.N., J.M. Pulhin, J. Barnett, G.D. Dabelko, G.K. Hovelsrud, M. Levy, Ú. Oswald Spring, and C.H. Vogel. 2014. "Human Security," in C.B. Field, V.R. Barros, D.J. Dokken, K.J. Mach, M.D. Mastrandrea, T.E. Bilir, M. Chatterjee, K.L. Ebi, Y.O. Estrada, R.C. Genova, B. Girma, E.S. Kissel, A.N. Levy, S. MacCracken, P.R. Mastrandrea, and L.L. White (eds.), *Climate Change 2014: Impacts, Adaptation, and Vulnerability. Part A: Global and Sectoral Aspects. Contribution of Working Group II to the Fifth Assessment Report of the Intergovernmental Panel on Climate Change* (pp. 755–791). Cambridge, United Kingdom and New York, NY: Cambridge University Press.

Araghi, Farshad. 2012. "The Invisible Hand and the Visible Foot: Peasants, Dispossession and Globalization," in Haroon Akram-Lodhi and Kay Cristobal (eds.), *Peasants and Globalization* (pp. 111–147). London/New York: Routledge.

Autesserre, Séverine. 2014. *Peaceland: Conflict Resolution and the Everyday Politics of International Intervention*. Cambridge: Cambridge University Press.

Axworthy, Lloyd. 2001. "Human Security and Global Governance: Putting People First," *Global Governance: A Review of Multilateralism and International Organizations* 7(1): 19–23.

Ayoob, Mohammed. 1997. "Defining Security: A Subaltern Realist Perspective," in Keith Krause and Michael Williams (eds.), *Critical Security Studies* (pp. 121–146). Minneapolis: University of Minnesota Press.

Bailey, John. 2014. *The Politics of Crime in Mexico: Democratic Governance in a Security Trap*. Boulder, CO: Lynne Rienner.

Barkawi, Tarak, and Mark Laffey. 2006. "The Postcolonial Moment in Security Studies," *Review of International Studies* 32(2): 329–352.

Baldwin, David A. 1980. "Interdependence and Power: A Conceptual Analysis," *International Organization* 34(4): 471–506.

Bellamy, Alex J. 2011. *Global Politics and the Responsibility to Protect: From Words to Deeds*. New York: Routledge.

Bellamy, Alex J., and Paul D. Williams. 2011. "The New Politics of Protection? Cote d'Ivoire, Libya, and the Responsibility to Protect," *International Affairs* 87: 825–850.

Bigo, Didier. 2002. "Security and Immigration: Toward a Critique of the Governmentality of Unease," *Alternatives* 27(1): 63–92.

Bigo, Didier. 2000. "When Two Become One: Internal and External Securitisations in Europe," in Morten Kelstrup and Michael C. Williams (eds.), *International Relations Theory and the Politics of European Integration, Power, Security, and Community* (pp. 171–205). London/New York: Routledge.

Bigo, Didier. 1996. *Polices en réseaux. L'expérience européenne* [Police in Networks: The European Experience]. Paris: Presses de Sciences Po.

Bigo, Didier, and Elspeth Guild (eds.). 2005. *Controlling Frontiers: Free Movement into and Within Europe*. Aldershot: Ashgate.

Bilgin, Pinar. 2020. "Security," in Arlene Tickner and Karen Smith (eds.), *International Relations from the Global South: Worlds of Difference* (pp. 181–196). London/New York: Routledge.

Bilgin, Pinar. 2002. "Beyond Statism in Security Studies? Human Agency and Security in the Middle East," *Review of International Affairs* 2: 100–118.
Black, David R. 2016. *A Decade of Human Security: Global Governance and New Multilateralisms*. London/New York: Routledge.
Bohm, Alexandra, and Garrett Wallace Brown. 2020. "R2P and Prevention: The International Community and Its Role in the Determinants of Mass Atrocity," *Global Responsibility to Protect* 13(1): 60–95.
Bonelli, Laurent. 2005. "Un ennemi anonyme et sans visage" [An Invisible, Faceless Enemy]. *Cultures & Conflits* 58: 101–130.
Booth, Ken (ed.). 2005. *Critical Security Studies and World Politics*. Boulder, CO: Lynne Rienner.
Booth, Ken. 1997. "Security and Self: Reflections of a Fallen Realist," in Keith Krause and Michael Williams (eds.), *Critical Security Studies* (pp. 83–119). Minneapolis: University of Minnesota Press.
Booth, Ken. 1991. "Security and Emancipation," *Review of International Studies* 17(4): 313–326.
Brodie, Janine. 2003. "Globalization, In/security, and the Paradoxes of the Social," in Isabella Bakker and Stephen Gill (eds.), *Power, Production and Social Reproduction: Human in/Security in the Global Political Economy* (pp. 47–65). Basingstoke: Palgrave Macmillan.
Browning, Christopher S., and Matt McDonald. 2013. "The Future of Critical Security Studies: Ethics and the Politics of Security," *European Journal of International Relations* 19(2): 235–255.
Bull, Hedley. 1977. *The Anarchical Society: A Study of Order in World Politics*. London: Macmillan.
Butler, Michael J. (ed.). 2019. *Securitization Revisited: Contemporary Applications and Insights*. London/New York: Routledge.
Buzan, Barry. 1997. "Rethinking Security after the Cold War," *Cooperation and Conflict* 32(1): 5–28.
Buzan, Barry. 1983. *People, States and Fear; The National Security Problem in International Relations*. Chapel Hill, NC: University of North Carolina Press.
Buzan, Barry, and Lene Hansen. 2010. "Defining–Redefining Security," in Robert A. Denemark (ed.), *The International Studies Encyclopedia*. New York: Wiley-Blackwell.
Buzan, Barry, and Ole Waever. 2003. *Regions and Powers: The Structure of International Power*. Cambridge: Cambridge University Press.
Buzan, Barry, Ole Wæver, and Jaap de Wilde. 1998. *Security: A New Framework for Analysis*. Boulder, CO: Lynne Rienner.
Carnegie, Paul, Victor T. King, and Magne Knudsen. 2021. "Human Security, Marginality and Precariousness in Southeast Asia," *International Journal of Asia Pacific Studies* 17(1): 1–28.
C.A.S.E. Collective. 2006. "Critical Approaches to Security in Europe: A Networked Manifesto," *Security Dialogue* 37(4): 443–487.
Ceyhan, Ayse, and Anastassia Tsoukala (eds.). 1997. "Contrôles: Frontières-Identités. Les enjeux autour de l'immigration et de l'asile" [The Control of Immigration: Myths and Reality], *Cultures & Conflits* 26–27: 7–14.
Chandler, David. 2010. "R2P or not R2P? More Statebuilding, Less Responsibility," *Global Responsibility to Protect* 2(1): 161–166.
Colantone, Italo, Rosario Crino, and Laura Ogliari. 2019. "Globalization and Mental Distress," *Journal of International Economics* 119: 181–207.
Collier, Paul. 2003. *Breaking the Conflict Trap: Civil War and Development Policy*. Washington, DC: World Bank Publications.
Commission on Human Security. 2003. "Human security Now: Protecting and Empowering People." New York: United Nations. Available online: https://digitallibrary.un.org/record/503749?ln=en&v=pdf. Last accessed 12 February 2024.

Davis, Diane E. 2009. "Non-state Armed Actors, New Imagined Communities, and Shifting Patterns of Sovereignty and Insecurity in the Modern World," *Contemporary Security Policy* 30(2): 221–245.

Deng, F.M., S. Kimaro, T. Lyons, D. Rothchild, and I.W. Zartman (eds.). 1996. *Sovereignty as Responsibility: Conflict Management in Africa*. Washington, DC: The Brookings Institution.

Devetak, Richard. 2007. "Globalization's Shadow: An Introduction to the Globalization of Political Violence," in Richard Devetak and Christopher Hughes (eds.), *The Globalization of Political Violence: Globalization's Shadow* (pp. 17–42). London/New York: Routledge.

Eichengreen, Barry. 2018. *The Populist Temptation: Economic Grievance and Political Reaction in the Modern Era*. New York: Oxford University Press.

Erskine, Toni. 2014. "Coalitions of the Willing and Responsibilities to Protect: Informal Associations, Enhanced Capacities, and Shared Moral Burdens," *Ethics & International Affairs* 28(1): 115–145.

Fierke, Karin M. 2015. *Critical Approaches to International Security* (2nd ed.). Cambridge: Polity.

Floyd, Rita. 2007. "Human Security and the Copenhagen School's Securitization Approach," *Human Security Journal* 5(37): 38–49.

Fontana, Iole. 2022. "The Human (In)security Trap: How European Border(ing) Practices Condemn Migrants to Vulnerability," *International Politics* 59(3): 465–484.

Freedman, Lawrence. 1998. "International Security: Changing Targets," *Foreign Policy* 110: 48–63.

Friedman, Thomas L. 2007. *The World is Flat: A Brief History of the Twenty-First Century*. New York: Picador/Farrar, Straus, and Giroux.

Fukuda-Parr, Sakiko. 2003. "New Threats to Human Security in the Era of Globalization," *Journal of Human Development* 4(2): 167–179.

Glenn, John. 1997. "The Interregnum: The South's Insecurity Dilemma," *Nations and Nationalism* 3(1): 45–63.

Gray, Felicity. 2022. "Relational R2P? Civilian-Led Prevention and Protection against Atrocity Crimes," *Global Responsibility to Protect* 14(3): 313–338.

Hampson, Fen Osler. 2012. "Human Security," in Paul D. Williams (ed.), *Security Studies: An Introduction* (pp. 301–316). London/New York: Routledge.

Hanlon, Robert J., and Kenneth Christie. 2016. *Freedom from Fear, Freedom from Want: An Introduction to Human Security*. Toronto: University of Toronto Press.

Hopgood, Stephen. 2014. "The Last Rites for Humanitarian Intervention: Darfur, Sri Lanka and R2P," *Global Responsibility to Protect* 6(2): 181–205.

Huysmans, Jef. 2006. *The Politics of Insecurity: Fear, Migration and Asylum in the EU*. New York: Routledge.

Huysmans, Jef. 2002. "Defining Social Constructivism in Security Studies: The Normative Dilemma of Writing Security," *Alternatives* 27: 41–62.

Huysmans, Jef. 2000. "Migration and the Politics of Security," in Sophie Body-Gendrot and Marco Martinello (eds.), *Minorities in European Cities: The Dynamics of Social Integration and Social Exclusion at the Neighborhood Level* (pp. 179–189). London: Macmillan.

International Commission on Intervention and State Sovereignty (ICISS). 2001. *The Responsibility to Protect*. Ottawa: International Development Research Centre.

Jackson, Robert. 1990. *Quasi-States: Sovereignty and International Relations and the Third World*. Cambridge: Cambridge University Press.

Jacob, Cecilia. 2019. "R2P as an Atrocity-Prevention Framework: Concepts and Institutionalization at the Global Level," in Cecilia Jacob and Martin Mennecke (eds.), *Implementing the Responsibility to Protect: A Future Agenda* (pp. 16–34). London/New York: Routledge.

Jones, Richard Wyn. 2018. "'Message in a Bottle'? Theory and Praxis in Critical Security Studies," in Michael Sheehan (ed.), *National and International Security* (pp. 461–482). London/New York: Routledge.
Jones, Richard Wyn. 2001. *Critical Theory and World Politics*. Boulder, CO: Lynne Rienner.
Jones, Richard Wyn. 1999. *Security, Strategy, and Critical Theory*. Boulder, CO: Lynne Rienner.
Jones, Richard Wyn. 1996. "Travel Without Maps: Thinking About Security After the Cold War," in Jane M. Davis (ed.), *Security Issues in the Post-Cold War World* (pp. 196–218). Cheltenham: Edward Elgar.
Kaldor, Mary. 2012. *New and Old Wars: Organized Violence in a Global Era* (3rd ed.). Stanford: Stanford University Press.
Kalleberg, Arne L. 2018. *Precarious Lives: Job Insecurity and Well-Being in Rich Democracies*. Hoboken, NJ: John Wiley & Sons.
Kaplan, Robert D. 1994. "The Coming Anarchy," *Atlantic Monthly* 273(2): 44–76.
Karakaya, Süveyda. 2018. "Globalization and Contentious Politics: A Comparative Analysis of Nonviolent and Violent Campaigns," *Conflict Management and Peace Science* 35(4): 315–335.
Katzenstein, Peter J. (ed.). 1996. *The Culture of National Security: Norms and Identity in World Politics*. New York: Columbia University Press.
Keohane, Robert, and Joseph S. Nye. 2001. *Power and Interdependence* (3rd ed.). Addison, Wesley, Longman.
King, Gary, and Christopher J.L. Murray. 2002. "Rethinking Human Security," *Political Science Quarterly* 116: 585–610.
Krause, Keith and Michael C. Williams (eds.). 1997. *Critical Security Studies*. Minneapolis: University of Minnesota Press.
Lacher, Hannes. 2003. "Putting the State in its Place: The Critique of State-Centrism and Its Limits," *Review of International Studies* 29(4): 521–541.
Madrueño-Aguilar, Rogelio. 2016. "Human Security and the New Global Threats: Discourse, Taxonomy and Implications," *Global Policy* 7(2): 156–173.
Masco, Joseph. 2014. *The Theater of Operations: National Security Affect from the Cold War to the War on Terror*. Durham, NC: Duke University Press.
McGrew, Anthony, and David Held. 2002. *Governing Globalization: Power, Authority and Global Governance*. London: Polity Press.
McSweeney, Bill. 1999. *Security, Identity, and Interests: A Sociology of International Relations*. Cambridge: Cambridge University Press.
McSweeney, Bill. 1996. "Identity and Security: Buzan and the Copenhagen School," *Review of International Studies* 22(1): 81–93.
Mittelman, James. 2010. *Hyperconflict: Globalization and Insecurity*. Stanford, CA: Stanford University Press.
Murdie, Amanda. 2017. "R2P, Human Rights, and the Perils of a Bad Human Rights Intervention," *Global Responsibility to Protect* 9(3): 267–293.
Mutimer, David Roger. 2009. "My Critique is Bigger than Yours: Constituting Exclusions in Critical Security Studies," *Studies in Social Justice* 3(1): 9–22.
Nunes, João. 2012. "Reclaiming the Political: Emancipation and Critique in Security Studies," *Security Dialogue* 43(4): 345–361.
Nurhasanah, Siti, Marthen Napang, and Syaiful Rohman. 2020. "Covid-19 as a Non-Traditional Threat to Human Security," *Journal of Strategic and Global Studies* 3(1): 54–68.
Oliver-Smith, Anthony. 2013. "Theorizing Vulnerability in a Globalized World: A Political Ecological Perspective 1," in Greg Bankoff, Georg Frerks, and Dorothea Hilhorst (eds.), *Mapping Vulnerability: Disasters, Development, and People* (pp. 10–24). London/New York: Routledge.

Orford, Anne. 2013. "Moral Internationalism and the Responsibility to Protect," *European Journal of International Law* 24(1): 83–108.

Panebianco, Stefania. 2022. "Human Security at the Mediterranean Borders: Humanitarian Discourse in the EU Periphery," *International Politics* 59(3): 428–448.

Paris, Roland. 2014. "The 'Responsibility to Protect' and the Structural Problems of Preventive Humanitarian Intervention," *International Peacekeeping* 21(5): 569–603.

Pattison, James. 2021. "The International Responsibility to Protect in a post-Liberal Order," *International Studies Quarterly* 65(4): 891–904.

Peoples, Columba, and Vaughn-Williams, Nick. 2015. *Critical Security Studies: An Introduction*. New York: Routledge.

Reike, Ruben, Serena K. Sharma, and Jennifer M. Welsh. 2015. "Conceptualizing the responsibility to prevent," in Serena K. Sharma and Jennifer M. Welsh (eds.), *The Responsibility to Prevent: Overcoming the Challenges of Atrocity Prevention* (pp. 21–37). London/New York: Routledge.

Rose, Nikolas, Pat O'Malley, and Mariana Valverde. 2006. "Governmentality," *Annual Review of Law and Social Science* 2: 83–104.

Rosenberg, Sheri P. 2009. "Responsibility to Protect: A Framework for Prevention," *Global Responsibility to Protect* 1: 442–477.

Sassen, Saskia. 2016. "The Global City: Strategic Site, New Frontier," in Marco Keiner and Willy A. Schmid (eds.), *Managing Urban Futures* (pp. 89–104). London/New York: Routledge.

Sassen, Saskia. 1999. *Globalization and its Discontents*. New York: The New Press.

Scott, James C. 2020. *Seeing Like a State: How Certain Schemes to Improve the Human Condition Have Failed*. New Haven, CT: Yale University Press.

Serrano, Mónica, and Thomas G. Weiss (eds.). 2014. *The International Politics of Human Rights: Rallying to the R2P Cause?* London/New York: Routledge.

Sharma, Sagar, and Monica Sharma. 2010. "Globalization, Threatened Identities, Coping and Well-Being," *Psychological Studies* 55: 313–322.

Sørensen, Georg. 2007. "After the Security Dilemma: The Challenges of Insecurity in Weak States and the Dilemma of Liberal Values," *Security Dialogue* 38(3): 357–378.

Steger, Manfred B., Roland Benedikter, Harald Pechlaner, and Ingrid Kofler. 2023. *Globalization*. Berkeley, CA: University of California Press.

Stiglitz, Joseph, and Robert M. Pike. 2004. "Globalization and its Discontents," *Canadian Journal of Sociology* 29(2): 321–324.

Ullman, Richard. 1983. "Redefining Security," *International Security* 8(1): 129–153.

United Nations Development Programme (UNDP). 2022. "New Threats to Human Security in the Anthropocene." 2022 Special Report on Human Security. United Nations: New York. Available online: https://hdr.undp.org/content/2022-special-report-human-security

Van Creveld, Martin. 1999. *The Rise and Decline of the State*. Cambridge: Cambridge University Press.

Vershbow, Alexander. 2016. "The Warsaw Summit and the New Security Environment." Keynote Address delivered at the Assembleia da Republica, Lisbon Portugal (23 June 2016). Available online: http://www.nato.int/cps/en/natohq/opinions_132747.htm. Last accessed 18 January 2024.

Walker, R.B.J. 1997. "The Subject of Security," in Keith Krause and Michael Williams (eds.), *Critical Security Studies* (pp. 61–81). Minneapolis: University of Minnesota Press.

Walt, Stephen. 2010. "Realism and Security," in Robert A. Denemark (ed.), *The International Studies Encyclopedia*. New York: Wiley-Blackwell.

Watson, Scott. 2011. "The 'Human' as Referent Object? Humanitarianism as Securitization," *Security Dialogue* 42(1): 3–20.

Weinstein, Jeremy M., John E. Porter, and Stuart E. Eizenstat. 2004. *On the Brink: Weak States and U.S. National Security*. Washington, DC: Center for Global Development.

Zartman, I. William. 2008. "Introduction: Toward the Resolution of International Conflicts," in William I. Zartman (ed.), *Peacemaking in International Conflict: Methods & Techniques* (Revised Edition) (pp. 3–22). Washington, DC: U.S. Institute of Peace Press.

Conclusion

Reconstructing R2P

Diagnosis

The catalyst for this research was R2P's failure. At first blush that failure presents itself as a well-chronicled inability to elicit and sustain a discernable change in support for humanitarian intervention. R2P was intended to provide redress for one of (if not the) biggest challenges confronting international society in the post–Cold War period: the lack of capacity and will for civilian protection. This failure appears almost self-evident as humanitarian crises characterized by mass atrocities and human suffering mount and intensify. The fleeting and elusive capacity and will of the international community to respond to such scenarios only adds additional credence and weight to this characterization.

Given R2P's clear intention to provide a mechanism for effective response to the widespread human suffering borne of complex political emergencies, the persistence of the "humanitarian intervention deficit" outlined here is undeniably damning. Debates over R2P's status relative to that objective have often been grounded in and informed by ideological positions strongly supportive of, or strongly opposed to, the merits of third-party intervention and global governance. After reconsidering the terms of this debate over the politics of R2P, I turn my attention to the major theoretical contribution of this research – namely, the revelation that the failure of R2P to date is bigger and more significant than a failure to marshal greater support and capacity for humanitarian intervention. In light of this finding, and as the preceding investigation suggests, R2P's failure has less to do with the political and ideological contestation enveloping it than with its "goodness of fit" relative to the social context which has prevailed for much of its lifespan.

R2P as ideological talisman

R2P has been roundly criticized as the latest in a long line of idealistic ventures advanced by liberal internationalists, even being famously dismissed as "much ado about nothing" (Reinold, 2010). From this perspective, whatever prospects existed for R2P to gain traction as a mechanism for civilian protection upon its

DOI: 10.4324/9781315105628-7

introduction nearly a quarter-century ago have seemingly evaporated. Instead, R2P teeters on the brink of irrelevance in an international system and society that remains dominated by the pragmatic brutality of *Realpolitik* and dogged by utilitarian calculations of self-regarding interest.

Buttressed by the persistence and proliferation of massive and widespread atrocities against civilians in Gaza, Ukraine, Yemen, Syria, and elsewhere, this line of critique has taken to portraying R2P not only as an exercise in idealism but the culmination of years of erosion in the international rule of law and human rights norms (Callamard, 2024). As the agents of the state continue not only to forego their broader obligations to ensure human well-being and fulfillment but act with violent impunity against the most vulnerable members of the international community – all while R2P gathers dust on the shelf – it is tempting to accept the premise that R2P is an idea whose time has passed, if it ever had arrived in the first place.

The apparent devolution of the civilian protection regime against the backdrop of horrific and systematic campaigns of mass atrocity perpetration lends itself to pessimism, even fatalism. It is hard to avoid falling prey to these sentiments in light of the stakes involved, both from a human and moral standpoint; indeed, such pessimism has been expressed by several of the most recent Special Advisors themselves (Barber, 2023). Further compounding the appeal of this pessimistic perspective is the dogged and dogmatic adherence of some of R2P's proponents to assertions of its radical and transformational effects on international society in the face of overwhelming evidence to the contrary (Glanville and Widmaier, 2020). Indeed, R2P has retained a cadre of devotees who are prone to the practice of redefining R2P's purpose to sustain (salvage?) arguments of and for its merits and potential even when forced to confront its abject failings. This obdurance in the face of a mounting tide of evidence to the contrary – i.e., evidence of widespread suffering, powerlessness, and, again, impunity – lends itself to another, different kind of trap. That trap is borne of zealous optimism rather than fatalistic pessimism, and is rooted in the convenient distance of the Derridean subject/object binary. This is a unique form of idealistic liberal hypocrisy defined in this case by the luxury of clinging to R2P on its intellectual merits even when, or because, it is having little to no practical effect on actual behavior or outcomes (Hehir, 2013).

Both the pessimistic ("realist") and optimistic ("liberal") interpretations of R2P's track record and future prospects reflect ideological positions steeped in ontological biases concerning R2P rather than any systematic appraisal of behavioral outcomes and/or prevailing discourses. As such both are equally unhelpful for evaluating R2P objectively and in full. They effectively neuter R2P's ideational substance and render it the latest casualty in the "grand debate" between realism and liberalism – reducing R2P not only to a doctrine of and for humanitarian intervention, but to a proxy for the internecine conflict within positivist and materialist IR theory.

R2P's detractors are unfailingly Ecclesiastian in their critique; indeed, arguments grounded in the allegedly unchanging nature of power, interests, and states are themselves unchanging and for that reason largely uninteresting. In their simplistic and false denials of the inevitable – social change – they also serve (and perhaps intend) to reify the status quo; a status quo which, in the case of civilian protection, is politically, legally, and ethically unacceptable. Conversely, R2P's staunchest defenders operate from a quasi-religious platform, treating R2P more as an article of faith than a political doctrine or policy instrument. Here we are reminded that the dangers of unfounded and overstated optimism are every bit as serious as those of persistent and unwarranted pessimism; when the latter are proved wrong, the outcome tends to be virtuous, whereas when the former are the result is at best disappointing, and at worst disastrous.

The argument advanced throughout this monograph seeks to avoid this trap, instead striving for an intellectually honest and critical portrayal of where, exactly, R2P went wrong. One need to look no further than one's favorite (biased and curated) news source for copious evidence refuting the claim that R2P in its current form and status represents a revolutionary breakthrough in the transformation of the international system. At the same time, one must look beyond R2P's abject failure as a mechanism of and for civilian protection to date in order to see the potential for precisely that transformation inherent in the original ambition of the ICISS – to fashion a new norm of and for civilian protection in the fullest sense.

R2P as (stagnant) norm

The present research began with the objective of investigating the question of why R2P has failed to solve the problem(s) of humanitarian intervention. However, upon close scrutiny of its impetus and origins, the resulting investigation wound up revealing a deeper underlying purpose inherent in the very construction of R2P. That purpose – the introduction of a new global norm of civilian protection and human security – was motivated by an incentive to supplant states as the primary source of, and authority for, security action (transference), and to supplant states as the primary referent in security thinking in favor of individuals (transcendence). This revelation uncovers a more fundamental and profound dimension to R2P's failure; it is not only or just a failed policy doctrine, but rather a failed attempt at the development and diffusion of a new norm.

To be clear, any claim that R2P has realized this ambition and attained the status of a norm in international society is patently false. As considered at length here, the track record of R2P's implementation and its inability to inspire a concomitant change in behavior – whether in the narrow purview of humanitarian intervention, or more broadly – serve to debunk that assertion (Barber, 2023). It is a basic social psychological principle that for an idea to attain the status of a norm in any given society (the "norm activation" model; see Schwartz, 1977) requires that the behavior of the majority of the actors in that society comport with, reflect, and reinforce that idea. This has evidently not transpired with respect to R2P, which due to a problematically close association with humanitarian intervention has instead stagnated along the path to normativity.

The inability of R2P to transform humanitarian intervention behavior serves as a powerful illustration of its failure to attain the status of viable international social norm. However, the humanitarian intervention deficit is not only or even primarily an illustration of that failure, but also and more importantly the fundamental underlying cause. As chronicled extensively here, the close association of R2P and humanitarian intervention – to the point of a reductive equivalency – is chiefly responsible for the interruption and stagnation of R2P's normative trajectory. After taking concrete form in the ICISS report, and attracting both broad (2005 World Summit) and pivotal (2006 UNSCR 1674) support, one can make a convincing case that R2P reached, and even transcended, the "tipping point" as specified in the norm life-cycle model (Finnemore and Sikkink, 1998). In light of the revisionism and resistance R2P encountered after crossing that threshold, the case that R2P has failed to consolidate as a norm and proceed through successive stages (diffusion, internalization) in the life cycle is every bit as convincing, if not more (Reinold, 2012; Evans, 2008).

In light of that failure, we are left to conclude that as a normative project R2P is currently trapped in a state of dynamic equilibrium (e.g., a "steady state"). This outcome is a stark contradiction in terms to the evolutionary trajectory typically associated with the norm life cycle, and explains the prevailing stagnancy of R2P and its inability to elicit changes in international political behavior concerning the provision of civilian protection and human security. Indeed, it is more accurate to say that upon its endorsement by the UN, R2P entered a prolonged period of stasis. Rejecting the fantastical perpetual motion machine-style account of an unbroken linear process of transmission and socialization, the theoretical notion of norm stagnation introduced here, and used to conceptualize and contextualize the "failure" of R2P, allows for a revision to the norm life-cycle model. That revision speaks to and accounts for an alternative, and abundantly possible, outcome that agents acting within an intersubjective context can (and do) resist, challenge, and recast any desired normative commitment that could meaningfully alter the prevailing status quo (Payne, 2001). To this end, as Gareth Evans (2008: 288) noted, states that had seemingly committed to R2P through the World Summit Outcomes document in 2005 soon thereafter displayed an "evident willingness…to deflate or undermine the new norm before it is fully consolidated and operational."

This critical (re)appraisal of, and modification to, the norm life cycle allows for a means of theoretically conceptualizing what happened to R2P on its journey toward normativity. It also provides the basis for a more honest (re) appraisal of the specific factors that contributed to derailing that journey. This stands in stark contrast to the circuitous and elaborate apologies for R2P that insist that R2P is still emerging as a norm, that it has changed thinking and will gradually change (or is gradually changing) practice, or even that red herrings such as disasters in Syria, Yemen, Ukraine, or now Gaza (obvious scenarios demanding, but failing to elicit, the invocation of R2P) are mere outliers and exceptions. All of these arguments have a similar form and function. They essentially start with an imagined and desired scenario – that is, an international system transformed politically, legally, ethically, and morally around a normative commitment to act decisively to uphold and promote the security and well-being of the individual – render it an emerging reality, and work backward from there.

As we know from the philosophy of science, arguments such as these are pseudo-scientific at best. They are rooted in dogma, undaunted by contradictory evidence, and unwilling to revisit, refashion, or reject claims and propositions which lack plausibility (Popper, 1963). They draw from a cross-pollination of liberal thought and constructivist ontology that unhelpfully conflates the progressive and positivist bent of the former with the intellectual concerns of the latter – namely, ideas and norms. Too often the consequence is a non-reflexive interpretation and treatment of those conceptual building blocks of constructivism that animates ideas and norms with the liberal logic of a linear and unbroken trajectory of progressive and positive change. The by-product are arguments and analyses of an ostensibly "constructivist" bent are in fact warmed-over exercises in liberalism, with ideas and norms often, if not always, assumed to represent positive contributions to society, reflective of the continual and unyielding conveyor belt of individual and social progress. This assumption has much to do with the benign neglect of R2P by its proponents, a neglect that in turn led to its stagnation within the norm life-cycle.

To the extent that the norm life-cycle model rests on the fallacious and erroneous presumption that norms will inevitably follow along a positive linear trajectory leading to their widespread, if not universal, diffusion across international society, and internalization in domestic society, it is a reflection of liberal thought masquerading as constructivism. As liberalism has always been drawn to ideas, the gravitational pull of constructivism for those with a demonstrable liberal bent in their thinking (conscious or otherwise) is not particularly surprising. But it is troubling, for a number of reasons – not least of which being that it undercuts, if not subverts, the unique analytical and intellectual appeal and benefit of constructivism. To single out and underscore the explanatory power of ideas and norms for their own sake is assuredly not a natural segue way to the conclusion that ideas and norms are always "positive" or socially beneficial in their substance and impact, nor to the conclusion that even those ideas and norms that may portend positive or socially beneficial impacts are necessarily and inevitably bound to continue doing so universally and in perpetuity (Hehir, 2018). Ideas and norms can be "bad." They can also be "good," but in spatially and temporally limited and delimited ways. And, as is the main contention here, norms can and do wither and fade – losing whatever traction they once had on their own, or being crowded out and supplanted by competing ideas and norms – as well as rebound in the event they regain conversance within society. It is in that inherent dynamism of intersubjectivity that the key to R2P's potential normative restoration lies.

Prescription

Approaching and appraising R2P as a normative enterprise allows for a more expansive and contextually sensitive interpretation of how and why it has failed. Revisiting the underlying aim of the ICISS to construct a new norm of civilian protection and human security via R2P affords us greater purchase in terms of what R2P's original purpose was. Appraising it through the lens of a revised norm life-cycle model also and by extension allows for a more accurate diagnosis of what went wrong along the way. The resulting diagnosis – a reductionist emphasis on the reaction dimension via the binding of R2P to humanitarian intervention – illuminates R2P's stagnation and slide toward irrelevance.

As this retrospective assessment of the emergence and development of R2P demonstrates, it is hard to deny that the radical (re)conceptualization of responsibility as well as the expansive and proactive approach to civilian protection articulated by the ICISS through R2P was premature and out of step with the prevailing dynamics of international society at the time. Demanding and portending a transfer of authority over security provision from the sovereign state to the international community, was, undoubtedly, an ambitious, if not outlandish, proposition upon its introduction. So too was a call for prioritizing the protection of the individual, even to the point of acting preemptively to address the underlying structural causes of their insecurity. The misalignment between R2P and international society that prevailed upon the latter's introduction was manifested in the resistance of recalcitrant states to these radical moves and all that they entailed.

Yet while that resistance clearly impeded R2P's evolution as a norm, obstructing its diffusion and preventing its internalization, it was epiphenomenal. The true cause of the misalignment between R2P and international society – the factor that explains, above all else, the lack of receptivity of international society to R2P as an aspirational norm – was the fateful miscalculation of R2P's norm entrepreneurs to equate it with humanitarian intervention. Abandoning R2P's normative agenda while at the same time tying its understanding and articulation of a collective obligation to prioritize the security and well-being of individuals to a long contested and highly sensitive domain of international political behavior proved a near fatal blow to R2P, rendering it to the point of indifference, if not irrelevance, within international society at-large.

However, the fact that R2P's evident lack of traction in contemporary international society is explained by its reduction to little more than a (failed) mechanism for humanitarian intervention provision means that its broader normative ambitions remain untested, and thus potentially viable. Returning to R2P's original purpose – constructing a new norm of human security that

transfers authority for security provision from states to the international community and ***transcends*** existing security thinking and practice – offers a way out of the "saving strangers" morass. Dispensing with the limited (and limiting) notion of R2P as a doctrine of and for humanitarian intervention reveals its complex and nuanced engagement with the foundational cornerstone of the international society of states (state sovereignty) as well as a clear embrace of the priorities and concerns of the human security agenda.

The ability to precisely diagnose the cause of R2P's current malady also opens up the possibility for remedy. That potential remedy to R2P's current stagnation was proposed here in two parts, both of which share as their source of inspiration a recognition that the broad remit of R2P's initial formulation provides the blueprint for its reconstruction as a norm. As discussed here, that "blueprint" rests on the ICISS's expansive understanding and translation of both responsibility and protection. R2P clearly defines security provision as a collective moral obligation of the international community, and offers a proactive translation of protection as prevention centered on individual well-being in the fullest sense.

If R2P's stagnation as a norm is chiefly attributable to the abandonment of this sweeping ambition in favor of a narrow and limiting focus on reacting to crisis events, then reanimating it requires returning to and embracing that ambition and its core ideas and insights. As this research reveals, the time for doing so is now. The nature of the argument advanced here, which acknowledges not only the evolution of ideas but the evolution of their social acceptability and legitimacy, reflects the possibilities inherent in the dynamic quality of a socially constructed reality. To this point, as the preceding analysis reveals, we are currently at an inflection point in international society concerning the need for and provision of human security, one suggestive of an emerging and foundational logic of appropriateness for a reconstructed R2P (March and Olsen, 1998).

Prognosis

Rather than an idea whose time has passed, R2P is better understood as an idea that was ahead of its time – or, perhaps better put, an idea whose time is now upon us. This is reflected by the convergence between the reconstructed and reanimated R2P outlined here and three distinct yet interrelated dynamics currently emergent within contemporary international society: the diminution of the state's authority and capacity as a security actor; the transformation of the global security landscape; and the mounting critique and rejection of Western (liberal) biases.

The diminished state

The idea at the time of R2P's introduction is that it would cajole states into living up to their collective (moral) responsibilities to provide for the security and well-being of their populations. To this end, the ICISS drew on the notion of sovereignty as responsibility in constructing the doctrine of R2P out of a hope and desire that it would serve a "naming and shaming" effect. As even a cursory understanding of international relations indicates, this bold gambit, like R2P itself, has failed. In the intervening two decades, the chief problem that R2P sought to rectify – the inability of states to live up to the responsibility concomitant to their own self-proclaimed and highly prized sovereign authority – has persisted, and even magnified.

Consequently, the song remains the same: nearly a quarter-century after the introduction of R2P, the state continues to lack a plausible and morally convincing argument for retaining its authority and responsibility as primary security actor. If anything, the argument for the predominance of the state in the security arena has grown weaker as the weakness of state – both as an abstract entity and in its tangible and physical manifestations – has been exposed in its responses to the COVID-19 pandemic and global climate change (Sears, 2020). To be sure, states still remain highly engaged in the processes of securitization, enjoying a commanding position in the definition and specification of a wide range of policy concerns such as migration, terrorism, reproduction, and human sexuality as "security issues" (Sjostedt, 2019). However, securitization – unlike actual security provision – is a process undertaken for largely self-serving political reasons, and is one that can have as much to do with the consolidation of authority as with the alleviation of vulnerability and risk (Floyd, 2024). Furthermore, it is a process that often draws on moralizing language (as opposed to actual moral deliberation) to exploit or increase political and societal divisions and usher in and sustain oppressive, exclusionary, or violent policies (Williams, 2011; McDonald, 2008).

The notion of any broad obligation to ensure and enhance the well-being of individuals and society is becoming lost amid the machinations of the state (both in the abstract and in actuality). As states engage in or contend with the manipulation of particularistic identity politics and the purposive induction of anxiety by political elites, its failure as a security actor becomes more acute and visible (Kaldor, 2012; Bigo, 1996). Indeed, these machinations work at cross-purposes with establishing both the objective and subjective condition(s) of security, instead fueling the so-called "security trap," wherein the state concentrates its coercive authority at the expense of the population at-large by fueling insecurity within that population (Fontana, 2022; C.A.S.E. Collective, 2006). In the end, the result is a *de facto* realization within contemporary international society of a possible outcome suggested by the architects of R2P a quarter-century ago: that it is no longer permissible or feasible for the state to enjoy a monopolistic position in the security arena. This mounting realization represents an important window of opportunity for R2P, reflecting a growing convergence between R2P's ideational core and contemporary international society.

Transformed security environment

The incapacity and in some cases seeming unwillingness of the state to effectively respond to "new" (or newly recognized) threats and challenges in ways that enhance the security and well-being of humanity make the questions of what the responsibility for protecting humanity is, and who possesses it, imperative. This imperative is growing in strength and recognition in light of the transboundary nature of many contemporary global security challenges, as well as their direct and mounting effects on individual humans and society at-large. In light of the state's inadequate responses, inattentiveness, and even in some instances conscious inaction when it comes to existential security threats such as climate change, forced displacement, and pandemic disease, one is left to conclude that the state has fallen prey to the "insecurity dilemma" – failing in its primary responsibilities to the public in ways that further underscore its lack of credibility as a security actor (Bilgin, 2020).

The chief by-product of this collision between transnational and transboundary threats and challenges to human security on one hand, and the diminished capacity and/or willingness of the state to respond to them on the other, is an endemic condition of human vulnerability experienced by an increasing proportion of the world's population (Weiss and Thakur, 2010). As we have seen here, a broader accounting for human vulnerability is a core feature of a reconstructed and rehabilitated R2P. One example of R2P's strength in this regard is its potential ability – via the prevention dimension – to dispense with the limited and limiting emphasis on responding to humanitarian crises, in favor of confronting the chronic and diffuse structural factors that sustain human insecurity and vulnerability. From the standpoint of security provision, disaggregating crisis events from enduring structural conditions has undermined R2P, introducing a limiting and false dichotomy both conceptually and practically. Conceptually, prioritizing reaction over prevention overlooks the glaringly obvious: namely, that humanitarian crises are almost always acute and high-profile manifestations of chronic and enduring cases of societal insecurity and state incapacity (Bohm and Brown, 2020). Practically, the emphasis on reaction at the expense of prevention is, in the language of the microeconomist, inefficient (Jacob, 2019).

Responding as a firefighter would to episodic conflagrations of humanitarian crises is fully understandable and even "rational," since crisis scenarios represent "low hanging fruit" within the context of an international society where tangible political and material commitments to alleviating human suffering are scarce (to put it mildly). Yet in returning to our earlier deconstruction of R2P's origins and underlying impetus, doing so reaffirms a "beggar-thy-neighbor" status quo at the expense of R2P's normative ambition of transferring the moral duty for security provision and transcending existing modes of security thinking and practice. To suggest that reacting to the former when they occur (recur) is more deserving of our attention and resources than is undertaking measures to prevent the latter is doing a disservice both from the standpoint of R2P's stated mandate of human protection and to its unstated normative agenda. It misses the mark at a moment in international society where that generalized condition of human vulnerability and insecurity is expanding and intensifying – in other words, when the need for human protection is undeniable and ubiquitous, if not universal (Illingworth, 2024).

Rejecting Western bias

The culturally bound and culturally specific platform on which R2P was established proved to be a critical element in its stagnation as a norm. As discussed in earlier chapters, a growing recognition of, and resistance to, this underlying (Western) bias has thwarted R2P's diffusion and internalization. This friction emerged despite – or perhaps because of – its transcendence of the "tipping point" through the advocacy and support of leading Western liberal states in the early 21st century. In fact, that advocacy and support convinced many postcolonial states and societies that R2P represented the latest in a long line of practices employed by Western liberal states to control the "global borderlands" and to reaffirm rather than transform the global status quo (Chandler, 2010; Duffield and Waddell, 2006).

The domination of the politics of R2P by Western liberal states has certainly proven problematic within an international social context characterized by an ever-greater number of individuals and groups that are wary of, if not outright hostile to, that dynamic. Yet the extent of Western liberal bias running through R2P has a deeper and more substantive manifestation, at least as it has been pursued and operationalized to date. As earlier chapters have chronicled at length, equating R2P with humanitarian crisis and intervention has shunted R2P toward the subject/object problem that has long typified Western thinking within the security realm. This agency-claiming problem assumes the posture of treating security as a "good" to be supplied to a passive recipient (the "object" of security concern) by a removed and omniscient source.

Humanitarian intervention stands out as a particularly compelling example of this problem, by disclaiming the subjectivity of the "strangers" whom it attempts to "save." In this way, the association of R2P with humanitarian intervention to the point of near-equivalence renders it a conspicuous target for those disaffected by "Western" narratives and practices – a growing disaffection reflected in the emergence and expansion of various transnational social movements (Milani and Laniado, 2023; Chase-Dunn et al., 2022). Such critics have rightly identified in R2P's predominant operationalization as a mechanism for facilitating intervention evidence of the narrow liberal internationalist propensity toward "helping victims" (Chandler, 2012). Isolating solely on one discrete and acute type of outward manifestation of the degradation of human existence has the effect of relegating the root causes of that degradation – what Radice (2016) calls "crises of humanity" – down the security agenda. The end result is the commandeering of a supposedly new innovation in security thinking and practice in a manner that reifies existing political, social, economic, and ecological orders and sustains and perpetuates dynamics of insecurity (Kashyap, 2023). This stands in direct and stark contrast to the broader human security emphasis on vulnerability and the prevention thereof through practices that contribute to societal resilience, individual empowerment, and self-securing agency. This emphasis in fact (re)positions R2P as post-interventionist and is more reflective of the holistic interpretation of security evident in many non-Western societies and individuals (Howe, 2018; Chandler, 2012).

Much ado about something

Upon reaching its tipping point via endorsement by the UNGA and UNSC in 2005 and 2006 (respectively), R2P was systematically mainstreamed into international discourse and practice (Brown, 2013). This proceeded to such an extent that other vocabularies for describing mass atrocities and gross violations of the security and rights of the human person – as well as and other ways of seeing and responding to them – were supplanted by R2P (Crossley, 2016). Yet at the same time it is important to recognize that normalization through cooptation by institutional discourses and practices is not the same thing as attaining normativity. The former is a directed and institutionally driven "top-down" practice whereas the latter is necessarily organic, societal, and "bottom-up." Rhetorical support, academic attention, and even UN endorsement are superficial reflections rather than substantive evidence of R2P's normativity (Reinold, 2010).

Systematically embedding R2P within the international system – including, most notably, granting the UNSC ultimate authority over its implementation – was undoubtedly seen as a way to facilitate its implementation through existing institutional frameworks. However, this reversion to the mean had the negative consequence of arresting the diffusion and internationalization of R2P as a new security norm, paving the road to its current stagnation. Rather than contributing to the twinned ideational projects of deepening (a centering of the focus of security on individuals and social groups) and broadening (an expanding of the scope of what constitutes a "security" issue or threat) underpinning the human security agenda, normalization shunted R2P back into the prevailing Westphalian-Weberian status quo.[1]

Notwithstanding R2P's current and prevailing stagnation, the present analysis allows for concluding on a note of cautious optimism. Following Reinold's (2010) admonition to subject the "R2P hype" to critical scrutiny and to ask probing questions about its viability as a norm reveals a very different picture regarding that viability today. Developments in contemporary international society reflected not only in changes such as the actual and perceived viability of states, the nature of threats, and the rejection of Western biases but also a net-positive global sentiment toward R2P (Scherzinger, 2023) provide the foundation for a possible intersubjective consensus about what R2P means. That foundation and meaning is itself steeped in an emerging recognition of R2P as something more, and something bigger, than a political-legal doctrine for "saving strangers" (Scherzinger, 2023).

R2P's emphasis on the inadequacy of states as vehicles for security provision, as well as the paralysis engendered by a strict adherence to state sovereignty in the security arena have proven to be prescient, if not prophetic. In highlighting this prescience, this book uncovers a potential path to renewed relevance for R2P not only as a policy device but as an international social norm. As the philosopher Jon Elster (1985) has noted, synergy between and among norms (existing and/or emerging) is vital for societal acceptance of new ideas, fashioning what he calls the "cement" of society. To the extent that R2P can be (re)constructed as a norm of, and for, human security – one convergent with other emerging norms in international society regarding security, sovereignty, and rights – the bold step of ICISS toward fashioning a cosmopolitan, post-Westphalian society via R2P may prove to be much ado about something after all.

Note

1 As Keranen (2016) observes, with respect to R2P, this reversion to the mean is evident on the rebuilding and prevention as well as reaction dimension.

Bibliography

Barber, Rebecca. 2023. "A Proposal for Advancing Implementation of the Responsibility to Protect," *Global Responsibility to Protect* 15(4): 361–391.

Bigo, Didier. 1996. *Polices en réseaux. L'expérience européenne* [Police in Networks: The European Experience]. Paris: Presses de Sciences Po.

Bilgin, Pinar. 2020. "Security," in Arlene Tickner and Karen Smith (eds.), *International Relations from the Global South: Worlds of Difference* (pp. 181–196). London/New York: Routledge.

Bohm, Alexandra, and Garrett Wallace Brown. 2020. "R2P and Prevention: The International Community and Its Role in the Determinants of Mass Atrocity," *Global Responsibility to Protect 13*(1): 60–95.

Brown, Chris. 2013. "The Antipolitical Theory of Responsibility to Protect," *Global Responsibility to Protect* 5(4): 423–442.

C.A.S.E. Collective. 2006. "Critical Approaches to Security in Europe: A Networked Manifesto," *Security Dialogue* 37(4): 443–487.

Callamard, Agnès. 2024. "Gaza and the End of the Rules-Based Order," *Foreign Affairs* (15 February). Available online: https://www.foreignaffairs.com/israel/gaza-and-end-rules-based-order. Last accessed 25 February 2024.

Chandler, David. 2012. "Resilience and Human Security: The Post-Interventionist Paradigm," *Security Dialogue* 43(3): 213–229.

Chandler, David. 2010. "R2P or not R2P? More Statebuilding, Less Responsibility," *Global Responsibility to Protect* 2(1): 161–166.

Chase-Dunn, Christopher, Roman Stäbler, Ian Breckenridge-Jackson, and Joel Herrera. 2022. "Articulating the Web of Transnational Social Movements," in Jack A. Goldstone, Leonid Grinin, and Andrey Korotayev (eds.), *Handbook of Revolutions in the 21st Century: The New Waves of Revolutions, and the Causes and Effects of Disruptive Political Change* (pp. 941–971). Cham: Springer International Publishing.

Crossley, Noële. 2016. *Evaluating the Responsibility to Protect: Mass Atrocity Prevention as a Consolidating Norm in International Society*. London/New York: Routledge.

Duffield, Mark, and Nicholas Waddell. 2006. "Securing Humans in a Dangerous World," *International Politics* 43: 1–23.

Elster, Jon. 1985. "Rationality, Morality, and Collective Action," *Ethics* 96(1): 136–155.

Evans, Gareth. 2008. "The Responsibility to Protect: An Idea Whose Time Has Come… and Gone?" *International Relations* 22(3): 283–298.

Finnemore, Martha, and Kathryn Sikkink. 1998. "International Norm Dynamics and Political Change," *International Organization* 52(4): 887–917.

Floyd, Rita. 2024. *The Duty to Secure: From Just to Mandatory Securitization.* Cambridge: Cambridge University Press.

Fontana, Iole. 2022. "The Human (In)security Trap: How European Border(ing) Practices Condemn Migrants to Vulnerability," *International Politics* 59(3): 465–484.

Glanville, Luke, and Wesley W. Widmaier. 2020. "R2P and the Benefits of Norm Ambiguity," in Charles T. Hunt and Phil Orchard (eds.), *Constructing the Responsibility to Protect: Contestation and Consolidation* (pp. 50–68). London/New York: Routledge.

Hehir, Aidan, 2018. "R2P and the Limits of Norms," in Aidan Hehir (ed.), *Hollow Norms and the Responsibility to Protect* (pp. 57–85). Basingstoke: Palgrave Macmillan.

Hehir, Aidan. 2013. "The Responsibility to Protect as the Apotheosis of Liberal Teleology," in Aidan Hehir and Robert Murray (eds.), *Libya, the Responsibility to Protect and the Future of Humanitarian Intervention* (pp. 34–57). London: Palgrave Macmillan.

Howe, Brendan. 2018. "Divergent Interpretations of the R2P and Human Security: Implications for Governance Challenges in Myanmar," *Korean Journal of Security Affairs* 23(1): 80–101.

Illingworth, Richard. 2024. *Strengthening the Responsibility to Protect: A Transitional Cosmopolitan Approach.* London/New York: Routledge.

Jacob, Cecilia. 2019. "R2P as an Atrocity-Prevention Framework: Concepts and Institutionalization at the Global Level," in Cecilia Jacob and Martin Mennecke (eds.), *Implementing the Responsibility to Protect: A Future Agenda* (pp. 16–34). London/New York: Routledge.

Kaldor, Mary. 2012. *New and Old Wars: Organized Violence in a Global Era* (3rd ed.). Stanford: Stanford University Press.

Kashyap, Rina. 2023. *The Political Economy of Security/Development in the Neoliberal Age: R2P and the UN.* Springer Nature.

Keranen, Outi. 2016. "What Happened to the Responsibility to Rebuild?" *Global Governance* 22(3): 331–348.

March, James G., and Johan P. Olsen. 1998. "The Institutional Dynamics of International Political Orders," *International Organization* 52(4): 943–969.

McDonald, Matt. 2008. "Securitization and the Construction of Security," *European Journal of International Relations* 14(4): 563–587.

Milani, Carlos R.S., and Ruthy Nadia Laniado. 2023. "Transnational Social Movements and the Globalization Agenda: A Methodological Approach Based on the Analysis of the World Social Forum," *Brazilian Political Science Review* 1: 10–39.

Payne, Rodger A. 2001. "Persuasion, Frames and Norm Construction," *European Journal of International Relations* 7(1): 37–61.

Popper, Karl R. 1963. *Conjectures and Refutations: The Growth of Scientific Knowledge.* New York: Basic Books.

Radice, Henry. 2016. "The Responsibility to Protect as Humanitarian Negotiation: A Space for the 'Politics of Humanity'?" *International Politics* 53(1): 101–117.

Reinold, Theresa. 2012. *Sovereignty and the Responsibility to Protect: The Power of Norms and the Norms of the Powerful.* London/New York: Routledge.

Reinold, Theresa. 2010. "The Responsibility to Protect–Much Ado about Nothing?" *Review of International Studies* 36(S1): 55–78.

Scherzinger, Johannes. 2023. "Unbowed, Unbent, Unbroken? Examining the Validity of the Responsibility to Protect," *Cooperation and Conflict* 58(1): 81–101.

Schwartz, Shalom H. 1977. "Normative Influences on Altruism," in Leonard Berkowitz (ed.), *Advances in Experimental Social Psychology*, vol. 10 (pp. 221–279). Academic Press.

Sears, Nathan Alexander. 2020. "Existential Security: Towards a Security Framework for the Survival of Humanity," *Global Policy* 11(2): 255–266.

Sjostedt, Roxanna. 2019. "Assessing Securitization Theory: Theoretical Discussions and Empirical Developments," in Michael J. Butler (ed.), *Securitization Revisited: Contemporary Applications and Insights* (pp. 28–46). London/New York: Routledge.

Weiss, Thomas G., and Ramesh Thakur. 2010. *Global Governance and the UN: An Unfinished Journey*. Bloomington, IN: Indiana University Press.

Williams, Michael C. 2011. "Securitization and the Liberalism of Fear," *Security Dialogue* 42(4–5): 453–463.

Index

Pages in *italics* refer to figures, pages in **bold** refer to tables, and pages followed by "n" refer to notes.